James Joyce:
New Perspectives

James Joyce:
New Perspectives

Edited by
Colin MacCabe
Professor of English Studies,
University of Strathclyde

THE HARVESTER PRESS · SUSSEX

INDIANA UNIVERSITY PRESS · BLOOMINGTON

This edition first published in Great Britain in 1982 by
THE HARVESTER PRESS LIMITED
Publisher: John Spiers
16 Ship Street, Brighton, Sussex

and in the USA by
INDIANA UNIVERSITY PRESS
Tenth and Morton Streets, Bloomington, Indiana

© The Harvester Press, 1982

British Library Cataloguing in Publication Data

James Joyce: new perspectives.
   1. Joyce, James, 1882–1941 – Criticsm
and interpretation
   I. MacCabe, Colin
   823'.912   PR6019.09Z/

   ISBN 0-7108-0028-2

Indiana University Press
Library of Congress card catalog number: 82-47941
ISBN 0-253-33176-5

Typeset in 10/12 Sabon by Inforum, Ltd, Portsmouth
Printed in Great Britain by
The Thetford Press Ltd, Thetford, Norfolk

Contents

Acknowledgements

The author and publishers wish to thank the following who have kindly given permission for the use of copyright material.

The Bodley Head and Random House Inc., for the extracts from *Ulysses*, U.S. copyright 1914, 1918 by Margaret Caroline Anderson and renewed 1942, 1946 by Nora Joseph Joyce, and Jonathan Cape Ltd on behalf of the Executors of the James Joyce Estate and The Viking Press Inc., for the extracts from *Dubliners*, originally published in 1916 in the U.S. by B.W. Huebsch Inc., copyright © 1967 by the Estate of James Joyce, and the extracts from *A Portrait of the Artist as a Young Man*, U.S. copyright © 1916 by B.W. Huebsch Inc., 1944 by Nora Joyce, copyright © 1964 by the Estate of James Joyce. We also thank Jonathan Cape Ltd on behalf of the Executors of the James Joyce Estate and the Society of Authors as literary representatives for the extracts from *Stephen Hero*.

Faber and Faber Ltd and The Viking Press Inc., for the extracts from *The Critical Writings of James Joyce* edited by Ellsworth Mason and Richard Ellmann, U.S. copyright © 1959 by Harriet Weaver and F. Lionel Monro, as administrators of the Estate of James Joyce, and the extracts from *Letters of James Joyce* edited by Richard Ellmann, U.S. copyright © 1966 by F. Lionel Monro as administrator of the Estate of James Joyce. The Society of Authors as the literary representatives of the Estate of James Joyce and The Viking Press Inc., for the extracts from *Finnegans Wake*, U.S. copyright © 1939 by James Joyce, © 1967 by George Joyce and Lucia Joyce.

Notes on Contributors

Fritz Senn lives near Zürich, Switzerland. He has been interested in Joyce for a long time, is connected with *A Wake Newslitter* and the *James Joyce Quarterly* as well as with the organisation of the Joyce Symposia. He has been visiting professor in the United States and is a trustee of the James Joyce Foundation.

Colin MacCabe is Professor of English Studies at Strathclyde University. His books include *James Joyce and the Revolution of the Word* and *Godard: Images, Sounds, Politics*.

Jean-Michel Rabaté, born in 1949 and former student at the Ecole Normale Supérieure, is a Professor of English Literature at the University of Dijon. He completed a Doctorat d'État on Joyce, Broch and Pound, and has published various articles on these authors. A forthcoming book on Joyce is to be published by L'Age d'Homme and he is currently finishing a book on the poetry of Ezra Pound.

Maud Ellmann is a lecturer at the University of Southampton. Her book, provisionally titled *Modernism and the Problem of the Subject* is to be published by The Harvester Press. She is also joint editor of the *Oxford Literary Review*.

Raymond Williams is the Judith E. Wilson Professor of Drama at Cambridge University and a Fellow of Jesus College. His books include *Culture and Society 1780–1950*, *The Long Revolution*, *Modern Tragedy* and *Drama from Ibsen to Brecht*.

Stephen Heath is a Fellow of Jesus College, Cambridge. His books include *The Nouveau Roman: A Study in the Practice of Writing*, *Vertige du déplacement*, *Questions of Cinema*, *The Sexual Fix*.

Patrick Parrinder is Reader in English at the University of Reading. His books include *Authors and Authority* (1977) and *Science Fiction: Its Criticism and Teaching* (1981). He is co-editor of *H.G. Wells's Literary Criticism* (Harvester, 1980) and has contributed to numerous periodicals including *Critical Quarterly*, the *Times Higher Education Supplement* and *James Joyce Broadsheet*.

Seamus Deane is Professor of Modern English and American Literature at University College, Dublin. He is the author of two volumes of poetry (*Gradual Wars* and *Rumours*), and of a forthcoming collection of essays on Modern Irish Literature (from Faber & Faber).

Maria Jolas lives in Paris and is the widow of Eugene Jolas, founder and editor of the international English-language review, *transition* (1927–38), in which 17 fragments of *Finnegans Wake* first appeared under the title of *Work in Progress*. Her personal contacts with James and Nora Joyce covered a period of 12 years.

Preface

In the academic year 1973–74, James Joyce was introduced as a special subject option in Part 2 of the Cambridge English Tripos. This decision was perhaps more significant than it would have been in any other department of English in Great Britain or the United States. It was in Cambridge, around *Scrutiny* magazine and finding particular force in the writings of F.R. Leavis, that a certain canon of modernist writing had been constituted which included T.S. Eliot, D.H. Lawrence and certain of the later poems of Yeats but which deliberately excluded Joyce. This exclusion was effectively complicit with and consolidated his rejection by the London literary world which is detailed in Patrick Parrinder's contribution to this volume. It was in the very influential review essay 'James Joyce and the Revolution of the Word' published in 1933 (*Scrutiny* vol. 2. no. 2 pp. 193–201) that Leavis concluded that Joyce had developed an unhealthy interest in language and it was this artificial interest in language which placed him outside the pale of concerned criticism.

However, it was never simply formal questions of language that were at stake in Joyce's writing. Joyce's deliberate aim had always been the writing, forging of an Irish consciousness which would throw off the twin yokes of British imperialism and Roman Catholicism. Such a project brought home to Joyce more clearly than the other modernists how such political liberation went hand in hand with questions of sexuality and cultural identity, questions which could not be considered independently of language. Pearse's vision of a 'pure' Gaelic culture and language which would oppose the 'impure' Saxon versions was for Joyce a simple illusion which would swap one oppression for another. As he wrote to his Brother Stanislaus in November 1906 about Gogarty's campaign against the 'venereal excess' of the English: 'I am nauseated by their lying drivel about pure men and pure women and spiritual love and love for ever: blatant lying in the face of the truth. I don't know much about the "saince" of the subject but I presume there are very few mortals in Europe who are not in danger of waking some morning and finding themselves syphilitic. The Irish consider England a sink: but, if cleanliness be important in this matter, what is Ireland?' (*Letters*, II: 191–2).

Joyce's concerns with questions of sexuality and cultural identity made him, in the aftermath of the sixties, perhaps the crucial author around whom to re-evaluate the whole impact and force of modernism. Such a re-evaluation was made possible in Cambridge by the Joyce paper. But it was not simply a re-evaluation of Joyce and the literary history of the first part of the twentieth century that was at stake in the work undertaken by both teachers and students. For this work involved a concomitant re-evaluation of the whole literary tradition and the relation of literary criticism to it. It would be idle to pretend that Joyce was the only focus of this wider re-evaluation but the reading of Joyce's texts was possibly the single most significant contribution to the energy and excitement that informed so much of the work in Cambridge throughout the seventies and which was to reach such acrimonious and sterile institutional conclusions at the beginning of the next decade.

It was just before these conclusions began to manifest themselves that I organised a circus of lectures to accompany the last year of the Joyce paper and which were delivered in the Lent term of 1980. This circus, and particularly the magisterial opening lecture by Fritz Senn, the greatest of European Joyce Scholars, seemed to sum up so many of the themes of the previous seven years' work that it warranted, particularly in the context of Joyce's approaching centenary, publication for a wider audience. For if Cambridge may seem too parochial a focus, the work gathered here has some claim to represent a renewed European interest in Joyce.

All but three of the essays published here were given as lectures in that circus. The exceptions are my own contribution on *Ulysses*, Patrick Parrinder's article on Joyce's rejection in England (both of which were given at an earlier circus of lectures that I organised in the Lent term of 1977) and Maria Jolas's reminiscences of Joyce's relations with women which were first published in 1980 in the Irish magazine *The Crane Bag* vol. 4. no. 1 to whom thanks are due for allowing its re-publication. Maria Jolas, whom I had had the extreme good fortune to meet while in Paris on sabbatical, had generously offered, despite her ninety years, to come to Cambridge to talk about her memories of Joyce in what would have been a memorable and fitting conclusion to the seven years' work on Joyce. Unfortunately this proved impossible to arrange.

One of the lectures given in the 1980 circus is not reproduced here: that given by Philip Gaskell which concentrated on the songs and music in *Ulysses* and the multi-media form of which did not lend itself to any simple written transcription. But it would not be right, even in such brief mention to the Cambridge Joyce paper, to omit recording the enthusiasm and effectiveness of his teaching and the contributions made by his expert bibliographical and musical knowledge.

Finally, I would like to thank Jean Leithead and Margaret Philips for their help in preparing the final typescript and Ben Brewster for his invaluable aid in proof-reading the text and compiling the index.

Strathclyde University, Glasgow.
2nd February, 1982

Abbreviations

The following abbreviations have been adopted in the text. With the exception of *The Odyssey* (see below), all numbers within the text refer to pages of the volume mentioned.

The Critical Writings of James Joyce, edited by Ellsworth Mason and Richard Ellmann (New York: Viking, 1959) (*CW*).

Dubliners, The Corrected Text with an Explanatory Note by Robert Scholes (London: Jonathan Cape, 1967) (*D*).

Exiles, A Play in Three Acts with the Author's own notes and an Introduction by Padraic Colum (London: Jonathan Cape, 1952) (*E*).

Finnegans Wake (London: Faber & Faber, 1964) (*FW*)

Letters of James Joyce vol. I edited by Stuart Gilbert (London: Faber & Faber, 1957); vols II and III edited by Richard Ellmann (London: Faber & Faber, 1966). (*Letters*, I, II, or III).

The Odyssey translated by Richmond Lattimore (New York, Evanston and London: Harper, 1967) (*O* followed by the book number in Roman numerals and the line number in Arabic numerals).

A Portrait of the Artist as a Young Man, The Definitive Text corrected from the Dublin Holograph by Chester G. Anderson and edited by Richard Ellmann (London: Jonathan Cape, 1968) (*P*).

Pound/Joyce; The Letters of Ezra Pound to James Joyce, with Pound's Essays on Joyce, edited and with commentary by Forrest Read (London: Faber & Faber, 1968) (*Pound/Joyce*).

James Joyce's Scribbledehobble, The Ur-Workbook for Finnegans Wake edited by Thomas E. Connolly (Oxford: Northwestern University Press, 1961) (*Scribbledehobble*).

Stephen Hero, edited with an introduction by Theodore Spencer. Revised edition with additional material and a Foreword by John J. Slocum and Herbert Cahoon (London: Jonathan Cape, 1956) (*SH*).

Ulysses (Harmondsworth: Penguin, 1971) (*U*).

INTRODUCTIONS

CHAPTER 1

Righting *Ulysses*

Fritz Senn

Early readers of *Ulysses* had a hard time just finding their way around the book, distinguishing between tale and talk, or separating either from thought. Joyce, in this respect behaving like a divine judge of sins, did not appear to differentiate much between 'thought, word and deed', as the Catechism and *A Portrait* (P: 151) put it. To us late-comers such distinctions have become much less problematic, and we have also learned that some distinctions are futile. A passage may well be a third-person report and yet suggest the articulations of some character who may not be articulating anything aloud. Joyce changes from one track to another without notice and on occasion moves happily along two or more at the same time.

Whoever makes an effort nowadays will usually step cautiously through the first three chapters, perhaps with a few tutorial nudges, then progress fairly well through the early Bloom parts and, in the course of this apprenticeship, pick up some basic knowhow which will help to cope with most of the looming extravagancies. At every turning there are stumbling blocks, irritations, erudite clusters, unannounced references, dislocations, and our attention is generally directed towards them. Much later, however, our interest may well return to other, less remarkable, parts which we overlooked in our first tentative navigation. We are now – to judge from a recent burst of studies in narrative technique – more and more fascinated also by the 'easy' passages. Many of the following samples are therefore taken from the Bloom chapters in the first half of the book, that is, before the novel changes its character so radically (as we have been told). Many of the novel's strident departures from habit (our habits as readers, perhaps, more than anything else) have been quietly foreshadowed in those muted openings. A schoolmaster of 1922 might well have objected or an editor interfered where now we would hardly care to stop.

At the beginning of the 'Hades' chapter, for example, Bloom

enters into the funeral carriage and sits 'in the vacant place':

> He pulled the door to after him and slammed it tight till it shut tight. (*U*: 88)

This will hardly confuse us on a first reading, though we might well focus on the strangely echoing 'tight'. Perhaps we can accept it as the awkwardness, and most likely the silence and constraint of social occasions like a funeral procession, being carried into the sentence itself. We can share Bloom's sense of decorum and his self-consciousness; treated almost as a non-person when he enters, he feels ill at ease. Which may also explain why he concentrates so intently on a less than perfect door mechanism.

Leopold Bloom is not an indiscriminate slammer of doors. Not long ago, at his own house and with competent ease, 'He pulled the halldoor to after him very quietly, more, till the footleaf dropped gently over the threshold . . .' (*U*: 59) – a similar statement for a similar action, with obvious differences (already, we notice, the book gently varies its own phrases). Leaving home, Bloom is methodical about creating an appearance ('Looked shut'), but does not, for good reason, actually shut the door. In the carriage the required shutting comes about only by a renewed effort. Both actions are repetitive, threefold, they take time, and in each case a 'till' points the way towards achievement.

But only the 'Hades' sentence is awkward, as though the act were made even more difficult by the others (we can assume) watching Bloom. The first 'tight' in the sentence is the odd one, and we can imagine an early editor insisting on its excision. For if it were justified in its place, then the following clause would be redundant. It is only today's modern reader, schooled in writers like Joyce, who has learned to appreciate stylistic inadvertance as an expression of clumsiness or a sign of inner turbulence.

What does emerge from this minuscule linguistic fluster is Bloom's perseverance. On the smallest possible scale he is what Joyce said of Odysseus, '. . . a jusqu'auboutist'[1]. As we can see from an earlier version, now called the Rosenbach Manuscript, Joyce had originally written: '. . . and slammed it twice till it shut tight',[2] a wholly unobjectionable phrasing. The substitution has changed a lot and introduced some nervousness. We might say, pedantically, that the first 'tight' will at the end come to mean '*not* tight', so that further efforts are needed. Or we might say the first adverb refers to appearance, the second to reality. The first one will be recognised, in hindsight, as a fumble, the last one as a hit. The second one makes us doubt the validity of its identical predecessor. Or, to try again, 'he slammed it tight' expresses an endeavour, 'till it shut tight' the fulfilment. That a trivial insistent act calls for such a lot of descriptive expenditure is not very surprising, for we are already dealing with eminently Ulyssean concerns and techniques. It is also not surprising that the rebarbative duplication does not translate itself very well. The French version of it is a simple sequence, 'Il tira la portière après lui, la claqua et reclaqua jusqu'à ce qu'elle tînt bon', like the Italian one: '. . . e lo sbatte finché non fu ben chiuso'; in German too the sentence is smoother, '. . . schlug sie fest zu, bis sie fest schloss', and renders a somewhat different action.[3]

Even in that 'initial style' of *Ulysses* a harmless word like 'tight' may stand for a disquieting semblance or for the reality of its meaning, and we have an early instance of the weaving and unweaving of a texture, a word retroactively changing its being. Furthermore the whole sentence, with its reiteration before a door gets finally shut, could be reinterpreted entirely if we were, as well we might, to comb the 'Hades' chapter for metaphors of death.

Much of *Ulysses* has to do with the deceptive identity of appearance. Close to the beginning of Book II there are two sentences of almost parallel construction. 'Gelid light and air were in the kitchen . . .' resembles, on its surface, the preceding: 'Kidneys were in his mind . . .' (*U*: 57). But clearly, kidneys are not in one's mind in quite the same sense that air is in one's kitchen. No reader has trouble adjusting to the minor discrepancy within the range of the idiom, in fact few readers will notice it at all. But if we turn to our control group, the translations, we will hardly find one rendering which retains the spurious parallelism. The target languages cannot, it seems, simply put kidneys into a mind. A Portuguese version is here representative for most of the others: 'Rins tinha em mente . . . Luz e ar gélidos havia na conzinna . . .'

It is perhaps in little low-key miracles like 'kidneys were in his mind' that *Ulyssess* departs from the smooth level of conventional novels. This occurs when Joyce shifts from Bloom's mind to his surroundings and allows us, for the first time, to locate him in space:

> Kidneys were in his mind as he moved about the kitchen softly, righting her breakfast things on the humpy tray. (*U*: 57)

Early readers probably balked at the abrupt possessive 'her' and its lack of an antecedent and, therefore, its pointed dependence on, precisely, 'his mind'. But we might still wonder for a moment what exactly Bloom is doing, 'righting' her things; the verb is not often used in such a non-figurative sense. Translators tend to settle for some kind of arrangement, a disposition of objects, unless they leave it at some vague 'preparation'; 'disposant . . .', 'sistemando . . .', 'dispondo . . .', 'preparandole . . .', 'richete . . .', 'zurechtmachte . . .', etc. In none of these samples do we get the impression of Bloom striving for some kind of satisfactory array which can then be called 'right', as the sequel bears out: 'Another slice of bread and butter: three, four: right. She didn't like her plate full. Right.' But while one can determine whether a door is shut tight or not, this 'right' of approval is far less objective (we may remember that Stephen Dedalus, in the first chapter of *A Portrait*, had a tough time learning its tricky applications). Standards differ. And in fact we never know if Bloom's judicious structuring of cup and plate, toast and cream actually satisfies 'her', for when the humpy tray – not the only defective gear in the house, as we will also have learned by that time – is served upstairs, both Molly Bloom and her husband have other arrangements to think of.

'Righting' is a particularly human activity, and a common one. Because it is the first endeavour of a new character, prototypical of him and of *Ulysses*, it may pay off to study the hand-righting. The sketch is characteristic, Bloom moves about a good deal righting things, literally and figuratively. He is concerned with a different spatial arrangement the next morning: 'So saying he skipped around nimbly, considering frankly, at the same time apologetic, to get on his companion's right, a habit of his, by the by, the right side being, in classical idiom, his tender Achilles' (*U*: 581). His ameliorative pains often go unappreciated: '. . . of course he prefers plottering about the house . . .' (*U*: 673), says Molly, not applauding. Bloom sees a dinge in John Henry Menton's hat and – this as the last thing Bloom does at the end of the introductory triad of chapters – instigates a remedy, with success, 'It's all right now, Martin Cunningham said' (*U*: 117), but little thanks. Bloom is always full of projects for civic improvements.

The 'Aeolus' chapter presents Bloom busy to right the conditions for an advertisement. The newspaper offices assemble a group of professionals whose functions are to prepare and edit news (including a letter for veterinary remedies), to set or proofread type. Within that chapter Bloom will self-edit a belated retort to Menton and fail at it (*U*: 123). The concealed activities of 'Aeolus' include one of the novel's main chains of mismanaged rectification, the naming of M'Intosh in the obituary report. This communicative misadventure was caused by Bloom supplying the right word which, written down, became the wrong name. One of the chapter's captions is 'ORTHOGRAPHICAL' (the right way of writing words). (This caption is missing from the Penguin edition of Ulysses. It should occur on p. 122 above the lines beginning 'Want to be sure of his spelling').

Bloom is not the only character who permutes objects towards a more satisfactory end. His own efforts are often wasted, but on his late return he comes up against an unexpected rearrangement of the furniture, 'alterations effected . . . to a more advantageous . . . position' (*U*: 626). This change, more difficult to ignore, leaves a lasting impression on his forehead.

As it happens, 'Ithaca' also arranges data and themes previously encountered, while at the same time supplementing new features and angles for the reader to take into account. The chapter in particular offers new recapitulations (scientific, statistical, categorical, budgetary, ritualistic, etc.) — 'recapitulate' (*U*: 649) means finding new unifying perspectives, appropriate headings (from *caput*, 'head', which, Bloom might agree, is perhaps the *mot juste*). In a purely figurative and wholly painless sense, the reader in turn is also 'knocking his sconce against' (*U*: 42) restructured realities.

Bloom is adept at mental rectification, which does not mean that he usually gets things right. Experience is forever conducted through, or reflected (is it perhaps refracted?) in, a mind which remains cautious and ready to adjust. A few minutes after his breakfast preparations we watch him rehearsing an address to Larry O'Rourke, pub keeper, trying out an alternative (inwardly), but opting for a simple salute (*U*: 60). Even before that he wonders how he compares in size to his cat — from her point of view (already a corrective change of view-point): 'Height of a tower?' He instantly checks himself: 'No, she can jump me' (*U*: 57). This No sets him off from his monocular fellow citizens. He can sense his wrongness, recognise his own limitations or the illusions he sometimes gives in to. After conjuring up a scene of the East, full of memories of the stage, of *Arabian Nights*, popular poetry and stereotypes, he deflates his own day dream: 'Probably not a bit like it really. Kind of stuff you read . . .' (*U*: 59). Such a corrective can even be taken up by the narrative itself, as in 'Eumaeus', when an earlier statement is abruptly cancelled with the same negation that Bloom often uses: '. . . No, it was the daughter of the mother in the washkitchen . . .' (*U*: 537), the narrative consciousness, as it were (and it has clear affinities with Bloom), having second thoughts and even going on to challenge all variant versions: '. . . if the whole thing wasn't a complete fabrication from start to finish.' By the time we have progressed this far in the book we know, or should know, that such caution applies fairly generally.

It is fitting that one of the apotheoses of the 'Circe' chapter has Bloom enthroned as a versatile Reformer and Righter of errors, mistakes and injustices (*U*: 455–464). On occasion his inclinations bore or irritate the others: '. . . he'd try to downface you that dying was living' (*U*: 328). In quick succession Bloom appreciates (in fact, like any good reader, interprets) Molly's erroneous but witty remark on Dollard's 'base barreltone' voice (*U*: 154), and then fumbles at a literary conceit of his own, a satirical sketch of a Laestrygonian eater: 'Born with a silver knife in his mouth' (*U*: 169). Then, typically unsatisfied, he corrects himself: 'Or no.' This time no improvement is at hand: 'Silver means born rich. Born with a knife. But then the allusion is lost.' Molly's accomplished witticism and Bloom's abortive one look like examples of what composing *Ulysses* must have been: hits and misses and hazards in the shaping of resistant material.

Explaining an eccentric word to his wife, 'metempsychosis', a word he first has to extract correctly from her garbled, tell-tale assimilation 'Met him pike hoses', Bloom shows Odyssean resilience. A first attempt, '. . . the transmigration of souls', is adequate but ill-adapted to the audience and leads to a rebuff. Undaunted, after some stalling he comes up with an alternative, embedded in simple instruction: 'Some people believe . . . that we go on living . . . They call it reincarnation. . .' His shrewd didactic sense prompts him to look for an illustration, and he picks the nymph over the bed for visual aid. But because of Molly's diminished attention and her sudden sensual response to the downstairs smells, most of Bloom's exertions are in vain (*U*: 66–7). Instead he is precipitated down to the kitchen. He retrieves the kidney (a real one, not just in his mind), and he is brought, along with the reader, to the chapter's starting point, the kitchen. At this point the narrative – after allowing Bloom an excursion into the world of classical reverberations (which, in the overall assignment of duties, is more Stephen's domain) – has adjusted itself and called him back to the appropriate mundane level.

Already it has proved impossible neatly to separate one character's corrective urge from the way in which the novel handles its many concerns. Like Bloom, it tends to counteract whatever it has been doing, contradict whatever it has been saying. We may now observe that the sentence which was here singled out as being somehow representative occurs within an opening where the author is softly moving about from one narrative stance to the next. He introduces, according to well-known convention, a character by means of some dominant trait, with the unconventional difference that it is a preference of taste:

Mr. Leopold Bloom ate with relish the inner organs of beasts and fowls.

This continues in the same vein thematically, but with a tonal drop from a formal 'ate with relish' to the homely translation 'liked'; from the stylised (even biblical) general to the itemised particular of a menu:

He liked thick giblet soup, nutty gizzards, a stuffed roast heart, liver slices friend with crustcrumbs, fried hencod's roes.

The details amount to one of the earliest catalogues in the novel, to which the third sentence adds one superlative item which will become, as it turns out, the final selection. But a new note of reflection and causality is also noticeable:

Most of all he liked grilled mutton kidneys which gave to his palate a fine tang of faintly scented urine.

The shifting of gears may be slight, but the narrative progression is not uniform, though it is not at all easy to pin down the faintly scented variations. With the second paragraph (already looked at), however, a strikingly new perspective comes into play:

Kidneys were in his mind as he moved about the kitchen. . . .

From this we can orient ourselves in two ways: we have, at last, a setting in the external world, and it becomes clear that all along we have been obliquely sharing what goes on in Bloom's mind as it was considering tasty alternatives for a breakfast meal. The next sentence, 'Gelid light and air were in the kitchen . . .', takes us completely outside, with a widening angle of vision, but by now we are assured of also being given impressions of Bloom: no doubt *he* now becomes aware of what is around him. But then a really unmistakable change of direction occurs with a first grammatical lapse, the elliptic:

> Made him feel a bit peckish.

This is the closest so far to how Bloom may actually phrase to himself something that he is unlikely to verbalise at the moment. But we have now been initiated to Bloom's rhythm and his cadences, even though we cannot as yet be sure that these are in fact his characteristic thought patterns. At this point the narrative veers again, back to a descriptive statement:

> The coals were reddening.

Formally this looks like a regression to the earlier type of sentence, the so-called objective, but (we have somehow learned by now) obviously not *just* objective. We sense what we cannot prove – that Bloom is now also looking at those coals. And once more we adjust the focus in the opening paragraph: the tending of the fire, presumably, caused Bloom to think (but, on our first run through, we couldn't realise that he *was* thinking this) about delicacies whose preparation depend on heat. And we might now try out too, moving from our minds to our tongues and palates, that second sentence again, that little festival of food fried or roasted, and to articulate it with our own vocal instruments. We will feel that, because of its obstacular consonant clusters, it is not a sentence that we can formulate without considerable lingual effort:

> He liked thick giblet soup, nutty gizzards, a stuffed roast heart, liver slices fried with crustcrumbs, fried hencod's roes.

Our lips get busy and our tongues have to do an awful lot of moving about the palate: we come in fact as close to imitating what happens when we taste and swallow – or when we imagine it very vividly. As deglutitory a sentence as ever there was. When the 'Sirens' chapter first appeared, readers were taken aback by its acoustic assimilations, the bold innovation of making language (as it seemed) conform to music. Few may have noticed that the technique is anticipated in a sentence which brings language as near to gustative articulation as seems possible – taste-speech. It is continued in that next saporific lump, 'grilled mutton kidneys', of the following sentence and, later on, extensively in 'Laestrygonians'.

After some initiatory jockeying of narrative slants, then, the style at last settles down, more or less, to the typical movements of the Bloom chapters, a blend of direct 'interior monologue'. 'Another slice of bread and butter, three, four: right . . .', narrated monologue, 'She didn't like her plate full', and third person report, 'He turned from the tray.' A complex arsenal of terminology has recently been marshalled to label the various modes with some show of precision and, as current discussions indicate, no narrative terms are likely to prove convincing enough to be above further righting and modification.

Irrespective of how we name then, a whole series of narrative relations has been conjugated already in about half a page. On a modest scale, most of the prominent stylistic excesses of the latter part of the novel have been subtly prepared for.

As though to corroborate the constant need for modulation, Bloom's cat exemplifies change on a prelinguistic level, proceeding on a similar principle of rhetorical variation for a strategic end. In three stages,

Mkgnao! . . . Mrkgnao! . . . Mrkrgnao!

there is continuity (a basic 'gnao' remains stable and, incidentally, looks like a Greek verb, though it isn't) as well as modification. The initial consonant structure – like the whole of *Ulysses* – gets more elaborate. Feline critics may interpret the increase of 'r's' as a gradual transition from plaintive plea to anticipatory purr, culminating in 'Gurrhr!'. Cat and author, in any case, adapt their style to new contexts.

Explicitly or not, as readers we have been composing the novel just as the author has done. 'Art', as a youthful Stephen Dedalus lectured long ago to an audience of one, '. . . is the human disposition of sensible or intelligible matter for an esthetic end' (*P*: 211). Writing, in particular, is a matter of arranging, adjusting, getting words right, revising. Joyce, one of the most obsessed righters of them all, chose words with care, scrupulously, from the outset; and in *Finnegans Wake*, as he told us, the words of the English Language were no longer the 'right' ones any more. He had already put them in some optimal order.[4] The shaping of Ulysses was a laborious development from short story to multidimensional epic. In 1915 an outline in Joyce's mind assigned 4, 15 and 3 chapters, respectively, to the book's three parts; these were then trimmed to a symmetrical arrangement in a triptych which balanced swelling disproportions. A detailed 'Schema' helped to shape the writing, but was also determined *by* the writing; but the Schema was righted into a final one, so that now we have at least two systems of authorial designs, and thereby a constant invitation to the critical reader to devise further metaschematic refinements.

We can now assess Joyce's indefatigable revisions by the many studies of the process, such as Michael Groden's *Ulysses in Progress*, and also by leafing through a score of facsimile volumes, with notes, drafts, fair copies, typescripts, corrections and proofs. But externally too, in writing after Easter 1916, Joyce was restoring central Dublin to its pristine state before the destruction: the General Post Office, O'Connell Street and much of the city furniture had to be fictionally re-erected.

No special virtue inheres in the clue 'righting' as picked up from an early passage; it calls up merely one more way of rereading, which would supplement all the other approaches. Righting, as developed here, is convenient shorthand for at least four interconnected processes: (a) characters in the book, mainly Bloom, amending their practices or conjectures in what they momentarily believe to be improvements; (b) Joyce revising and retouching his own handiwork; (c) the reader/critic adjusting to the text; and (d) the book itself tending towards ameliorative diversity. We can almost personify the novel, in a metaphorical shift, as though it had its own self-critical consciousness, were 'selfrighting the balance' of its own being. This later quote is brought back from *Finnegans Wake* (471), the self-righting literary work *par excellence*: it never lets you forget its inevitable wrongness, which it signals, and aims to correct, by its glaring heterography and its lexicological and syntactic fusions. It may also be called, with equal justice, the first self-wronging book: 'Wringlings upon wronglings . . .' (*FW* 367).

The *Wake* of course no longer keeps writing apart from righting, nor right from rite, nor either from wright(ing). Evidence abounds: '. . . the rite words by the rote order' (*FW*: 167), 'righting his name . . .' (*F W*: 422), 'the wright side . . .' (*F W*: 597), 'you could wright anny pippap passage . . .' (*F W*: 301) and so on. But *Finnegans Wake* is far removed in time and concept from a straightforward sentence introducing Bloom which was wrought no later than 1918. And yet the sound-connected activities have something in common and take over ritual overtones in the luxuriating novel which begins with an elaborate rite on top of a Martello tower, which is then counter-pointed in Bloom's lowly kitchen. The rite, we learn, is the poet's rest; and the book rests precariously for a moment with a later rectified account of the day's deeds given in terms of Jewish observa-tions and rites (*U*: 649–50).

But no claim is made here that Joyce intended to implement all such potential readings; these are in fact already the subjective rightings of one particular reader. In Joycean critical practice, read-ers tend to rewright the text; this is called interpretation. Readers returning from *Ulysses* and *Finnegans Wake* can be irreversibly conditioned, prone to retouch the earliest works in ingenious ways the young author may never have thought of, to realign the short stories or *A Portrait* in accordance with themes later encountered or discovered through cognitive skills later acquired. After *Ulysses*, the 'faints and worms' of 'The Sisters' (*D*: 7) become very intriguing, multilayered things, not at all constricted by whatever the original intentions may have been.

The homophone 'wright', enlisted here in this retroactive way, is cognate with 'work' and such Greek words as 'en*erg*y', '*org*an', or even 'dem*iurg*os': the reader's function becomes that of a *demiurgos* (from *demos*, people, and *ergos*, workman). In the *Odyssey* (XVII, 383) the term is applied to seers, healers, joiners, and even singers; Greek philosophers applied it to a creator, either divine or, later, a subordinate craftsman (it surfaces in *Ulysses* in this capacity: the ground '. . . sounds solid: made by the mallet of *Los Demiurgos*' (*U*: 43). Readers are mediators who shape, or forge, the matter at hand.

Moving about and righting entails a lot of inceptive groping, trial and error, possibly false steps. Success is never guaranteed. Bloom may never get his advertisement from Keyes. His very profession deals with improvement. Remedies are promised but not invariably effected. The home, even with Catesby's cork lino or Plumtree's Potted Meat, may become neither 'bright and cheery' (*U*: 353) nor 'an abode of bliss' (*U*: 76).

We have no reason to believe that our interpretations work much better than Plumtree's potted meat. What we regard and present as essential, remains dubious and, at best, incomplete. We tend to rephrase *Ulysses* in our own favourite terms (witness this performance). Awareness of this tendency might militate against the rigidity with which we single out, at times, arbitrary aspects or glorify one particular scene, image, symbol, act or analogy as though it moved, like Mr Deasy's history, to one great, nameable goal.

The righting urge is always present in the reader – to give or find direction, to align elements, to complete; the urge has been felt even by the dreary criticism of the middle period which streamlined *Ulysses* to some kind of dismal diagnosis (as often as not tied to 'paralysis') and managed to disregard the myriadmindedness of the work in favour of some privileged cure for Bloom or Stephen.

That *Ulysses* variegates forms of righting would not put it into a special class, but merely into a long tradition, often called humanist. What makes *Ulysses* different in kind is that the processes are not just described but integrated, acted out, and that the book seems to want to redress, emend, adjust, itself continually, and that it involves the reader in these processes.

Even righting *Ulysses* in the elementary sense of rescuing the text from the errors and falsifications which its complicated gestation made inevitable is a tricky task demanding expert skills. It is being undertaken right now, with the help of computers, so that in a few more years we may finally have a text which resembles best what the author wanted us to read. In the meantime it is small comfort to know that the *Odyssey*, too, differs essentially and irretrievably from whatever it was that a Greek poet made up around the eighth century B.C. Every Homeric critic presents a variant account of the author, or authors, compilers, and the genesis of the epic, including Athenian and Alexandrinian editors and commentators. A scholar like Victor Bérard moreover considered the whole epic a cross-cultural assimilation of Phoenician nautic lore to Greek notions, a Hellenising of some earlier material. And every translation of the poem that we use adds its own priorities and adjustments. The *Odyssey* belongs to a group of tales which take as their theme the restoration, through vengeance, of some lost order, a particularly violent form of righting which Joyce toned down considerably. The same is true of *Hamlet* (here, too, as with all of Shakespeare's plays, the text can never be authoritative) and of Don Giovanni; in each case the new order brought about differs from the old one.

Some corrective touches in the novel are structural or have thematic impact. The Bloom chapters revise much of the Telemachiad, and with the advent of Bloom we get new points of view for confirmation, or for questioning, at any rate for our comparison. Parallax will stalk into the book a bit later as an instance of Bloom's curiosity and as a concept, but it has been applied from the beginning, in the narrative shifts or in the setting off of Stephen's musing against Mulligan's posing. The first chapter elevates common things like teeth, navels, or the sea into classical Greek. In the fourth chapter Bloom tries to render a Greek word into ordinary English (which Molly has done already, through ignorance). For him a navel is something in which dirt gets rolled up (*U*: 86), not some Homeric-Delphic *omphalos* (*U*: 24).

The best known example of parallax is the cloud which turns, first, Stephen's mood (*U*: 15) and then affects Bloom, 50 pages and a few minutes of actual time later (*U*: 63). Parallax, an apparent displacement, allows scientists to measure with Euclidian precision distances that could never be traversed; it here allows readers to objectify the cloud itself and measure character differences. It is thus all the more instructive to ponder the novel's prime instance of a scientific method of verification, a matutinal cloud, which is also duly noted in the 'Ithaca', the book's most scientific report (*U*: 587). Clouds are something that can never be fixed with accuracy, they change both shape and their position, are one of nature's least stable items, so that they have become proverbial notations for dreamy lack of determination. No accumulation of parallactic information can pinpoint that cloud, or any other. They fit the 'Proteus' chapter because of their mutability; and one famous cloud, especially, is lifted from a play where it exemplifies change, gullibility and the mind's projective capabilities, 'Ay, very like a whale' (*U*: 46). Such an early nebulous cluster shows *Ulysses* already counteracting itself, scientific procedure and imaginative flexibility holding each other in check.

Each Ulyssean chapter re-processes its material according to a different programme and new priorities. Our attempts even to describe what each chapter 'is' never quite succeed. We still have not yet assimilated a performance like 'Oxen of the Sun', a jerky array of fake-historical re-rightings modelled on the styles of particular authors or periods, but with anachronistic checks working against facile systematisation. The chapter induces us to recreate, paraphrase, extract a text to our own liking. There is a strong temptation to talk about its action in the manner of what we have become used to, say, of the 'Hades' chapter, to expound what the characters do,

what exactly they may be saying or thinking. The final pages of
'Oxen' are perhaps the most sustained challenge to our adjustive
skills. No reader absorbs them as they are. We accommodate each
phrase within some plausible context. What in fact we usually do is
to translate it into a kind of script – precisely what it is not. A phrase
like 'The least tholice' (*U*: 424) remains irksome until it is seen as a
variant of 'The Leith police dismisseth us' immediately preceding;
and we feel more at ease when we are given the 'right' information
that this latter sentence is, not some provincial aside, but a standard
enunciation test for one's sobriety (Bloom's '. . . liver slices fried with
crustcrumbs', incidentally, might serve the same purpose). So we
may deduce that someone present (and we are provoked into finding
out who) has playfully worked in this line and that someone else is
offering a variant, perhaps drunkenly incapable or merely pretend-
ing. In some such way we change the debased quotation into its
'correct' form and setting, which of course still does not account for
the specific whatness of 'least tholice', which needs further adjust-
ment. What we have done could conveniently be presented by the
typographical layout which characterises the 'Circe' chapter:

1) NAME OF SPEAKER (in capital letters)
2) (*parenthetical stage direction, in italics, indicating speaker's gestures
or mannerisms*)
3) The least tholice.

But 'Circe' would most likely conjure up a transient scene in a police
station, perhaps even in County Leith. And in 'Circe' as well as in
'Oxen' we would have to speculate on whether the words given are
actually spoken or not. We would have to argue, in fact, about every
single item in the above transcription, but we would agree that *some*
such rearrangement is implied when we try to come to terms with the
elusive lines.

By having subsequent chapters (often parts within them) reright-
ing what went before, *Ulysses* demonstrates our own practice as
readers. When we talk about the 'Sirens' chapter we usually take the
music out and report *on* it, or report on the characters' problems, or
talk *about* its music. In effect and for practical purposes, we all
punctuate 'Penelope' by parcelling out its components or themes for
critical retailing. But let us descend again, from interpretative
restructuring to the ordinary business of simply reading the novel
correctly on the factual level. At one time no-one could do it, and

even today it remains so hard that most readers, and conscientious scholars, ask for assistance. Within 60 years we have, collectively, learned a great deal, and still not enough. Where else in literary criticism would one find a whole volume which sets out to do nothing but rectify wrong readings, that is, not tenuous interpretations, but demonstrable falsifications of the text at some elementary level. A Dutch scholar, Paul P.J. Van Caspel, has undertaken the task in *Bloomers on the Liffey*[5], and the task, unfortunately, is necessary. Van Caspel's list could even be expanded (most of us probably have a list of our own); weeding out the hard-core errors in *Notes for Joyce* alone would be a sizeable venture. In his useful though somewhat disproportionate strictures, however, Van Caspel just stops short of asking why *Ulysses*, of all novels, has caused such numerous sloppy and faulty readings. This seems to be one of its characteristics, in fact *Ulysses* is almost defined by the way it provokes misreadings at each of its levels; it does indeed deceive, puzzle, mystify, trick, mislead its readers. (Its own characters, after all, misread in the same way.)

Many errors are forgivable enough, although perhaps not their perpetuation. It was easy to suppose, on first experience, that 'Married to Bloom, to greaseaseabloom' (*U*: 259) and similar hints at the beginning of 'Sirens' means that the two barmaids in the Ormond hotel are making fun of Bloom passing by outside: they aren't and he isn't. But it takes a lot of exegetical and topographical rummaging to show this. A reader unfamiliar with Dublin also cannot tell whether some paragraphs in 'Wandering Rocks' are interpolated from elsewhere or not. Passing 'Farrell's statue' and then 'Gray's statue' (*U*: 95), how can we possibly know that the first statue is *by* and the second *of* the person named? For a long time it seemed understood that the two women whom Stephen sees coming down to Sandymount strand (*U*: 43) are midwives, named Florence MacCabe and Anne Kearns. Or when documents came to sight which showed that Oliver Gogarty had rented and paid for the Martello tower in Sandycove it seemed necessary to point out that Joyce altered a fact for the fiction: in the book Stephen, and not Gogarty-Mulligan, pays the rent. And perhaps he does. But who is to say that Stephen's 'It is mine. I paid the rent' (*U*: 26) recalls his own deed and status, and not something Mulligan has said or might say? We always have to sort out voices in a regress of quotations, to distinguish external saying from internal thought, all amidst pitfalls we never thought of. (Regarding sandy towers on the coast of Dublin, how many tourists have been directed to the Martello tower in Sandy*mount* by helpful locals, it being much closer to the city than Sandy*cove*? Quite a few, but even more have been offered the wrong tower in a documentary book.[6])

In the sex life of the Blooms, we read, '. . . something changed. Could never like it again after Rudy' (*U*: 167). *Who* never like it? The French translators (who could have approached the author if they liked) say: 'Elle ne s'y plaisait plus'; the Italian version opts for Bloom: 'Non ci ho mai preso gusto . . .' We may settle this question, perhaps, by recourse to further parallactic evidence, but even parallax may cloud the issue.

Translators have to put their cards on the table. What would one do with 'loom of the moon' (*U*: 55)? Is 'loom' something Penelopean to weave on (as most translators have decided), connected with a following 'toil' (from *texere*, weave): or else something dimly visible and looming – perhaps taken up by 'shining' in the next line? You pays your money . . . A simple question like 'Who is the long fellow running for the mayoralty . . . ?' (*U*: 313), though not ambiguous when spoken, is tricky in print. The Italian translation, 'Chi è quel lungo manigoldo che è candidato sindaco?', is wrong: the long fellow (Long John Fanning, not named), is not running for office, but backing candidates. But all wrong readings at least tell us something about *Ulysses*, and the examples given in particular about the hazards of identification. It is from the 'Cyclops' chapter where traps of naming or grammatical agreement become thematic concerns.

Stephen's dictum about Shakespeare's errors as portals of discovery (*U*: 190) seems to apply to the most humble readers. To define any reading as absolutely wrong may be futile, especially when semantic, homophonic and etymological coincidences are freely enlisted. 'Ties', which Stephen borrows from Mulligan (*U*: 37) are something to wear for decoration; but every loan is also a bond. Bloom watches, from the funeral carriage, a woman's nose 'whiteflattened against the pane', later he eats his lunch while '. . . stuck on the pane two flies buzzed' (*U*: 88, 175). Both of these are window panes and nothing else, and yet the themes in residence, love and death, also cause pain. In 'Hades' Bloom remembers the man in charge of the protestant cemetery: 'His garden Major Gamble calls Mount Jerome' (*U*: 110). The name was not invented but merely exploited by Joyce, who fitted it into his arrangement of mortality and thereby gave the reader a chance – never an obligation – to see in it yet one more circuitous reminder of death. 'Desolation', a weighty word forming a whole paragraph (*U*: 63), has nothing to do with Latin *sol*, sun, but with *solus*, alone. Yet this is the moment when that remarkable cloud begins to 'cover the sun slowly wholly' and Bloom's morning becomes in fact de-sunned for a while. *Finnegans Wake* will later purposefully take such accidental concurrencies of etymology in its semantic stride. One didactic value of *Ulysses* lies in its capacity to alert our senses, to train our skills, to confront us with decisions which no authority can make for us. Readings like the above are frank falsifications of the text, but they can be recircuited into patterns which are not entirely extraneous.

Since all the processes so far described, including the process of 'meaning', *are* processes they would be best expressed by active verbs. The pivotal sentence of Bloom's breakfast arrangements depends, not on 'things', 'breakfast', 'tray' or 'kitchen', but on the actions of moving and righting. As critical readers, we might take up the hint and do what we can to counteract the Western mind's tendency towards objects, things, nouns, categories.

Processes elude us while things can be handled, ordered, administered, categorised, classified, filed away, as nouns. Perhaps all we can do, given the nominal bias of our language habits, is to signal, from time to time, that we are dealing essentially, not with rigid substances, but with dynamic doings, relatings, meanings or rightings. Our own categories are necessary, but they remain *our own* categories. And perhaps we can guard against talking of structures, schemas, themes, narratives, etc., as though these were solid fixtures and not somehow encapsulated doings. Remeber only those once-fashionable interpretations which consisted in a run through the text, as with a Geiger counter, marking out passages which were termed epiphanies or symbols, as though these were things. That method of interpretation has outlived its usefulness, but the continued reification of terms like allusion, pun, or parody (all essentially actions) has a similarly deadening effect.

Much sterile arguing concerns what *Ulysses* 'is'; whether Bloom for instance 'is' or else 'is not' a Jew. To claim that *Ulysses* is a novel is as correct and inconclusive as to claim that Joyce is a Dubliner, an exile, a symbolist, a humorist, a perhapsed catholic, or a case of particular neurosis. If such formulas as '*Ulysses* is X; M'Intosh is Y; this is a symbol of Z . . .' could give way to phrasing like '*Ulysses* behaves in part like X', we would at least avoid the semblance of laying down a law. Verbs like 'This passage/phrase/chapter . . . performs, provokes, incites, questions . . .' frankly admit to their purely metaphorical function as convenient illustrations and could less misleadingly pose as the momentous truths which nominal fixations have a way of projecting.

Verbs have the added advantage of being formally less fixed, of changing with different persons, numbers, voices, moods. Their tenses reveal that they change with time, which in itself qualifies them for *Ulysses*; they don't even suggest the stability vitiating some otherwise valuable criticism. In its most naive, pedestrian sense, time infuses *Ulysses*. It is not just that the action naturally evolves in time; nor that we are made aware of clocks and watches, of a funeral looming at eleven, and a visit at four; nor that simultaneity is emphasised; nor that several times and cultures (the present, the characters' pasts, Irish history, Homeric, Semitic, Christian, Shakespearean ages, etc.) are conflated; nor even that the novel goes out of its diurnal way to compress centuries of linguistic growth into one chapter. *Ulysses* literally (in its letters) changes with the time the reading takes, and these temporal changes affect the reader. Bloom catches short his images of the East, the 'Kind of stuff you read: in the track of the sun' (*U*: 59). At this stage we can do little more than connect the phrases with Bloom's ideas of travelling around the earth in front of the sun. Hundreds of pages later we find out that Bloom actually has read something of the sort; his library contains the book *In the Track of the Sun* (*U*: 630). The earlier passage can then no longer remain what it has been (but it is questionable whether a first reader should already be short-circuited to Bloom's bookshelf by a well-meaning, interfering commentator).

That 'bowl of lather' in the book's first line is *not* a chalice, as *Notes for Joyce* misinforms its public.[7] But the bowl – in a manner of speaking – *will be* transformed into the chalice of the Mass just a few moments and three lines later, as soon as Buck Mulligan distinctly switches on his priestly role – just as the bowl will be reduced back to mere matter when it again becomes a 'nickel shaving bowl' (*U*: 17). This may amount to the tiniest qualitative difference in phrasing, but it is a vital one within the text's protean lifestyle.

The effect of delayed recognition is a Wakean feature. When we first come upon 'Pinck poncks that bail for seeks alicence' (*F W*: 32), we may play around with pick, pock, ping-pong, bail, licences, Alice, perhaps Belle Alliance, and many other things (and try to right them on our humpy tray). But we will not hear 'the bell for Sechseläuten', not until we come to the end of the first book, in Anna Livia's 'Pingpong! There's the Belle for Sexaloitez!' (*F W*: 213) and even then the meaning will only emerge if we have been told that 'Sechse-läuten' (as its name is) is an annual spring rite, when winter is driven out and the bells start ringing ('läuten') at six o'clock again in Zürich (where Joyce often attended the festival). Without such information a reader is still left with sexy bells loitering and a number of guesses. Once primed with that knowledge, the reader on a recircling tour will tackle the earlier sentence by changing it into an echo of something which it precedes.

Such temporal rightings occur in *Ulysses* too. (In a way, this whole essay is one.) 'O, lust . . .', initially, is simply lust; but the sequel, '. . . our refuge and our strength' (*U*: 423), transforms the beginning into a prayer and the whole into a blasphemous parallel reading. *Ulysses* changes, on re-reading, its letters and words and generates more configurations that could ever be recognised a first time, and it changes even more so if, between readings, one has visited Dublin, studied Aristotle or music hall songs, or taken a course in semiotics. It also changes because our previous moving about makes us aware of more contexts and alignments. Furthermore the book also seems to provide a narcissistic comment on its own idiosyncrasies (or should we say, with a verb 'its own behaving'?). In the 'Aeolus' chapter, Professor MacHugh steadies his glasses '. . . to a new focus' (*U*: 142). This further instance of righting is applicable to the chapter itself with its new technique and different perspectives which require the reader to adjust his own focus. 'Righting' has been treated here as such a narcissistic touch.

Temporal expediency should not be disregarded in the classroom or in guidebooks or notes. Not all information is equally helpful at all times, for certain insights would only confuse the novice and are better detained for opportune passages. Some relations simply do not 'make sense' at first, such as presenting the first chapter right away as some analogy to Homer and Telemachus. A student has many good reasons for remaining unconvinced and finding the correspondences forced. But later it might be a rewarding exercise to treat the whole chapter, for the sake of an argument, as though it were nothing but some adaptation from the Greek, or a continuation of *A Portrait*, or a re-enactment of the Mass, or a choreography of roles. It may be didactically useful to extract some kind of narrative 'norm' from the early chapters against which later extravagancies can be measured. But by the same token, a subsequent corrective reading can also help unmask such an empirical norm as yet another convention, no more and no less artificial and arbitrary than any that follow. Interpretations, too, have to be timed or, to return to the grammatical analogy, conjugated through the tenses and moods.

The model of some sort of conjugation helps to highlight a few facets of *Ulysses*, such as its gradual departure from the indicative mood (closer to reality) early on to more subjunctive, conditional, conjunctive, or optative ones, expressing wishes, hypotheses, contingencies, mere conjectures. The chapters of the second half seem based on various suppositions, *what if . . ,*, and Molly's monologue would in part be a return to the indicative mood.

But *Ulysses* never conforms very smoothly. At least one chapter, 'Ithaca', yields more inert data than verbs. In its diabolical advocation of substances and its accumulation of solid, factual information, measurements, statistics and inventories like department store catalogues, it reminds us more of things than of processes. Never are finite verbs less frequent than in this orgy of nominal fixation. We are aware of much abstract verbiage and of little syntax. Even visually the chapter is a series of separate blocks. It glorifies the Western mind's trust in systematisation and its proclivity to freeze, take apart, order and pigeonhole experience. One could redistribute most of the contents of the chapter in some different order (according to subject matter or even alphabetically) without violating its administrative spirit as much as one would similarly falsify the mood of 'Sirens' or 'Circe'.

And yet the 'Ithaca' chapter, almost more than any other, invites us to process the material it presents in such arid abundance. Even Joyce implied this when he confessed to Frank Budgen that the chapter, his favourite, was 'the ugly duckling of the book'. Ugly ducklings are notorious for changing into something one would not expect. Our trial run here is a sequence in which Bloom and Stephen urinate side by side in the back garden. Information is accumulated on issues we would never think of investigating, such as the position or visibility of 'their organs of micturition'. After learning that their gazes are elevated to what must be a lighted window, we may find the next question difficult to account for: 'Similarly?' It is far from clear which action may be similar to what other action, and we would never predict the kind of answer that is offered, in the terms of classical sciences like ballistics and physiology:

> Similarly?
>   The trajectories of their, first sequent, then simultaneous, urinations were dissimilar: Bloom's longer, less irruent, in the incomplete form of the bifurcated penultimate alphabetical letter who in his ultimate year at High School (1880) had been capable of attaining the point of greatest altitude against the whole concurrent strength of the institution, 210 scholars: Stephen's higher, more sibilant, who in the ultimate hours of the previous day had augmented by diuretic consumption an insistent vesical pressure. (*U*: 624)

In sorting out the data, we gain little insight by concentrating on the verbs: '. . . were . . . had been capable of attaining . . . had augmented', they perform mere ancillary or copulative functions. What the almost 40 substantives and adjectives do, is, primarily, to spawn more questions. It takes time – not much perhaps, but nevertheless time – just to figure out what it all means. And we may wonder how the whole tangential sketch fits into the narrative framework. Perhaps this is something like a scientific transcript of what goes on in the mind of, presumably, Bloom. We may sense the silence of the occasion and even that strange constraint of male timidity which often goes with it. In such a moment Bloom might compare the jets in front of him, and his memory might lead to a juvenile achievement and Bloom's only Olympic feat we hear of in the whole book, a veritable victory over strong competition. This allows for a Homeric sideglance too: Odysseus beating all competing suitors at wielding the bow. Bloom's interest in causality is prominent in general, so that here too he might relate Stephen's previous drinking with his present performance. But this is not what the text says, only what we can possibly extrapolate from it. There must be other ways to account for the why and the wherefore of the sequence; again the point is simply that reading means giving some kind of account, we bring back (or perhaps tra-ject) the passage back to some of the norms it questions.

This we can do be releasing the verbs from their nominal wraps, obvious enough with 'urination' or 'consumption'. A trajectory has to do with something thrown (*Ulysses* takes great interest in everything 'thrown away', and in making water). We can extract motion from 'irruent' or 'insistent', and noise from 'sibilant', which may in fact lead us to reconsider even 'dissimilar' and its circumambient esses for acoustic effect. Above all we can savour the reticent beauty of a participle, Bloom having triumphed over '. . . the whole *concurrent* strength' of his High School, in a word which runs many meanings together.

The two curves, the main topic of the paragraph, are laid out, so to speak, for inspection and comparison and for us to wonder what else these graphs may tell us about the protagonists, the symbolic relationships or the novel itself. The two oddly misplaced relative clauses link the present urination to Bloom's remote past (by association) and Stephen's recent past (by causality). But a future is codetermined too: altitude is an attainment of youth. Bloom, 24 years from his apogee, may be conscious of his waning powers, and we may find ourselves transferring a word like 'strength' to a different context (just as we do when Molly Bloom thinks of 'the strength those engines have in them like big giants . . .' (*U*: 675–6)).

Scientific terminology purports to be accurate as well as non-distractive. The passage strives for this but does not quite succeed; against its overt intentions it suggests spurious patterns. Stephen's higher trajectory connects with 'altitude', but only coincidentally with 'High School'. Is there any meaningful relation between the conspicious clutter of '. . . ultimate year . . . ultimate hours of the previous day' and the intrusive 'penultimate letter'? A ghostly configuration of ultimacy arises, to be relegated, most likely, to some more remote level of significance, but vaguely disturbing in the foreground. Many such polysyllabic signposts in the 'Ithaca' chapter seem more useful as markers for the various subsections than for instant communication.

And how to accommodate that gratuitous 'bifurcated penultimate alphabetical letter', worked in, it seems, to illustrate a shape (but incompletely at that)? It waits for further co-ordination among the primary concerns of the passage. It is up to us to speculate, at some further remove, that Stephen's and Bloom's ways will soon bifurcate. Incomplete form characterises much in the lives of the characters, it is a strategy of the text and demands the readers' supplementation (there is thus also a return to a remote beginning, 'The Sisters', with incomplete sentences and deficient information – the first injunction to readers is to complete the forms). And we happen to be in the book's penultimate chapter. Homer's works were divided, by later editors, into 24 books designated by the 24 letters of the Greek alphabet. The penultimate book of the *Odyssey* concerns itself with the recognition of Odysseus and Penelope: the corresponding scene in *Ulysses* is close at hand. But in the Greek the second last letter was *Psi* and not Y. By grace of English homophony, however, the sound of the penultimate letter is identical with a potent interrogative: this 'why' is behind Bloom's curiosity, and it introduces many of the questions in the chapter, including many a reader will ask on top of it. The urge to look into cause, motive, reason, purpose, etc. was perfected by the Greeks, among them thinkers like Pythagoras, a man who held forth about numbers, triangles and heavenly bodies, as well as about metempsychosis. He might well be the patron saint of 'Ithaca' (one could not, in those times, go through High School without hearing about him). He never, as far as we know, lectured on micturition, but because he used the letter Y to illustrate the divergent paths of virtue and vice, it came to be known as the 'letter of Pythagoras'. All of which may have very little to do with the passage except that the text by its odd concatenations seems to provoke a search for centrifugal justification.

But – to return to the matter at hand – what exactly did happen at that unique exploit which Bloom recalls, his attaining 'the point of greatest altitude against the whole concurrent strength of the institution, 210 scholars'? Raleigh states succinctly that 'Bloom wins a contest by urinating higher than any of his 210 classmates'.[8] How did they organise those contests, back in 1880, in the limited area of a Dublin school? surely not by lining up 210 athletes, vesically ready at the word 'go' – that is, not simultaneously. Then perhaps 'sequently', with markings on a wall (and with no spoilsport cleaning staff to intervene)? Such was in fact the practice at British schools, but if we accept that version, then the contest was not, strictly speaking, 'concurrent'. We cannot trust the vocabulary which makes such a show of being objective. And once distrust has set in – and it is general all over 'Ithaca' – confidence is basically undermined: we are thrown back to guesswork, precisely what the elaborate wording strains to eliminate. What *really* (the chapter fills us in on reality) took place? The school presumably *had* 210 (or perhaps 211, counting Bloom extra) students at one time; which looks like a verifiable fact, but the stylisation of them as 'scholars' itself throws some odd light on it. It is just conceivable that a smaller group of boys discovered at one time Bloom's prowess (habitual or accidental), and that someone offered a remark that Bloom must be the champion of the whole bleeding school, and that some such memory, in the pedantic deadpan nature of 'Ithaca' (which has not been programmed to register irony, levity or hyperbole) would become objectified. This would be similar to Bloom's having been 'baptised', as another paragraph has it, '. . . under a pump in the village of Swords' (*U*: 603). One thing all the Nostos chapters do is to question the relationship between a report and the event itself.

The passage poses as an answer, but it offers solutions to questions we would never have asked in the first place. Whatever our interest focuses on, we will have to interpret and sort out, supply the verbs of action. As it happens, High School pupils often encounter the symbol Y (a bit less often than its companion X, which is scattered all over *Ulysses*): inevitably and kinetically it stands for something to be figured out. The teacher insists that it be righted, translated into some satisfactory arrangement of letters and numbers which is then called the solution.

The preceding chapter, 'Eumaeus', has prepared us for the chanciness of equations: '. . . as to who he in reality was let XX equal my right name and address, as Mr Algebra remarks *passim*' (*U*: 578). Mr Algebra and his colleagues have taken over the later chapters and spare no efforts, but theirs have to be supplemented by ours. Innumerable new sets of approaches, different systems of reprocessing, alternative points of view (some entirely irrational), but none of the new equations are solutions, the meaning, if any, seems to consist in the equating processes.

The retarded sting of 'Ithaca' lies in the defamiliarised terminology, which diversifies itself into the language of emotion, values, decisions and doings, of verbs simple and complex. One such verb is laboriously introduced, but not named, in grammatical paraphrases: '. . . the natural grammatical transition by inversion involving no alteration of sense of an aorist preterite proposition (parsed as masculine subject, monosyllabic onomatopoeic transitive verb with direct feminine object) from the active voice into its correlative aorist preterite proposition (parsed as feminine subject, auxiliary verb and quasimonosyllabic onomatopoeic past participle with complementary masculine agent)' (*U*: 655). Molly will translate that one later on, in plain words (*U*: 701). Joyce elaborately and deviously works in the conjugation of a verb around which some of the off-stage action of *Ulysses* turns. From hints such as these many critics have concentrated, perhaps rightly, on conjugal relations and, perhaps less rightly, on conjugal imperatives.

Here the emphasis is on conjugation itself, one of many names for a dynamic process. *Ulysses* refuses to stay put. Once we know what it *is* we are sure to be wrong. The nominal inertia of the 'Ithaca' chapter, the book's most solid fixation on the surface of it, vexes us into re-conjugating, yoking and joining, its elements and treating anew whatever went before. In the beginning was the verb, and it energises everything from breakfast preparation and morning shave through all the fumbles and trials of Bloomsday and night down to Molly's final turnings, and even more the lettered choreography of the next work, the 'reconjungation of nodebinding ayes' of *Finnegans Wake* (*F W*: 143), a book with one humpy character and much moving about, many 'curios of signs' (*F W*: 18) in wrong writing, blatantly in need to be righted by its own re-formations and the rightings of every mutable reader.

Notes

1   'But once at the war the conscientious objector became a jusqu'aboutist. When the others wanted to abandon the siege he insisted on staying . . .' Frank Budgen, *James Joyce and the Making of 'Ulysses'* (London: Oxford University Press, 1972), 16–17.

2   James Joyce, *Ulysses: A Facsimile of the Manuscript* (London: Faber & Faber, 1975), 'Hades', p. 1.

3   The one exception seems to be the Danish translation by Mogens Boisen. In its first edition of 1949, the wording was: 'Han trak døren til efter sig og smækkede den, saa at den cluttede tæt.' In the revision of 1970, this had become, more accurately, '. . . og smækkede den tæt, til den lukkede tæt.'

4   'No, . . . I have the words already. What I am seeking is the perfect order of words in the sentence. There is an order in every way appropriate.' Budgen, *op. cit*. p. 20. By 1918 the perfect order for the sentence under discussion was 'Perfumes of embraces assailed him. His hungered flesh obscurely, mutely craved to adore.' (*Ulysses: A Facsimile*, op. cit., 'Lestrygonians', p. 15) In the final text this was to become, more perfectly righted, 'Perfume of embraces all him assailed. With hungered flesh obscurely, he mutely craved to adore' (*U*: 168).

5   Paul P.J. Van Caspel, *Bloomers on the Liffey: Eisegetical Readings of James Joyce's Ulysses Part II* (Groningen, 1980) 292 pages, A dissertation.

6   Cyril Pearl, *Dublin in Bloomtime* (London: Angus & Robertson, 1969). Page 17 shows a picture of 'The Martello Tower at Sandymount', which is correct, but not that Joyce lived there 'from 9th September to 19th September 1904'; he lived in the tower at Sandycove, where *Ulysses* opens.

7 Don Gifford with Robert J. Seidman, *Notes for Joyce* (New York: Dutton, 1974), p. 6.
8 John Henry Raleigh, *The Chronicle of Leopold and Molly Bloom: Ulysses as Narrative* (Berkeley: University of California Press, 1977), p. 39.

CHAPTER 2

An Introduction to *Finnegans Wake**

Colin MacCabe

Context

In 1922, on his fortieth birthday, James Joyce's *Ulysses* was published. The fruit of seven years' work, Joyce had started the book as an unknown English teacher in Trieste and had completed it as an acknowledged major author in Paris. Ezra Pound's efforts on his behalf had ensured that both *A Portrait of the Artist as a Young Man*, Joyce's first novel, and the early drafts of *Ulysses* had been enthusiastically received in London literary circles. The public acclaim that Joyce now enjoyed was accompanied by financial security because Harriet Shaw Weaver, who had published *A Portrait*, made him a regular allowance. It was in these favourable circumstances that Joyce began to write a book which was to take him 17 years to complete and which, once published, was to be almost universally castigated as the product of charlatanism or insanity (or both). This is the book that we know as *Finnegans Wake*. Although a huge number of scholarly studies have since been written, explicating the text with reference sometimes to Joyce's life, sometimes to the books he read, sometimes to the languages he spoke, and very frequently with reference to all three and more, *Finnegans Wake*, nevertheless, remains inaccessible to most readers.

In *Finnegans Wake* Joyce attempted to write a book which would take all history and knowledge for its subject matter and the workings of the dreaming mind for its form. If one takes a page at random from *Finnegans Wake*, one may find reference to subjects as disparate as chemistry, Irish mythology, philosophy, American history, details from Joyce's life, all woven together in a language which constantly creates new words by fusing and shortening old ones or by borrowing from the many European languages that Joyce knew. The result of this deformation of language is that every word carries

* Originally published in the British Council Series *Notes for Literature*

more than one meaning and each sentence opens out onto an infinity
of interpretations. Joyce explained his method to a friend when he
said: 'In writing of the night, I really could not, I felt I could not, use
words in their ordinary connections. Used that way they do not
express how things are in the night, in the different stages – conscious, then semi-conscious, then unconscious.'[1] The difficulty of the
language is compounded by difficulty of divining what story this
extraordinary language is recounting. Figures change name and
transform themselves into their opposites, appear and disappear
without any obvious rationality. Joyce's claim for his method was
that it enabled the articulation of areas of experience which were
barred from conventional language and plot. He told Miss Weaver:
'One great part of every human existence is passed in a state which
cannot be rendered sensible by the use of wideawake language,
cutanddry grammar and goahead plot.'[2]

Many critics have complained that Joyce's last book marks a
major change from his earlier work and that his interest in language
had become a self-indulgent aberration. But such criticism ignores
the fact that from his earliest work, Joyce was obsessed with language, with its structure and its effects. Above all his writing focusses
on the methods by which identity is produced in language. The
opening passage of *A Portrait* demonstrates this production:

> 'Once upon a time and a very good time it was there was a moocow
> coming down along the road and this moo-cow that was coming down
> along the road met a nicens little boy named baby tuckoo. . . .
> His father told him that story: his father looked at him through a glass:
> he had a hairy face.
> He was baby tuckoo. The moocow came down the road where Betty
> Byrne lived: she sold lemon platt.
> *O, the wild rose blossoms*
> *On the little green place*.
> He sang that song. That was his song.
> *O, the green wothe botheth*.
> When you wet the bed, first it is warm then it gets cold. His mother put
> on the oilsheet. That had the queer smell.
> His mother had a nicer smell than his father. She played on the piano the
> sailor's hornpipe for him to dance. He danced:
> *Tralala lala*
> *Tralala tralaladdy*
> *Tralala lala*
> *Tralala lala*. (P: 7)

In this passage we move from the paternal narrator who tells us a story and fixes an identity (the listening child realises that he is baby tuckoo and that he can locate himself in a definite spatio-temporal identity) to the mother's voice in which stories are dissolved into the sounds, smells and sensations of the body. It is the deformation of language in 'O, the green wothe botheth' that signals the transition to a world where the material of language (the sound of *Tralala*) has dominance over meaning. The identity of the story gets lost in the confused and disparate experiences of the body. While the father fixes with his eye, the mother displaces into the world of the ear. On the one hand we find the self and the father, the authority of meaning and society and, on the other hand, we find the body and the mother, the subversion of sound and desire. This movement from identity to infancy is one that we repeat each night as we enter the timeless world of dreams where words become things and we reverse the process each morning as we wake to the temporal continuity of meaning. Language changes its nature in the passage between these two realms. A normal syntax and morphology (cutanddry grammar) is appropriate to the normality of stories (goahead plot) but as soon as we begin to pay attention to the material constituents of words in either the spoken or written form then we find ourselves slipping into the world of desire. And this eruption of the material of language is not confined to the sleeping life or dreams. Jokes and verbal slips are the most obvious example in our waking life when another order of language interrupts the normal flow of communication. When Joyce claimed that in *Finnegans Wake* he was investigating a 'great part of every human existence' which escaped normal linguistic relations, he was not simply claiming to represent accurately a sleeping mind but rather to be investigating a vital dimension of our being which, although more evident in dreams, insists in our waking life as well. His earlier works and their experiments with narrative and language made the writing of *Finnegans Wake* possible but both his methods and his topics remain remarkably constant throughout his adult life as we can see in the extract that we looked at from *A Portrait*.

The importance of the opposition between the invisible language of the story and the material language of desire is evident throughout *Finnegans Wake* but it is towards the end as Anna Livia, both mother and river, flows to her death that it is stated in one of its simplest forms. As Anna thinks back over her past life, she remembers how much her husband (the ubiquitous figure who is indicated by the letters HCE) wanted a daughter, hoping for a female in the family who would believe his stories, who would give to him the respect that he feels is his due. But the father is inevitably disappointed for the mother teaches her daughter that beneath the stories and the identities lies the world of letters and desire. While the father tells the son stories, the mother teaches the daughter the alphabet: 'If you spun your yarns to him on the swishbarque waves I was spelling my yearns to her over cottage cake' (*F W*: 620). The father's yarns (stories) are displaced by the mother's yearns (desires); telling gives way to spelling. It is this struggle between meaning and sound, between story and language, between male and female that *Finnegans Wake* enacts, introducing the reader to a world in which his or her own language can suddenly reveal new desires beneath old meanings as the material of language forms and reforms.

If the language attempts to investigate the processes by which we are constructed in the world of sense and syntax, the stories that we piece together from the mosaic of the *Wake* constantly return us to the place of that construction: the family. As the text throws out references to the world's religions and philosophies, to geography and astronomy, we come back again and again to the most banal and local of all problems. What is the nature of the obscure sexual offence that the father, HCE, is charged with? And is he guilty? Only the mother Anna Livia Plurabelle, ALP, seems to know the definitive answers to these questions. The mother has written or will write (tenses become interchangeable in the timeless world of the *Wake*) a letter which will explain all but the letter is difficult to identify and decipher. It was dictated to one of her sons, Shem, a writer of ill repute, who is likely to have altered the contents, and may have been delivered by her other son, Shaun, a nauseating worldly success. The two brothers are engaged in a constant conflict, often occasioned by sexual rivalry. In some obscure way their sister, Issy, might hold the solution to the problems of her father and brothers but she refuses to say anything at all serious as she is quite content to gaze endlessly at herself in the mirror.

If language, the family and sexuality provide three of the emphases of Joyce's last work, there is a fourth which is as important: death. Indeed the title of the book, *Finnegans Wake*, makes clear this concern. The immediate reference is to a song of almost identical title (only an apostrophe differentiates them): *Finnegan's Wake*. This tells the story of an Irish bricklayer who went to work one morning with a terrible hangover and, as a result, fell off his ladder. His friends presume that he is dead and take him home to 'wake' him, that is to spend the night before the funeral drinking beside the dead body. During the wake a fight breaks out and a bottle of whiskey breaks by Tim's head. No sooner has some whiskey trickled into his mouth than he revives and joins in the fun of his own funeral (which thus becomes a *'funferal'* (*F W*: 120)). The ambiguity of the 'wake' of Joyce's title, which refers both to part of the funeral process (Finnegan's wake) and to the general awakening of all the Finnegans (Finnegans wake without an apostrophe), indicates the inseparability of life and death in the world of language. To come to life, to recognise one's separate existence, is also to allow the possibility of its termination, its end. *Finnegans Wake* not only puns on two meanings of 'wake' but the first word contains both an end ('fin' is French for 'end') and a new beginning ('egan' tells us that everything will start 'again'). And this process will be the negation (negans) of the ordinary processes of language, an attention to the trace ('wake' in its third sense) left by the passage of language. The clarity of communication will be disturbed by the material trace of the letter that any communication leaves in its wake.

Death and sexuality, the construction of language within the family drama, Joyce's text is no self-indulgent whim but an engagement with the very matter of our being. In his attempt to break away from the 'evidences' of conventional narrative with its fixed causality and temporality, two Italian thinkers, Giordano Bruno and Giambattista Vico, were of profound importance in the writing of *Finnegans Wake*. In understanding the importance of these figures it is not enough to sketch the positive features of their thought, one must also understand what Joyce is avoiding by his use of these theorists, what presuppositions he is denying.

Giordano Bruno was a philosopher of the Italian Renaissance. After becoming a Dominican friar he flirted with the varieties of Protestant reformism as well as interesting himself in hermetic philosophy. His unorthodox beliefs and his final death at the stake as a heretic in 1600 had interested Joyce from an early age. Bruno's principle of the 'coincidence of contraries' denied the existence of absolute identities in the universe. Bruno argued that oppositions collapsed into unities at their extremes, thus extreme heat and extreme cold were held to be indistinguishable, and all identities were, therefore, provisional. Bruno joined this belief to a belief in an infinite universe composed of an infinity of worlds. There is an obvious level at which such theories offer some explanations of both the constant transformation of characters into their opposites in *Finnegans Wake* and the infinite worlds opened up by the 'dream within a dream' structure of the text. But to understand Joyce as simply providing an artistic gloss to the theories of an obscure philosopher is to minimise crucially the importance of the *Wake*. Bruno is important insofar as he provides a philosophical trellis on which the philosophical and linguistic presuppositions of identity can be unpicked. At one level of consciousness we claim an identity and stability both for ourselves and our objects of perception. But such identities can only be produced by a process of differentiation in which other identities are rejected. This rejection, however, presupposes that other identities are possible. The paradoxical feature of identity is that its conditions of existence allow the possibility of its very contradiction. It is this play of identity that Joyce investigates in the *Wake* where language no longer has to presuppose non-contradiction and everybody becomes everybody else in an infinite series of substitutions and juxtapositions which never attain some imaginary finality but constantly break, reform and start again.

Giambattista Vico is, arguably, even more important to the structure and content of *Finnegans Wake*. His name occurs (in suitably distorted form) in the opening sentence of the book as does a reference to his cyclical theory of history. A Neapolitan philosopher of the eighteenth century, Vico was one of the first to propose a general theory of historical change. He held that history was a cyclical process in which civilisation proceeded from a theocratic to an aristocratic to a democratic age and that, at the end of the democratic age, civilisation passed through a short period of destruction, the *ricorso*, which recommenced the cycle.

The very plan of *Finnegans Wake*, with its three long books and a short concluding one, bears witness to Vico's importance. It is not only Vico's historical theories which figure in the *Wake*, there is also much play with his account of the birth of language and civilisation. According to Vico, primitive man, surprised in the sexual act by a clap of thunder, is stricken with fear and guilt at what he imagines is the angered voice of God. He retires into a cave to conceal his activities and it is this act which inaugurates civilisation. Language arises when man attempts to reproduce the sound of thunder with his own vocal organs. Once again, however, it would be wrong to understand Joyce's use of Vico as the artistic illustration of philosophical theses. What Vico's theory offers is both an initial articulation of language, sexuality and society and, more importantly, a theory to oppose to dominant historicist accounts of history. Historicism understands the historical process to be subordinate to a dominant principle, which can only be understood in terms of the 'end' to which it is progressing. When Stephen Dedalus and Mr Deasy discuss history in the second chapter of *Ulysses*, Mr Deasy claims that 'All history moves towards one great goal, the manifestation of God' (*U*: 40). This historicism imposes on the individual a meaning in which he is already defined. Stephen refuses such a meaning and identity when he claims that God is simply a noise in the street, the undifferentiated sound from which we fabricate meaning. It is by plunging into this sound that we can unmake the meanings imposed on us and awake from the nightmare of history into the dream of language. By insisting on the infinite repeatability of any moment, by refusing a progression to history, one can refuse the ready-made identities offered to us in order to investigate the reality of the processes that construct us. By denying an end to history, we can participate in the infinite varieties of the present. Bruno and Vico are used in *Finnegans Wake* to aid the deconstruction of identity into difference and to replace progress with repetition. But if Joyce used these thinkers it was largely to displace the dominant conceptions of the everyday novel of identity and temporality and not because they hold some intrinsic truth.

The text

To attempt a summary of the events of *Finnegans Wake* is both necessary and misleading. Necessary in that there are strands of narrative that we can follow through the text, misleading in that such narratives are always dispersed into other narratives. In an essay of this length it is only possible to look at one of the seventeen chapters of the *Wake*, and I have chosen chapter 7 of Book 1, the portrait of Shem the Penman, as one of the more immediately accessible sections of the text. The six chapters that lead up to it have taken us through both a synopsis of all the themes of the book (chapter 1) and then through a series of accounts of HCE's obscure and unmentionable crime and his trial (chapters 2–4). The letter which is so crucial to an understanding of all the issues at stake is discussed in chapter 5. Chapter 6 is composed of a set of questions and answers about the characters discussed in the letter and ends with a question about Shem. The whole of chapter 7 (the one we shall consider in a little more detail) is devoted to Shem the writer and at the end of this chapter he gives way to his mother, Anna Livia, whose life and activities are discussed in chapter 8. Book 2 transfers the scene from the whole city of Dublin to a particular public house in Chapelizod, one of Dublin's suburbs. In chapter 1 the children play outside the pub and in chapter 2 they have been put to bed in one of the rooms above the bar where they conduct their nightlessons, lessons which intermingle academic subjects with the discovery of sexuality. Chapter 3 takes place in the bar over which the children are sleeping. Customers and publican (HCE) gossip the evening away and when they have all left the innkeeper falls asleep on the floor in a drunken stupor and dreams about the story of Tristram and Iseult, this dream composing the major topic of chapter 4. Book 3 finds the innkeeper asleep in bed and chapters 1–3 deal with Shaun in his various manifestations as man of the world. At the end of chapter 3 Shaun dissolves into the voices of other characters and in chapter 4 the father and mother, woken by the cries of one of the children, make rather unsatisfactory love as dawn breaks. Book 4 sees the coming of dawn and the start of a new cycle. The mother Anna Livia is now old and looks back over her past life before she dissolves into the sea of death which starts the cycle again.

The portrait of Shem (*F W*: 169–95) is unflattering in the extreme. He is accused of endless crimes and perversions. The officious tone of the opening sentences suggests that it is the rival brother, Shaun, speaking. Shaun, a pillar of society and an exemplar of moral rectitude, accuses Shem of refusing to be a proper member of society. To this end Shaun employs every kind of racist and anti-semitic slur. Shem is accused of being a sham and a forger, never able to be himself, to assume a definite identity, but constantly imitating others in his writing. His immense pride goes together with an absolute refusal to join in the patriotic struggle which would offer him the chance of achieving true manhood. Instead he prefers to occupy himself with the affairs of women. Shaun describes the particularly obscene process by which Shem's books are composed (we will look in detail at this description) and how Shem was arrested because of his books. After we have read the details of the arrest, we find ourselves at a trial where Shaun, in the person of Justius, tries Shem, in the person of Mercius. Mercius is accused of irreligion, of corrupting women, of squandering money and, most importantly, of being mad. It would seem that Mercius (Shem) is going to be unable to answer the last charge (the quintessential accusation aimed at those who refuse to conform), but, at the last moment, Anna Livia speaks through his mouth and evades Justius' (Shaun's) accusations. The process by which the mother speaks through the son reduplicates the whole effort of writing *Finnegans Wake*, in which the mother is finally given a voice. Shaun's demand that Shem identify himself, the policeman's request for identification, is avoided by a throwing into doubt of sexual identity. The apparatus by which the police of identity control the progress of history can be undercut by the assertion of an interminable, never complete, bi-sexuality.

If this imperfect summary indicates some of the drift of the chapter on Shem, we can now look, in a little more detail, at the description of Shem's method of writing. The lines in question occur after an explanation, in Latin, of the alchemical operations by which the body's waste matter is transformed into ink with the aid of a perverted religious prayer:

> Then, pious Eneas, conformant to the fulminant firman which enjoins on the tremylose terrian that, when the call comes, he shall produce nichthemerically from his unheavenly body a no uncertain quantity of obscene matter not protected by copriright in the United States of Ourania or bedeed and bedood and bedang and bedung to him, with this double dye, brought to blood heat, gallic acid on iron ore, through the bowels of his misery, flashly, faithly, nastily, appropriately, this Esuan Menschavik and the first till last alshemist wrote over every square inch of the only foolscap available, his own body, till by its corrosive sublimation one continuous present tense integument slowly unfolded all marryvoising moodmoulded cyclewheeling history (thereby, he said, reflecting from his own individual person life unlivable, transaccidentated through the slow fires of consciousness into a dividual chaos, perilous, potent, common to allflesh, human only, mortal) but with each word that would not pass away the squidself which he had squirtscreened from the crystalline world waned chagreenold and doriangrayer in its dudhud. (*F W* : 185–6)

We can get an initial perspective on how this sentence functions by examining earlier versions which occur in Joyce's notebooks.[3] The first, very short, draft of chapter 7 contains some preliminary suggestions, in Latin, of the equation between writing and excretion which the final text insists on but there is no hint of the English passage we are considering. In the next draft, however, we can read: 'With the dye he wrote minutely, appropriately over every part of the only foolscap available, his own body, till integument slowly unfolded universal history & that self which he hid from the world grew darker & darker in outlook.' Joyce then started to revise the sentence (all additions are italicised): 'With the *double* dye he wrote minutely, appropriately over every part of the only foolscap available, his own body, till *one* integument slowly unfolded universal history *the reflection from his individual person of life unlivable transaccidentated in the slow fire of consciousness into a dividual chaos, perilous, potent, common to all flesh, mortal only*, & that self which he hid from the world grew darker & darker in *its* outlook.'

In the first version of the sentence we are given an account of how the writer produces his work. The sentence is not syntactically difficult or lexically complex with the exception of the word 'integument' which means a 'covering' or 'skin' and which refers here to the parchment, the material, on which the text is written. The text itself is, of course, *Finnegans Wake* (a universal and atemporal history) but it is also earlier manuscripts. There is no question of understanding writing as an aesthetic production of a disembodied and creative mind; to write is to engage in a transaction between body and language, word and flesh. It is not surprising that this activity may seem to resemble the small infant's play with all the parts and productions of his body for throughout *Finnegans Wake* adult behaviour is never far distant from children's play and phantasy. But if the writer is transforming his body into the text we are reading, his self, hidden from the world, is becoming more and more pessimistic. The first editions emphasise that Joyce is working with a 'double dye' (both ink and excrement) which he is transforming into the 'one integument' that we are reading. The major addition to the text ('the reflections' to 'mortal only') is one of the clearest statements of the process that produces *Finnegans Wake*. The text starts from the 'unlivable' life of the 'individual' and 'transaccidents' it into a 'dividual chaos'. The invented word 'transaccidentated' refers to the Catholic Mass and to the doctrine of *transubstantiation* which holds that the consecrated bread has been transformed into the body of Christ. The Church explains this process with reference to the Aristotelian distinction between the essential nature of a thing (its substance) and the inessential features (its accidents). After the consecration in the Mass, the bread is merely an 'accident' while the 'substance' is Christ's body. Joyce's writing also involves a transformation of the body but there is no question of an appeal to any ultimate 'substance'. Shem's whole life is a series of accidents, both in the modern sense of 'unfortunate and arbitrary events' and in the philosophical sense that Shem is all inessential features ('accidents') without any essential identity ('substance'). Through concentrating on the 'accidental', the writing unmakes the 'individual' to investigate the 'dividual chaos' that constitutes the 'unlivable life'. The presuppositions of identity are displaced to reveal the divisions from which we are all fabricated into unity.

In the text's final version we find that Joyce has added a proper name ('Eneas'), a demonstrative phrase ('this Esuan Menschavik') and a definite description ('the first till last alshemist') to expand the pronoun 'he' at the beginning of the sentence. The first proper name is modified by a clause governed by a present participle modelled on the Latin ('conformant . . .'). This clause in turn contains a relative clause ('which enjoins . . .') which contains within it a further subordinate clause ('that . . . he shall . . . or bedeed . . .') which is itself modified by an adverbial clause of time ('when the call comes'). The effect of this syntactic complexity is that one has a tendency to read each clause or phrase in a variety of relations with surrounding groups of words. Without seriously transgressing the rules of English syntax at any stage, Joyce so confuses the reader that although each grammatical step will be followed, the phrases and words begin to function outside any grammatical relationship, taking on a multitude of meanings.[4] At the same time Joyce repeats, with variations, the main theme of the sentence as well as introducing topics from elsewhere in the book. Vico's thunder God makes an appearance in 'fulminant firman' (through the Latin *fulmen*, a thunderbolt). His command equates the 'call of nature' which reminds one of the necessity of excretion with the writer's 'call' or vocation. A further term is added to this equation with the introduction of a set of chemical references which link writing to digestion. The first meaning one might attach to 'tremylose' would be *tremulous*, fearful, but the -ose suffix is a biochemical suffix indicating a sugar. Similarly 'nichthemerically' suggests some bio-chemical process although the 'nicht' refers both to the nocturnal (night) and the negative (through the German *nicht*, not) features of the writing of *Finnegans Wake*.

The reference to copyright and the United States of America refer to Joyce's own law suits in that country where *Ulysses* was both condemned as obscene and published without Joyce's permission. It thus provides more details of Shem's life but the presence of 'anus' in 'Ourania' and 'copro' (Greek for dung) in 'copriright' insist on the presence of the body in all Shem's activities.

The opening phrase of the final version ('Then, pious Eneas') illustrates a common device of the *Wake* in quoting famous phrases from European literature in a context which robs them of their sense. The phrase is used frequently in Virgil's epic, the *Aeneid*, where it functions in the narrative as an indication that one part of the action is finished and another is about to begin. Within the *Wake* such a phrase merely emphasises that we are reading a narrative which has no ability to distinguish between ends and beginnings as everything is written in an atemporal present. The other description conferred on Shem ('this Esuan Menschavik') confirms the charge that Shem is a loser in the game of life as it identifies him with Esau (who lost his birthright to Isaac) and the Mensheviks (who lost to the Bolsheviks in the Russian Revolution).

If we now turn to the end of the sentence and look at the transformation from the first draft to the final version then we find once again that the simple meaning has been multiplied through a series of lexical coinages and literary references. The original version claims that there is a correspondence between the degeneration of the artist's self and the production of the book from the material of his body. The final version states that the words that he is producing will not disappear and that the self which he had tried to hide behind the skirts of women and squirts of ink ('squirtscreened') is becoming sadder and older as it is affected by the book. In the coinage 'doriangrayer', there is a reference to Oscar Wilde's *The Picture of Dorian Gray*, a story of a beautiful young man whose picture ages although he, himself, remains young. In its confusion of art and life, of body and representation, Wilde's story is also Joyce's. What *Finnegans Wake* suggests is that it is the story of us all and that if we wish to read this story of ourselves then we must enter into an experience of language more radical than any offered by the literary tradition.

This reading of a sentence from *Finnegans Wake* is not in any way exhaustive. All I have indicated is some of the processes by which *Finnegans Wake* involves the reader in a complicated network of signification which is never completed. *Finnegans Wake* does not ask

for an interpretation that will identify it but for another set of
elements to continue its work.

Notes

1   Max Eastman, *The Literary Mind* (New York: Scribner's, 1931), p. 101,
    quoted in Richard Ellmann, *James Joyce* (London: Oxford University
    Press, 1959), p. 559.
2   Ellmann *op. cit.*, p. 597.
3   David Hayman, *A First-Draft Version of Finnegans Wake* (Austin:
    University of Texas Press, 1963), p. 112, 118–9.
4   For a more detailed consideration of the linguistic procedures adopted
    by Joyce see Colin MacCabe, 'Joyce and Chomsky: The Body and
    Language', *James Joyce Broadsheet*, Vol. 1. No. 2, June 1980.

READINGS

CHAPTER 3

Silence in *Dubliners*

Jean-Michel Rabaté

So this is *Dubliners*.

Hush! Caution! Echoland!

The scene: Dbln, a besieged city; war has been going on for years, walls have been erected around it, critics have dug underground, undermining, hoping to bring back a fossil or some skeleton from the crypt of the author's past. Well, all be dumbed! (Silent) A password, thanks. Shall I try the password, voicing the mute word of power all would wish to hear?

When I was still fumbling around the doors, hesitating, searching for a new mode of access to this text, I had only a handful of questions to start with, prompted in part by Hermann Broch's readings of Joyce, in part by a reflection on the difference between the silence of the analyst and the silence of the priest during confession. Now that I am trying to thread my little wire of commentary through the many previous interpretations of *Dubliners*, I would like to point out that such an initial discouragement (why not keep silent, or else turn to the more rewarding mysteries of *Finnegans Wake*?) is a move which has been calculated by the strategies of the text.

The question of the silence of interpretation is built within the text, prepared and foreseen in the deceptive game it plays with the reader. This, as I see it, is the primary function of the silences of the text. For there are different kinds of silences: silence can mean the inversion of speech, its mirror, that which structures its resonance, since without silence, speech becomes a mere noise, a meaningless clatter; silence can reveal a gap, a blank space in the text, that can be accounted for in terms of the characters who betray themselves by slips, lapsus, omissions; or in terms of the general economy of the text, silence being the void element which ensures displacement, hence circulation. Silence can finally appear as the end, the limit, the death of speech, its paralysis. There, silence joins both the mute symptoms (Eveline's aphasia is a good example of this in *Dubliners*) and the work of Thanatos inscribed in the production of writing.

The problematics of silence can offer an approach which would go beyond the facile antagonism between the surface realism of the stories and the suggestions, allusions and quasi-symbolist tactics of inferring by cross-references. The only way to gain a broader perspective is to introduce the silent process of reading into the text. Thus one can keep in mind the insistent ethical function of the stories (Joyce knew he was writing a 'chapter of the moral history of my country' (*Letters*, II: 134)) and their political relevance, see these as confronted with the construction of a real Irish capital through literature ('Is it not possible for a few persons of character and culture to make Dublin a capital such as Christiania has become?' (*Letters*, II: 105)), a construction which opposes any capitalistic exploitation. The mirror held up to the Irish may well be nicely polished, it is not dependent on a theory of pure mimesis, nor of purely symbolist implications. *Dubliners* is not, on the other hand, a direct consequence of Joyce's current theories of aesthetics, such as Stephen expounds them; it is rather the theory itself, in its wider sense, which is mirrored in the text, where it is coupled with the utmost degree of precision and particularity, in the pragmatics of writing which deconstructs the voices of the characters, narrators, commentators, and paves the way toward the constitution of another rhetoric of silences, the silences of the writing being caught up by the silent reading-writing which transforms a collection of short stories into a text.

My question will then become: in what sense does this book offer a theory of its own interpretation, of its reading, of possible meta-discourses about its textuality? In what way is there the temptation of an identification, with what aspects of the text, and to what effects? If, finally, *Dubliners* rules out any final recourse to a meta-language, what are the consequences for the ethics and the politics of reading?

I shall start with two theoretical or critical preliminaries. For Broch, who wrote a penetrating review of *Ulysses* in 'James Joyce and the Present Time',[1] Joyce like Hofmannsthal reveals through his hatred of cliches the traces of what Broch calls a 'Chandos experience', taking this term from Hofmannsthal's fictional letter in which a young and gifted Lord tells Bacon that he cannot write any more, nor even speak, after a breakdown of the natural relationship between signifier and signified. Thus, for Hermann Broch, *Dubliners* and *Ulysses* manifest the mutism of a world condemned to silence by the destruction of centred values, in the very hypertrophy of their growth. *Dubliners* marks the reversal from pure individual and sympomatic aphasia to the process of recovering the void; it is to be considered between Lord Chandos' Letter (1902) and Wittgenstein's *Tractatus* (begun in 1911). Ezra Pound, too, points out the ethical and political import of *Dubliners*, from a different point of view. He praises the clear hard prose, which eschews unnecessary detail: 'he carefully avoids telling you a lot that you don't want to know' (*Pound/Joyce*: 28). These stories, which are all defined by the special quality of their 'vivid waiting' for some impossible escape, render Dublin universal; however, according to Pound, Joyce has not yet surpassed his Flaubertian model of *Trois contes*.

But the reference to Flaubert is decisive since it enables the critic to stress the ideological relevance of the work. Like Flaubert, who believes that the collapse of France in 1870 might have been avoided if only people had read his books, Joyce also thinks that his 'diagnosis' might have been useful to his country in turmoil. In Pound's words, this becomes: 'If more people had read *The Portrait* and certain stories in Mr. Joyce's *Dubliners* there might have been less recent trouble in Ireland' (*Pound/Joyce*: 90). I shall have to come back to Joyce's use of Flaubert, and to remark on the limitations of Pound's interpretation; it nevertheless throws a double light on the text of *Dubliners*, which constantly hesitates between the status of a cure, a diagnosis, and that of a symptom, produced by the same causes it attempts to heal. Such an oscillation will become apparent if we try to apply the famous phrase of 'silence, exile, and cunning' (*P*: 251) to *Dubliners*.

The theme of exile has been the focus of critical attention, while 'silence' seems to have embarrassed everyone. Firstly, the order of the terms in this well-known triad poses a problem; when Stephen decides to be an artist, a 'priest of eternal imagination' (*P*: 225), he selects these three weapons as the only tools he can use against the encroachments of home, fatherland and Church. If the order is chronological, the initial silence defines his refusal to take part in the political and linguistic wrangles of Dublin until he exiles himself, and moves to Paris for a start. But then *cunning* cannot be simply considered as the third step in this movement towards greater intellectual freedom, if this freedom is available elsewhere. Could it be that Joyce implies a more logical correspondence between the two triads, silence referring to the family, exile to nationalism, and cunning to the perverse and religious refusal of religion? I shall, in fact, suggest strong affinities between silence and paternity, but as these three 'nets' are constantly overlapping, especially in the Dublin of *Dubliners*, it must then be that all three concepts or attitudes work together indissociably and simultaneously. All the dreams of exile to the East in *Dubliners* are part of a ruse which employs silence in different modes of revelation. I shall thus commence by an approach via the silent ruses of interpretation, centred around the notions of perversity, heresy and orthodoxy, and then move on to an analysis of the exile of 'performance' in the enunciative strategies of the text, until finally everything will appear hinged on the silent name of the capitalised Father.

I

'The Sisters' offers the real starting-point, for it is more than just the first story in the collection, but provides an elaborate introduction to the discourses of *Dubliners*. What strikes one from the first page is the deliberate suspension of a number of terms: the identity of the dead priest is disclosed through a series of hesitating, unfinished sentences, and even the 'now' of the initial paragraph is not related to a precise chronology (it is not directly linked to the supper scene which follows). Several signifiers are given, almost too soon, without explanation (paralysis, simony, gnomon), while the real messenger who brings the news of the priest's decease has already made up his mind as to the signification of the event, but deliberately withholds his own conclusions. 'I'll tell you my opinion . . .' but he never really affords more than hints of a possible perversion. This continuous suspension of meanings introduces a whole series of unfinished sentences, marked by dots: all of Old Cotter's remarks, except for one (*D*: 7–8); the end of the boy's dream (*D*: 12); the aunt's questions (*D*: 14); and finally the answers given by Eliza ('But still . . .') and her conclusion ('there was something gone wrong with him . . .') (*D*: 16–17).

We must be aware that the child is not a narrator, but an interpreter, who also believes that Old Cotter knows more than he does, while constantly suspecting the validity of his informations (he has to read the card pinned on the door to be persuaded that the priest is actually dead). The story begins *in medias res*, so that the child may supply the reader with a figure mirroring his own interpretative process. In this process, the child has to come to terms with hints or allusions (Old Cotter *alludes* to the boy as a child, which angers him), from which he attempts to make sense: 'I puzzled my head to extract meaning from his unfinished sentences' (*D*: 9). As he imagines that the face of the dead priest follows him in the dark, it becomes obvious that the symbolic realm of interpretation exhibits its gaps which are soon filled by imaginary fantasies. These contaminate the interpretative process with suggestions of sacrilegious communion. Now the roles of the priest and of the old man appear as opposite points of view on the very process of reading.

For, in fact, in the child's view, the meaning only hinted at by Old Cotter through his silences has to be identified with the dream itself. Indeed, the dream supplies meanings which all develop the suspended signifiers of the first paragraph. The face wishes to utter something to the child but fails: 'It began to confess to me in a murmuring voice and I wondered why it smiled continually and why the lips were so moist with spittle. But then I remembered that it had died of paralysis and I felt that I too was smiling feebly as if to absolve the simoniac of his sin' (*P*: 9). The absence of 'gnomon' will be accounted for later, what matters here is the exchange of sacerdotal functions between the boy and the priest. He confesses the priest, whose voice is heard, but not his words, and the perverse enjoyment of the scene in such a 'pleasant and vicious region' derives from the inversion of the roles and the transmission of the frozen smile from the priest to the boy. The next time the dream is mentioned, in a flash-back, it again is accompanied by speculations about Old Cotter's sentences, and the memories are themselves cut short: ' – in Persia, I thought. . . . But I could not remember the end of the dream' (*D*: 12).

The strange complicity between the priest and the child, which is stressed in his recollections of their conversation, enhances two important points: unlike Mr Cotter, the reverend Flynn explained to the boy the *meanings* of different ceremonies, of the sacraments and institutions. He also obviously got pleasure from these lessons, and in the parody of the *puer senex* theme, we find the repetition of the uncanny smile which becomes an obscene leer. So, on the one hand, we witness a perverse and seductive exchange of sacraments within an order of faith that appears utterly absurd (until the intricate questions of the catechism are debunked in 'Grace'); on the other hand, we find a theory which obstinately refuses to give away its key: 'I have my own theory about it, he said. I think it was one of those . . . peculiar cases. . . . But it's hard to say . . .' (*D*: 8). I would be tempted to read here the disjunction between *orthodoxy*, defined as a theory without a meaning, and *perversity*, as a game of signifiers whose meaning is uncertain.

In order to define this use of the concept of orthodoxy, it might be helpful to consider the very 'orthodox' approach to the Church by Stephen in a passage of *Ulysses* in which he sees the Church triumphing over all heresies: 'The proud potent titles clanged over Stephen's memory the triumph of their brazen bells: *et unam sanctam catholicam et apostolicam ecclesiam*: the slow growth and change of rite and dogma like his own rare thoughts, a chemistry of stars. . . . A horde of heresies fleeing with mitres awry . . .' (*U*: 27).

Orthodoxy in such a picture is not simply the 'right opinion', it is concerned with authority in a special, theological sense, linking it with the idea of tradition, blending the voices of the singers in Stephen's image, and also slowly adding rites and dogmas to the canon. Cardinal Newman is probably the best exponent of such a view of orthodoxy; beside the fact that he is highly praised by Joyce as a prose-writer, he gives a very consistent definition of orthodoxy in his writings. For Newman, the particularity of heresy is to appeal to the Scriptures alone and to disdain tradition; in this separation of dogma from living faith, the heresiarchs separate themselves from the body of the true Church. It is known that he began his theological researches with an examination of the heresy of Arius, and founded his main conclusions on this case, which figures in Stephen's list of heresies, 'The handful of bishops who supported Arius did not make any appeal to an uninterrupted tradition in their favour. They did but profess to argue from Scripture and from the nature of the case.'[2] Orthodoxy is not dependent on Revelation alone or on Tradition alone, it is the right authority deriving from an exact balance between Scripture and Tradition.

It would then remain to prove that the perversion of such an orthodoxy always stems from a reliance on the written word, or a dismissal of oral tradition. The maternal function of heresy is clearer in *Ulysses* than in *Dubliners*, but I must, for the moment, postpone the articulation of the process of writing with the maternal world. In *Dubliners*, nevertheless, the disjunction between orthodoxy and perversity roughly delimits the world of the absent father and that of the mother's smothering attentions. This can be borne out by a comparison with another passage from 'A Painful Case'. There is in Mr Duffy a companion to Mr Cotter, since he too seems in favour of a separation of the sexes and ages ('let a young lad run about and play with young lads of his own age and not be . . .' says Mr Cotter (*D*: 8) which appears less drastic than Mr Duffy's denial of love and friendship, but asserts the same pedagogical repression). He too has a 'theory', while Mrs Sinico listens to him, probably as amused by the patter of his aphorisms as the reverend was by the halting answers of the boy: 'Sometimes in return for his theories she gave out some fact of her own life. With almost maternal solicitude she urged him to let his nature open to the full; she became his confessor' (*D*: 123). But when she tries to act out the implications of what he has left unsaid, as she reads in his refusal of intimacy a longing for closer contact, he undercuts such a gross misunderstanding of his own sentences, and takes refuge in theoretical equanimity: an enunciated compilation of wisdom without a voice ('he heard the strange impersonal voice which he recognized as his own, insisting on the soul's incurable loneliness' (*D*: 124)). When Mrs Sinico presses his hand, he flees, essentially fearing the distortion of an interpretation of his own voice: 'Her interpretation of his words disillusioned him' (*D*: 124).

The discrepancy between theory and the interpretation of symptoms acquires tragic overtones in this story, while in 'The Sisters' it essentially describes the particular infinity of the process. Such an infinity is mentioned by the child when he adds that he used to enjoy Old Cotter's endless stories before, probably before he had met the priest: the faints and worms can be adequately replaced by the responses of the Mass. But what he finally hears during his long silence in the last scene after the visit to the corpse, is either the empty gossip of his aunt, or Nannie and Eliza, the ill-fated 'Sisters' of destiny, or the silence of the empty chalice: 'She stopped suddenly as if to listen. I too listened; but there was no sound in the house' (*D*: 17). This will be taken up by the final silence which surrounds Mr Duffy after Mrs Sinico's death ('He could hear nothing: the night was perfectly silent. He listened again: perfectly silent. He felt that he was alone' (*D*: 131)). The endlessness of the other narratives relies on such a victorious silence, and this is the real link between the stories in *Dubliners* and those of *Finnegans Wake*. When Joyce reordered his notes for the *Work of Progress*, he mentioned the 'story of the invalid pensioner' in a context of 'desperate story-telling': 'Arabian nights, serial stories, tales within tales, to be continued, desperate story-telling, one caps another to reproduce a rambling mock-heroic tale . . .' (*Scribbledehobble*: 25).

While the masculine theory rests on the gnomic utterance of clichés with no proper conclusions, and which in their denunciation of bad 'effects' are akin to the pompous trivialities of a Polonius, the perversity of the dead symbolic father defines the incompleteness of a gnomon, a significant inadequacy. A gnomon is not only the pointer on a sun-dial, but more specifically 'that part of a parallelogram which remains after a similar parallelogram is taken away from one of its corners,' in the Euclid. The absent corner hints at the gaping lack revealed not only by the paralysis of the priest, but also by the disjuncture between symptoms and their interpretation. Although the boy is urged by his uncle to 'learn to box his corner' (*D*: 8–9) – which also alludes to the confession-box in which the priest has been found laughing silently – this foolish assertion of the subject's autonomy and self-reliance is contradicted by the series of dichotomies the child faces. The 'lighted *square* of window' (*D*: 7; my emphasis) has not disclosed such a gnomon yet: it would have taken *two* candles set at the head of the corpse to project a shadow visible from the outside. What the child saw in his fascinated gaze was simply the lack of an expected lack, since death has already begun its 'work', but without visible external signs. 'We would see a sign . . .' these signs, never ascertainable although working behind the square, are set into motion through the words only.

The words 'paralysis', 'simony' and 'gnomon' become thus inexorably connected through an etymological chain of associations. Gnomon implies interpretation and *Greek* geometry, but is placed curiously beside catechism. Joyce has an illuminating remark in a letter of April 1905: 'While I was attending the Greek mass here last Sunday it seemed to me that my story *The Sisters* was rather remarkable. The Greek mass is strange. The altar is not visible but at times the priest opens the gates and shows himself. . . . The Greek priest has been taking a great eyeful out of me: two haruspices' (*Letters*, II: 86–7). The connection Joyce implicitly states is striking, suggesting that the very exposure of a sacrament can become the exposure of the person in what can be termed simony. The series of parallel lines intersecting one another can thus describe the figure of the interlocking signifiers. We know, for instance, that Simon Magus, who was the first to try to buy the power to transmit the Holy Ghost from the Apostles, was also a Samaritan prophet, adored as the first God by the members of his sect. They also coupled him with a goddess named Helena, who was said to have been created by his thought. In his teachings can be found the sources of most subsequent heresies spreading Gnosticism through the early Church. He bears witness to the extent to which the messianic Judeo-Christian heresies had been Hellenised. Thus *Persia* in the boy's dream also calls up the strong Manichean tendencies of the Simonite heresies, while adding another dimension of exoticism to the composite figure of such a 'Jewgreek', like Bloom, incestuous and suspected of being homosexual, but really in need of a son.

In the same way, *paralysis* etymologically conveys an idea of dissolution, of an unbinding (*para-lyein*: to release, to unbind) which is coupled with an anguishing immobility, while *paresis* means 'to let fall'. The priest's paralysis is both a dropping of some holy vessel (a chalice) in a parapraxis (a slip or lapsus), and the untying of the knots which paradoxically constrict the cramped movements of the protagonists. The fall itself, the 'felix culpa' of original sin links the boy's perverted innocence (it must have been 'the boy's fault' in some version of the incident) to the heresy of the condemned priest. In echo to this, Mr Duffy laments the ruin of their confessional (the meeting place to which Mrs Sinico came) and fears another 'collapse' (*D*: 124) of his feminine confessor − the first collapse he implicitly alludes to being the gesture of Mrs Sinico when she kissed his hand!

If Mr Duffy shrinks away, Old Cotter would prefer to cut off, to lop away the gangrened limbs, appearing thus as a real 'Old cutter'. For the orthodoxy divides in order to anathematise through the particular injunction of lacerated sentences, in a series of performative utterances which stop abruptly before the end. The imitation of Christ is transformed into an apotropaic strategy, such as Stephen practices in the *Portrait* when he tries to become a saint: 'His eyes shunned every encounter with the eyes of women. From time to time also he balked them by a sudden effort of the will, as by lifting them suddenly in the middle of an unfinished sentence and closing the book' (*P*: 154). But in *Dubliners*, the maternal tissue of the city, is corrupted at its very core by an absent and mute centre (indeed, the priest was never heard in the house: 'You wouldn't hear him in the house any more than now' (*D*: 15), now that he is dead) reforms, spreads over and re-forms, over the incision, which is sutured, overgrown with new tissue. This could be why the shop window notice usually reads '*Umbrellas Re-covered*' (*D*: 10). The umbrellas are inscribed both in the series of veils, curtains, clothes such as the great-coat in which the priest is smothered, priestly vestments which blur the difference, and in the series of parodic phallic substitutes, culminating with O'Madden Burke's gesture as a final law-giver, 'poised upon his umbrella' (*D*: 168). In this city of lost property, one cannot recover an absent penis, but the phallus is there as a signifier of the lack to be recovered. The catacombs and the catechism organise a space of echoes (*kata-echein*) which allows for the puns on 'faints' and 'faint', 'not long' and 'I longed' on the first page of 'The Sisters', since the idle play of the signifiers prepares for the silent and deadly work of Thanatos in the text.

The recovering of the text by itself when it doubles back in this way describes the necessary process of rereading and mirrors the points where it attaches itself inextricably to ambiguous signifiers, that are floating without mooring. One of these is the term of 'resignation' used for the priest: 'He was quite resigned. . . . He looks quite resigned' (*D*: 14). The signs on his truculent face reveal that this resignation acquires a double edge; the resigned priest has been suspended, so that he is retired and excluded, has resigned his function after his failure to perform his duties. He then assumes the part of the unwilling heretic, perverse precisely because he did not choose to be apart, but obeyed the unconscious law of the symptom. The word 'resigned' yields then another hint, pointing towards 'sign'. What this double sign (of the cross) leaves open is the symbolic transference of his attributes to the boy, whose life, too, is 'crossed' by the symptom:

> And then his life was, you might say, crossed.
> – Yes, said my aunt. He was a disappointed man. You could see that.
> A silence took possession of the little room, and, under cover of it I approached the table and tasted my sherry . . . (*D*: 16).

The child who has refused the crackers because he would have made too much noise eating them now indulges in this silent communion. Eliza was 'disappointed' (*D*: 13) at his refusal, but this devious acceptance of the wine instead of the Eucharist is another 'crossing' of someone's wish. In the first version, the verb used by Joyce to show their first movement when coming into the room was 'We crossed ourselves'; the cross was there as a sign, not the sign of the cross, but the crossing of the sign, through the cancellation of a symbol. The silence of confession, from which the priest has been debarred, superposes the 'latticed ear of a priest' (*P*:225) on that of a boy. The priest was 're-signed' because of the crossing between the empty symbol and the transmission of esoteric and perverse powers to someone who is called a 'Rosicrucian' (*D*: 9).

The confession is the process of perverse crossing which breeds a rose on a cross in Dublin. This is why Old Cotter vigorously prohibits the boy's confession ('I wouldn't like children of mine . . . to have much to say to a man like that') and utters this unique complete sentence just after he has 'spat rudely into the grate' (*D*: 8). The forceful projection of his spittle of course contrasts with the soft oozing of the priest's dribble. The familiar notion of contamination through a poisonous humour can help to explain the curious reversal of the situation of confession. The priest's teaching could have infected the ears of all possible listeners, contaminating by synecdoche the whole of the town. There was a medieval theory of which Joyce was aware which held that heresies could actually poison the atmosphere of a city, as a kind of polluted air (*pestilentia*) penetrating men's viscera.[3] The contagion generated by this infection would surely condemn everyone to excommunication, just as when Henri de Clairvaux found the city of Toulouse so infected with Cathar heresies that no healthy part remained.

The metaphor then develops into that of the cancer, the perverse parasite preying on the whole of the organism, and for which the only cure is the amputation of the diseased member. But this cancer is not visible yet, since it still proliferates beneath the skin. The antagonistic forces of division and proliferation can be seen at play in the famous expression used by Saint Paul who left the formulae that were to be repeated over and over during the later struggles of the Church against heresies:

> Study to shew thyself approved unto God, a workman that needeth not to be ashamed, rightly *dividing* the word of truth. But shun profane and vain babblings: for they will increase unto more ungodliness. And their word will eat as doth a *canker*: of whom is Hymenæus and Philetus (by way of parenthesis, they were followers of Menander, who was very close to Simon Magus in his origin and doctrine); who concerning the truth have erred, saying that the *resurrection* is past already. . . . (2nd Epistle to Timothy, 2: 15–18; my italics).

Truth implies a certain concern for division, whereas heresy thrives as perversion on the body of dogma; nowhere is perversion more virulent than in a discourse which attempts to articulate the truth of the subject in his own division, and this is where psychoanalysis and religion exhibit their common logic, a logic Joyce merely displaces, or rather warps.

In his reversal of the pattern of confession, Joyce tends to imply that the cancerous contamination of perversion can be effected by the simple silent act of hearing a confession. The poisoned ear of the murdered king in *Hamlet* becomes the imaginary conch which would magnify parabolically the principle of perversity in the text. To define perversion by simony, and simony by perversion points to the idea that the emptying of the symbolic power stems from a denegation* of the locus of the Other**, and thus the difference which constitutes the subject as subject of his desire tends to be displaced, duplicated. The child's wish was utterly dependent on that of the old priest, who had reduced it to a distorted image of his own frustrated desire. Perversion appears then firstly as a certain confusion on the one hand of duplication, and on the other of division and difference. This entails a derision of the signifiers of the Other's desire. Thus the pervert erects codes, maxims, laws, so as to dodge

* The term *dénégation* is used here in a direct transcription of the French in order to emphasise the difference between the simple negation of an event and the more complicated psychic process, described in Freud's essay *Die Verneinung* (1925, *The Complete Psychological Works of Sigmund Freud*, vol. XIX, p. 235–9), in which an event is both consciously denied, and in that denial, accepted at another level. The obvious term that one might use for such a process is *disavowal* but this word is standardly used to translate the process which Freud terms *Verleugnung* in which the split between conscious acceptance and unconscious denial of an event issues in a psychotic symptom (see *From the History of an Infantile Neurosis (1918 [1914]) ibid* vol. XVII, p. 85). Negation, which is the more literal translation of *Verneinung*, fails to bring out the complicated play of denial and acceptance which characterises the neurotic. – Ed.

** The child encounters language issuing from the beings that surround it, and whereas it can identify these beings as others similar to itself, there is also within them another agency at work enabling them to speak language and marking them as having submitted to the Law. It is this mysterious element of the beings surrounding the child that Lacan has called the *big Other* (the capital letter marking the irreducible difference between this realm of being and the realm of the imaginary where the other simply appears as the mirror image of the self). The big Other can be equated with the unconscious present in all those who have learnt to speak language, and it is this unconscious which forms the basis for the child's interrogation of its parent's desires. The world of difference which erupts into the child's imaginary world with the recognition of the phallus is caught through a series of key terms related to the big Other and whose internalisation as the *Name of the Father* guarantee the stability of the symbolic order. – Ed past them all the better, and to get around them. Getting round them, he also turns round in them: such is the significance of the meeting with the pervert in 'An Encounter'. In such a vicious circle, the loss of the object is atoned for by the loss of meaning, and there is an indefinite turning back of drives towards their sources. But paradoxically, perversion constantly needs the outcrop of sense, its generation as well as the reference to desire and the Law.

I do not mean that Joyce is a 'pervert' in a trivial sense, he rather appears as a neurotic who imagines himself to be a pervert in order to assure the continuity of his enjoyment.[4] He was also aware both of his ethical posture and of the perverse nature of his drives in writing. He deplores at one point that he has not expressed the beauty and glamour of Dublin, for he has started idealising it by comparison with Rome, and he knows he cannot help distorting the picture: 'I am sure I should find again what you call the Holy Ghost sitting in the ink-bottle and the perverse devil of my literary conscience sitting on the hump of my pen' (*Letters*, II: 166). But other writers must be judged according to ethical standards: 'Maupassant writes very well, of course, but I am afraid that his moral sense is rather obtuse' (*Letters*, II: 99).

II

Perversion cannot be reduced to parody, and this is how we can, I think, start to distinguish between the strategies of Flaubert (and possibly of Pound), and those of Joyce. Both Flaubert and Joyce have met the problems of censorship, but while *Madame Bovary* and *Ulysses* were attacked on grounds of immorality and obscenity, *Dubliners* was thought litigious, libellous: more perverse than obscene, more subversive than immoral. This can be read in the games the text plays with silence, and it is clear that the first truncated warning given by Old Cotter ('When children see things like that, you know, it has an effect . . .' *D*: 9) has been read too literally by the printers. Joyce had been naive enough to reveal the 'enormity' of 'An Encounter' to his publisher, and the same suspicion creeps back in his relationship with Roberts, the second publisher he went to see in Dublin: 'Roberts I saw again. He asked me very narrowly was there sodomy also in *The Sisters* and what was "simony" and if the priest was suspended only for the breaking of the chalice. He asked me also was there more in *The Dead* than appeared' (*Letters*, II: 305–6). Everything becomes potentially dangerous, and the fear one is exposed to is paralleled by a desire to name the alleged perversion – a perversion for which, of course, 'sodomy' is totally inadequate.

As with Flaubert, a maximum of legibility, of transparence, is coupled with the insinuation of a perversion at work within the signifiers of the text. But Flaubert stops this process before it attacks the structure of the subject. I shall rapidly analyse some parts of *Un Coeur Simple* to substantiate my point, and I shall select three moments which are also three moments of silence. Firstly, a silence spreads over all the objects to stress their weight, their sensual volume, and corresponds to instants of diffuse happiness for a Félicité who is not cut off from the others; she still has to identify with Virginie (The Virgin) and Victor (the defeated heroism and exoticism meeting death). This takes place at Trouville in the Summer, when it is too hot to leave the room: 'L'éblouissante clarté du dehors plaquait des barres de lumière entre les lames des jalousies. Aucun bruit dans le village. En bas, sur le trottoir, personne. Ce silence épandu augmentait la tranquillité des choses. Au loin, les marteaux des calfats tamponnaient des carènes. . . . '[5] After Félicité's complete immersion into the only dominant discourse available, that of religion, her fixation on the parakeet which has been offered to her reveals the limitation of her perception and the dwindling of her circle of reference: 'Le petit cercle de ses idées se rétrécit encore, et le carillon des cloches, le mugissement des boeufs, n'existaient plus. Tous les êtres fonctionnaient avec le silence des fantômes. Un seul bruit arrivait maintenant à ses oreilles, la voix du perroquet.'[6] The parakeet, Loulou, an obvious parody of the paraclete or Holy Ghost, is there posed as 'son and lover', until the last epiphany which affords the finale of the text, shows her death when she imagines a gigantic parakeet hovering over her head and soaring from the religious procession. This epiphany, like those of *Dubliners*, is a logical denouement, which allows her no other possibility of escape. Slowly crushed in the spiralling metaphor, she has to conclude parodically that the voice of God and the answers she hallucinates are one: 'Le Père, pour s'énoncer, n'avait pu choisir une colombe, puisque ces bêtes-là n'ont pas de voix, mais plutôt un des ancêtres de Loulou.'[7] This deduction could have been made by Bouvard and Pécuchet, but here it stresses the sacrilegious innocence of her desperation. The effects of perversion in Flaubert's text turn around the problematics of utterance, of enunciation, and in this way Félicité appears as the precursor of Eveline, to whom she may have lent the episode with Victor, when he sails away, like Frank; but these textual effects remain at the level of parody, not because they are limited to an exploration of 'style', but because the reader cannot but identify with Félicité's consciousness. The story soars up towards this derisive climax, from which the only fall back to the real happens outside the text. In *Dubliners*, there is no hysterical identification, but the strategy of silences, not so ordered in their progression, escapes from the brittle dialectics of stylistic parody. Perversity flies from the Pigeon House to the Ballast Office, leaving a deaf Nannie or a mute Eveline in a lurch of the structure – since 'c'est le Pigeon' (*P*: 47) (it is the pigeon or Holy Ghost) of paternity which could alone hold the missing key.

To follow along these lines, *Dubliners* can be divided more simply than Joyce suggests with his four-part pre-Viconian scheme of growth from childhood to adolescence, maturity and the anarchy of public life. The text falls into two main moments; the first one explores the blind alleys of the possible strategies of interpretation, up to 'The Boarding House'; the second part, starting with 'A Little Cloud', hinges around a study of roles and performances, and in fact explores what I would call *enunciation* for short. 'Grace', which was meant to be the conclusion of the book in its first stage, ties all the strands together, as it unites the themes of confession, of interpretation and of performative utterance. The two significant titles would be *Encounter* to name the first part, an encounter with an Other denied and reduced precisely because it denies and reduces the Other, and *Counterparts* for the second: the system of balances and oppositions encompassing the blocked gestures of the first part and providing them with an endless circulation within the city of paralysis.

Silence means in the first part a teasing seduction to hermeneutics; the moments of interpretation are generally underlined in the text, as in 'Araby' ('I could interpret these signs' (*D*: 34) which foreshadows the final revelation). Lenehan is likewise deliberately ambiguous, since to 'save himself' (*D*: 55) he leaves his expressions open to several interpretations; he also tries to read signs of reassurance in others' gestures or physique. 'An Encounter' offers the most blatant clues: the narrator fixes a distant aim, the Pigeon House, and is obviously looking for signs, such as the green eyes his phantasy lends to Norwegian sailors and which he finds in the pervert's face. He has failed to decipher 'the legend' on the boat (D: 23), and remains unclear about his own motivations ('. . . for I had some confused notion . . .' (D: 23)). The unfinished sentence is similar to the omission of the end of the first boy's dream.

Every time, the interpretation abolishes itself in a moment of silence, either the missing centre of the perverse speech about castigation, this absent secret or mystery never to be disclosed, or the untold action such as the suggested masturbation of the man, which is conveyed by a facile trick of the narration, for the boy has more or less been hypnotised: '—I say! Look what he's doing! As I neither answered nor raised my eyes Mahony exclaimed again: – I say. . . . He's a queer old josser!' (D: 26). The plot contrived in order to achieve some measure of freedom or escape only results in a paltry stratagem, when the boys change their names, and an embarrassed silence. The cunning move is similar to the ruse of Ulysses facing the Cyclops, but here it remains insignificant. In the same way, Corley has been 'too hairy' (D: 54) to tell his name to the girl he wants to exploit, and this master trickster exhibits the coin of simony in a silent gesture of monstration which gives Lenehan the status of a perverse disciple.

The silence felt in 'Araby' ('I recognised a silence like that which pervades a church after a service' (D: 35)) assails the speakers as it invades Dublin: Eveline's speechlessness is formulated in 'silent fervent prayer', (D: 42) and recognition is lost; she cannot even give a 'sign' (D: 43) to Frank. In 'The Boarding House', the complicity between the mother and Polly issues in a 'persistent silence' (D: 68) which cannot be misunderstood, it is the impetus behind the decisive gesture of the end. Mrs Mooney's moral cleaver will no doubt cut through the hesitation of Bob Doran as it would do through tender meat. What Polly is waiting for in the end is not told, for she herself has forgotten that she was waiting for something: the castrated body of a man ready to accept all the ties of marriage is a direct anticipation of Tom Kernan's fall, and is to be followed by Doran's degradation in *Ulysses*. Both go down the stairs to be met with the loss of some property, be it simply money, freedom and respect, or a corner of the tongue.

Thus, in what I recognise as the second moment, we move towards a definition of failure through the inadequacy of some performance; silence is then constitutive of a discourse, not simply covered or revealed by a discourse. Enunciation refers not simply to direct speech, but assumes the sense of producing meaningful signs in a performance, be it singing or writing. What obviously links the fates of Little Chandler and Farrington is their inability to write. In Chandler's case, the main issue is his blindness to the real process of writing: he cannot think of any mediation between an imaginative mood, a certain psychological state, and the finished product, the idealised book of poems. He accordingly lives in the world of the clichés of romantic bad taste, and finally cannot even read the hortatory consolation afforded by Byron's juvenilia.

Farrington, on the other hand, must find substitutes for whatever violence he feels threatening to disrupt his servile copying. It is not a mere accident when he repeats the first name in the contract he has to write out. The repetition of 'Bernard Bernard' (*D*: 100) is structurally similar to the repetition of the same verse sung by old Maria (*D*: 118). Death-drives are branched into repetitive parapraxes, until the pure repetition is identified with the silence of death, as we saw in Mr Duffy's case. Death is then not a voice repeating itself, but the 'laborious drone of the engine reiterating the syllables of her name' (*D*: 131). The deadly work of the signifiers now seem to undermine the names of the dead, and this appears in 'Ivy Day in the Committee Room'.

It is in this story that the disjuncture between enunciated and enunciation is brought to the fore in a masterwork of political analysis and it is emphasised by the intricate punctuation that the text develops through its silences. Pauses and silences mark the appearance and disappearance of the characters ('the room was silent again' seems to be a Leitmotiv). For silence maps out the presuppositions of the speakers, their unspoken discourses and their modes of expression expose them much more than their empty speeches; Crofton's arrival releases the longer and most sustained speech by Mr Henchy, and his silence is twofold: 'He was silent for two reasons. The first reason, sufficient in itself, was that he had nothing to say; the second reason was that he considered his companions beneath him' (*D*: 146). The void of the enunciated word is not really sufficient, for we have to understand what matters most is the *a priori* position of superiority he assigns to himself. Enunciation can reveal this position, without any material being spoken. All the while, this empty enunciated word is the object of the competition between the speakers, who all turn to Crofton and try to gain his mute support. Crofton is addressed twice directly by Henchy, but refuses to side with him, and does not assent either to O'Connor's pleading asides; only the cork popping out of the bottle can give him the cue. And what he adds to the debate is only the term of 'gentleman', which will become the object of the derision of 'Grace'.

In the same way, the adverb 'argumentatively' (D: 148) used to qualify the unfinished sentence of Mr Lyons about the dubious morality of King Edward VII acquires an ironic significance since the same argument of 'let bygones be bygones' buries it in the silence of betrayal and denial. Denial has to be taken in its religious sense here, for it is such a denial that Joyce betrays, slyly putting perversion to work against itself. The final silences which greet the beginning and the end of the bathetic poem on Parnell culminate in the deflation of Mr Crofton's final reply. The absence of any standard standpoint from which to judge this poem leaves the reader teased and speechless, with no discourse at his disposal. The 'clever' piece by Henchy is suspended in a vacuum of political interpretation, since the name of Parnell has been deprived of all political force and turned into a myth, the myth of the dismembered Father devoured and mourned by the parricidal sons. Crofton's silence resting on the assumption of superiority but unable to voice anything more than the void appears then as the only place the text prepares for the reader – after all, the Conservatives had not 'betrayed' Parnell! – a place no one can accept.

Names and enunciative strategies are intricately connected in these last stories, but 'Counterparts' provides the example that is easiest to analyse. The first thing the reader witnesses is a violent shout: 'Farrington!' which sets the dominant tone of aggression. Being called by his name from the outside, he remains 'the man' as a subject of enunciation. But he apparently never utters anything original, we learn that he infuriated Mr Alleyne by mimicking his Ulster accent, as he will later mimic the flat accent of his terrified son, until he finds the felicitous reply which almost escapes his lips. He is then alluded to as the 'consignor' (D: 102) when he gains his only real victory, derisory as it is: he pawns his watch for six shillings instead of merely five. From then on, he seems to be the subject of his own speech, because he appears capable of narrating the incident, repeating it as he amplifies its nature. He stands the drinks as 'Farrington', for his utterance has transformed a spontaneous witticism which was almost a slip of the tongue ('could he not not keep his tongue in his cheek?' (D: 102)) into a decisive retort, now seeming a 'smart . . . thing' (D: 103). What passes unmentioned, of course, is that his answer was the release of an impotent rage, the first symptom of which was the paralysis of the hand when he could not write. The circle of his downfall is rounded when, in the last part of the story, he is again called 'the man', as he forfeits even his role as a father (*D*: 109).

But the story of 'Grace' affords the real conclusion to the problematics of enunciation: from the slip of the cut or hurt tongue to the divine performative utterance of the Pope's proclamation of infallibility, the whole gamut of speech-acts is depicted, ascending the ladder which goes from the infelicities to the 'happy' results. Even such a minor character as Mr Fogarty helps to define 'grace' in terms of personal appearance, and contributes to its connection with utterance: 'He bore himself with a certain grace, complimented little children and spoke with a neat enunciation' (*D*: 188), and later: 'He enunciated the word and then drank gravely' (*D*: 190). The text begins to insist on its own metaphoricity, which is brought to the fore twice. The first 'metaphor', 'we're all going to wash the pot' (*D*: 184) brings in the theme of confession, while the second, comparing a priest to a 'spiritual accountant' (*D*: 198) introduces to simony. Both are linked with enunciation: 'He uttered the metaphor with a certain homely energy and, encouraged by his own voice, proceeded' (*D*: 184). The energy of Martin Cunningham's efforts to lead his friend towards salvation is relayed by the 'resonant assurance' of Father Purdon, who asks for permission to use his dominant trope: 'If he might use the metaphor. . . .' (*D*: 197) This rhetorical precaution is of course superfluous, but shows that we are invited to difficult readings with possible ruses and tricks (such as the deliberate distortion of the Biblical quotation): 'It was one of the most difficult texts in all the Scriptures, he said, to interpret properly' (D: 197). In this devious way, Joyce warns us to read the satire along the lines of Dantean exegesis, and progression from Hell to Purgatory and Paradise.

This circular structure links the inverted progress towards a parodic Paradiso for the bankrupt petty-bourgeois of Dublin to the doomed circularity of confession. The forceful tautology of the doctrine of infallibility ('not one of them ever preached *ex cathedra* a word of false doctrine . . . because when the Pope speaks *ex cathedra* . . . he is infallible' (*D*: 191) stand out as the key-stone of the edifice of empty discourse ('until at last the Pope himself stood up and declared infallibility a dogma of the Church *ex cathedra*' (*D*: 192)). It is Mrs Kernan's role to underline the feminine transmission of such a doctrine: on the one hand she refrains from telling the 'gentlemen' that her husband's tongue would not suffer by being shortened (*D*: 178), while on the other hand she feigns 'pity' for the priest who would have to listen to their confession (*D*: 194). The gap in the tongue signifies the first fall, the inscription of the *gnomon* within the apparatus of enunciation. And the fact that their conversation drifts towards the Council of 1870 reveals that it sets up a trap, with which his friends attempt to get at Kernan through his recanted heresy. John MacHale who, in Mr Cunningham's narration, suddenly stands up and shouts '*Credo*', conveys the hysterical contagion of the performative power of authority and orthodoxy – it is the detail 'with the voice of a lion' (*D*: 192) which seems so catching here. The other cardinal (Döllinger in fact) is disqualified, excommunicated: this is a strategy which pushes Mr Kernan towards the utterance of such a 'Credo'. In order to continue speaking with an equivalent authority, he must utter 'the word of belief and submission' (*D*: 192) with the others, but also find his marginal freedom – he then adds another performative verb, fetishistically selecting the most trivial item of pomp: 'I bar the candles!' (*D*: 194). He thus manages to create a similar effect ('conscious of having created an effect on his audience' (*D*: 194)) which duplicates the unconscious parody of the historical Council with its 'farcical gravity'.

The barred tongue opens to the barring of the phallic substitutes. What remains is only the 'retreat business and confession' (*D*: 194), and their acceptance of a world where business is business. Thus both the Pope and the English King are two focal points helping to expose the undermining of utterance in the void of discourses. The English capital demanded by Mr Henchy, and which enables him to condone King Edward's past lapses, and the spiritual accounts which can palliate the most outrageous distortions of the sacred texts and even excuse the aberrations of those 'old popes' who were not precisely 'up to the knocker' (*D*: 190), both thrive on the same death and prostitution of values. From this point of view, there remains the possibility of ethical judgements. This will disappear with 'The Dead.'

III

'The Dead' is the supplement to the series of stories of *Dubliners* which, added one year after the completion of the rest, not only mirrors the earlier stories, but modifies them retroactively, pushing them into a new mode of writing. Its function is similar to that of the Penelope chapter in *Ulysses*, with the difference that Gretta's secret has been repressed for so long that it cannot really be voiced, so that her voice only resounds muffled through the memories and desires of her husband.

The three aggressions by women, all of whom 'discompose' (*D*: 203) Gabriel, bring about a new askesis, which puts off the work of perversion, because the subject enjoys his own dissolution. This can be examined through a study of the uses of silence as a musical pause in the narration. There are different moments of silence which enhance the progressive undoing of the subject. Firstly, a silence greets Lily's bitter retort (*D*: 203), a silence which is then mirrored negatively in the silence by which the three young ladies snub Mr Browne (*D*: 209). Gabriel is silent when he fails to answer Miss Ivors (*D*: 214) after which he concentrates on the preparation for his speech: 'He . . . took no part in the conversation with which the table covered Lily's removal of the plates' (*D*: 226). Even this conversation, lively as it appears, reveals its weak points and allows for the lurking menace of death to hush the gossips, as when someone mentions the monks who sleep in their coffins: 'As the subject had grown lugubrious, it was buried in a silence of the table' (*D*: 230). The uneasy silence of this parodic last supper is transformed into the general silence marking the signal for Gabriel's speech. His empty rhetoric sours on the background of a willingness to forget the silence of vanished ghosts.

When Gretta, entranced, listens to the song Bartell d'Arcy finally sings, Gabriel tries to arrest her movement in a permanent vision which is blind to the musical qualities of the scene, precisely because he asks the wrong question of the symbolical meaning of such a picture: he wonders 'what is a woman standing on the stairs in the shadow, listening to distant music, a symbol of' (*D*: 240). The sense he is groping for is of course the deferred meaning he has promised to tell Gretta, this hidden truth which allows him to cope with the task of sewing clichés together to entertain his aunts. This truth can in fact never be uttered, for in the destruction of the symbol, it is exposed as a sham.

Like Tom Kernan, Gabriel refuses the candle offered by the porter, preferring the complicity of shadows to 'that handsome article' (*D*: 247); he prepares a little scenario of seduction, in which he would be the master of the revels, ready to 'overmaster' (D: 248) his wife when she seems aloof. It is not simply that he cannot hold a candle to the secret and past love betwen Michael Furey and Gretta, but rather that he fears that the simple light of a candle could pale the fire he feels in his blood. It might also be that he unconsciously fears that their tête-á-tête would look like a mortuary vigil, a wake, watched from the outside by some unknown and wistful youth.

For the music of desire is also one of hackneyed phrases quoted from old letters; the silence of his lust is curiously linked with the ineffability of her name: '*Why is it that words like these seem to me so dull and cold? Is it because there is no word tender enough to be your name?* Like distant music these words that he had written years before were borne towards him from the past' (D: 244). It is well-known that Joyce quotes from one of his letters to Nora, but it must be stressed that the context of this 'model' is one of dejection and also of an utter failure to speak; Joyce wrote in September 1904:

> The energy which is required for carrying on conversations seems to have left me lately and I find myself constantly slipping into silence. . . . I know that when I meet you next our lips will become mute. . . . And yet why should I be ashamed of words? . . . What is it that prevents me unless it be that no word is tender enough to be your name? (*Letters*, II: 56)

Gretta's bare and artless enunciation of a fact that pierced her yields the symbolic otherness for which Gabriel was vainly looking in his own past.

Thus silence assumes a double function in 'The Dead', and it is for instance such a silence which explains Gabriel's misunderstanding of Gretta's mood. The same expression as in 'The Sisters' is used: 'Under cover of her silence' (D: 246) he indulges in his erotic fantasies, while such a silence is echoed twice in the following paragraph. The mounting tension toward physical desire is contrasted sharply with the desexualised truth of Gretta's past love, an infinite love because it has been unbounded by the death of Michael, and the climax of their misunderstanding comes when she tells him: 'You are a very generous person' (D: 249) as he entangles himself in sordid details. When she breaks down, he approaches her and passes a mirror: 'he caught sight of himself in full length . . . the face whose expression always puzzled him when he saw it in a mirror and his glimmering gilt-rimmed eye-glasses.' (D: 249) The mention of the mirror is strategic here; first, it duplicates itself, towards the imaginary fascination for the image of the self, captured in the smaller mirrors of his spectacles which screen him from the real as visual goloshes. This glance is still caught in the generality of the series of glances which *always* startle Gabriel, and appears as an indulgence. When the couple he visualises comes to the fore, the mirror is shattered: 'While he had been full of memories of their secret life together, full of tenderness and joy and desire, she had been comparing him in her mind with another. A shameful consciousness of his own person assailed him.' He can now reinterpret the 'pitiable fatuous fellow he had caught a glimpse of in the mirror' (*D*: 251), a mirror in which Gretta had looked rapidly at herself only to go beyond it.

But then the duplication gives way to division, to splitting, to the fading of the subject, an evanescent Gabriel becomes the frozen stone guest who comes in symptoms to disturb the banquet of his desires, to paraphrase Lacan. He understands that he has to play the role of the Other in relation to his wife, an Other absolutely cut off from any hearing; the generous ear he lends to his wife brings no real atonement. His tears of remorse, similar to those of Little Chandler, betray only his self-indulgence: 'Generous tears filled Gabriel's eyes' (*D*: 255). The generosity of impossible love brings no analytic position: he only listens to the fall of snow, that is of a natural descent, without a subject. The generous is then swallowed up by the general ('Snow was general all over Ireland'), a general of death whose last charge rounds off everything. Gabriel is poised between the pleasure of his own disappearance ('His own identity was fading out into a grey impalpable world: the solid world itself which these dead had one time reared and lived in was dissolving and dwindling,' and the anguish of such a 'bitter ending'; a delicate balance is established between the reversed signifiers of 'swoon' and 'snow' in their slow downfall (*D*: 255–6)): potentiality dissolves into entropy.

The last oceanic silence which concludes 'The Dead' cannot be reduced by interpretation; in its rhythmic beauty, it calls up an ecstasy such as *The Portrait* describes with 'the soft peace of silent spaces of fading tenuous sky above the waters, of oceanic silence' (*P*: 230) before the conclusion of *Finnegans Wake*. The dissolution of the subject implies an infinite interpretation, not reducible to the antagonisms between East and West. The critical controversy around the value of 'westward' (*D*: 255) seems a little idle; what Joyce simply suggests is that a cycle has been completed since perversion has exhausted its own possibilities. The pure annihilation of differences proposes to the subject the empty place of the other and silent listener, 'playing possum', as Earwicker will have to do to save himself in the *Wake*. The symbolic structure has been so violently fractured for Gabriel, that we are left gazing at the empty mirror of the sky, in much the same way as we stand as readers metamorphosed into a horned and paralytic Shakespeare at the end of the 'Circe' episode in *Ulysses*.

Silence is not a mere symptom then, it defines the vanishing point of all assertion, exhibits the empty space which the writing of the text constantly re-covers and recovers, in its multiplication. The 'few light taps upon the pane' made by the snow are echoed in *Finnegans Wake* by the taps of the branches on the shutters expressed by the recurrent 'Zinzin' motif.

> – Now we're gettin it. Tune in and pick up the forain counties! Hello!
> – Zinzin.
> – Hello! Tittit! Tell your title?
> – Abride!
> – Hellohello! Ballymacarett! Am I thru' Iss? Miss? True?
> – Tit! What is the ti . . ?
> 　　　　　　　　SILENCE.　　　　　　　　(*F W*: 500–1)

In the *Wake*, the recurrent 'Silence' incorporates the same symptom into an historical movement, it marks the tabula rasa of the last stage of a Viconian ricorso: 'and all's set for restart after the silence' (*F W*: 382). This dialectical silence breaks with the silences of *Dubliners*; the metaphor of confession which applied to 'Grace' (with the 'washing of the pot') does not apply to the 'Dead'. Gretta feels no regret, no contrition, she never 'confesses' to Gabriel, hence the impression of strangeness of her diction; moreover, she may not have told everything, as Gabriel suddenly realises. As with Anna Livia, washing not the pots and kettles of supper but the dirty linen of the capital, the only silence which produces the space of otherness necessary to the weaving of the serial stories will be that of an almost inaudible murmur, the deep flow of the river of time.

The first fourteen stories try to set up the possibility of an ethical discourse criticising the paralysis of Dublin; this is finally left outside the scope of the subject's discourse in 'The Dead', as in *Finnegans Wake*. Like Wittgenstein, Joyce tends to affirm the salvation of ethics through silence, since with the loss of any meta-language, one can only show, not enunciate the possibility of direct action or of mythical contemplation. This is why there is a real break and a real loss in the last silence in Anna's final monologue, and not a mere expectancy of the restart for a new beginning. There a certain 'tacebimus' can found the ethics of critical reading. Maurice Blanchot remarks in his introduction to *Lautréamont and Sade* that Heidegger has compared the poems of Hölderlin to a bell held up in a still air, which a soft snow, falling on it, could make vibrate; likewise, the commentary should not be more than a little snow, sounding or ringing this ancient bell.

Finally, the text approaches the region where a supreme silence reigns, returning to the original condition from which it emerges. The space of our reading is suspended between these two blanks, which are necessary to understand our position as subjects of a desire to read, a desire which can be that of losing oneself in the difference of the written signs. This process, indefinitely postponing the absolute loss of the self, manifests itself in fiction as an equivalent of the work of mourning, especially when the text is absorbed by its re-enacting the killing and the burial of the dead father, like *Finnegans Wake*. At this point reader and author lose their identities to fuse with the general system of the textual unconscious, a concept which is necessary to facilitate a reading of the *Wake* but for which there is no space in this essay.

The constant re-reading of Joyce's works by his later texts yields some clues to the symbolic strategies he employs, and such is the case with the parody of all the titles of the stories in *Finnegans Wake*. This comes after the description of the way Shem writes over his own body with his excrements, thereby displaying universal history in this 'dividual chaos' (*F W*: 186) All the stories are then quoted, and their grouping is interesting, since it does not follow the order of the book. The first to be mentioned is 'Ivy Day . . .' ('circling the square, for the deathfête of Saint Ignaceous Poisonivy, of the Fickle Crowd' (*F W*: 186.)) and it is the only title to be so developed as to seem to refer to the *Wake* itself. Saint Ignatius has replaced Parnell, but their wake is held by the same fickle crowd of politicians.

Then twelve stories are jammed together in one paragraph, and play the role of the twelve jurymen, here answering the call of 'constable Sistersen' (alluding of course to the Sisters). The police inquest into this 'painful sake' does not forget the 'fun the concerned outgift of the dead med dirt' (*F W*: 187) and seems to have spotted a case of murder, a murder which is then distorted at the beginning of the following paragraph in: 'What mother?' (*F W*: 187) The two stories of 'Ivy Day' and 'A Mother' have thus been carefully isolated, the first seems to define the general structure of the quadrature of the circle, the last the problematics of the murdering mother. The shaunish figure of Justius who appears to defend the rights of the father's law addresses the shemish heresiarch directly, but also speaks to 'himother', to himself made other through the mother's alterity. It is very fitting that he too refuses a 'confession' and advises his brother to 'conceal himself' (*F W*: 188): 'You will need all the elements in the river to clean you over it all and a fortifine popespriestpower bull of attender to booth' (*F W*: 188).

I have already commented on enunciation in 'Ivy Day', but have not yet touched on 'A Mother'. This is one of the key-stories in that it shows a mother who is ready to jeopardise or even destroy her daughter's musical career because of her obstination in enforcing the law of a contract she has drawn herself. She has married Mr Kearney out of spite and to silence the slander of her friends, but she soon capitalises on his name: she seizes the opportunity to introduce her daughter into nationalist circles to promote her piano-playing. In this story we find the unique example of a father who is depicted as a 'model': 'For his part he was a model father' (*D*: 154). We soon realise that this comes from the perspective of Mrs Kearney, who really acts in his place, but still needs the moral caution of an abstract paternal function: 'She respected her husband in the same way as she respected the General Post Office, as something large, secure and fixed; and though she knew the small number of his talents she appreciated his abstract value as a male' (*D*: 159). He is conspicuously silent during the whole scene of crisis, and seems only capable of getting a cab, after his wife has shouted him to do so. Perhaps he is also capable of an epiphany, like the clock of the Ballast Office in Dublin! But undoubtedly his role prepares for the figure of the gigantic Finn, buried in the landscape of Phoenix Park. His name and his real absence are indispensable for the mother to become 'A' Mother, another symptom of paralysis; and the echoes of Lot's wife turned into an 'angry stone image' (*D*: 168) add a mythological layer to the signification of her frozen gestures.

Mrs Kearney insists on the literal respect of an abstract law, taking no account of the other codes, of economic, political, cultural, human concerns. She manifests the drive to a reduction of character to type, and *Finnegans Wake* will develop itself in the proliferation of such stereotypes. To stress the link between *Dubliners* and *Finnegans Wake*, a link attested by the note-books, I would be tempted to say that the Father hesitates between the paralysis of heresy and sexual sin – this would be best figured out by the GPI, or syphilitic 'general paralysis of the insane'[8] affecting Father Flynn, and the paralysis of mute orthodoxy, the GPO, or General Post Office, the pure ballast of an empty symbolic structure, defining the void centre of the capital 'to the wustworts of a Finntown's generous poet's office' (*F W*: 265). The shift from 'i' to 'o' could describe the range of the IOUs the father bequeath to their sisters and sons alike. This could also explain why Father Flynn had told the boy that the works of the Fathers were as bulky as the Post Office Directory, and why Gabriel proudly announces his arrival to his aunts with these words: 'Here I am as right as the mail . . .' (*D*: 201). Shaun the Post and Shem the Penman are there implicitly portrayed in the gnomon of the Father, squaring the circle of a city with a corner less or too much.

For the gnomon itself will have to be identified as the Name of the Father, a name ruling the silences, exiles and ruses of Noman; Outis or Ulysses: 'First you were Nomad, next you were Namar, now you're Numah and it's soon you'll be Nomon' (*F W*: 374).

Notes

1 Hermann Broch, 'James Joyce und die Gegenwart' in *Dichten und Erkennen*, Essays I (Zürich: Rhein-Verlag, 1955), p. 183–210.
2 John Henry Newman, *Essays Critical*, I, p. 128, quoted by Günter Biemer in *Newman on Tradition*, translated by K. Smith (London: Burns & Oates, 1967), p. 90.
3 I am much indebted here to the fascinating paper by R.I. Moore on 'Heresy as Disease' in *The Concept of Heresy in the Middle Ages (11th–13th C.)* (The Hague: Leuven University Press, 1976), p. 1–11, as well as to the other papers in this collection. This conception of heresy as disease seems to be shared implicitly by Mr Tate, the English master in *A Portrait*, when he discloses his diagnosis of Stephen's paper: 'This fellow has heresy in his essay' (*P*: 81). Heresy is never far from dogma, in the same way as 'canker' and 'cancer' contribute an ironic epitaph to Wolsey's grave in Leicester Abbey (*P*: 10).
4 For a more detailed consideration of the relation between neurosis and perversion in Joyce see Colin MacCabe, *James Joyce and the Revolution of the Word* (London: Macmillan 1979), p. 32–8, 104–29.

5 Gustave Flaubert, *Trois contes, Oeuvres Complètes* vol. 2 (Paris: Seuil, 1964), p. 169.
6 *Ibid.*, p. 175.
7 *Ibid.*, p. 176.
8 See the recent summary of this Joycean ghost by Matthew Hodgart, *James Joyce, A Student's Guide* (London: Routledge & Kegan Paul, 1978), p. 45–6, as well as the new material provided by John Garvin, *James Joyce's Disunited Kingdom and the Irish Dimension* (London: Macmillan, 1976), p. 37–45.

CHAPTER 4

Polytropic Man:
Paternity, Identity and Naming in
The Odyssey and
A Portrait of the Artist as a Young Man

Maud Ellmann

and Rouse found they spoke of Elias
in telling the tales of Odysseus   ΟΥ ΤΙΣ

ΟΥ ΤΙΣ

'I am noman, my name is noman'
But Wanjina is, shall we say, Ouan Jin
or the man with an education
and whose mouth was removed by his father
         because he made too many *things*
whereby cluttered the bushman's baggage
vide the expedition of Frobenius' pupils about 1938
            to Auss'ralia
Ouan Jin spoke and thereby created the named
           thereby making clutter

         Ezra Pound, 'Canto 74'[1]

Part I

1

Wondjina created the world of things by uttering their names. He haunts *The Pisan Cantos*, which lament his fate as if the poem's speaker felt embroiled in this namer's destiny. In his onomastic zeal, Wondjina named and made so many things it seemed the world could not contain his nomenclature. His father removed his mouth to stop the 'clutter'.

But the scourge does not conclude with this dismemberment. The name itself decays without a namer. Wondjina's silence creeps into the very fabric of the text, disfiguring the body of the name. Wondjina's own name splits into Ouan Jin, to bear the scar of his dismemberment.

Let us notice, also, how Odysseus sneaks into the poem's argument, under the same alias by which he gave the slip to that ungracious host, the Cyclops: 'I am noman, my name is noman'. As if to match the namer's mutilation, the poem stutters on Odysseus's name. His name, indeed, is lost among its aliases – or its 'Eliases', if we prefer the text's own idiom. From 'Odysseus' to 'ΟΫ ΤΙΣ' to 'noman', we behold an odyssey to anonymity.

Pound's version of Wondjina's fall introduces many of the problems of identity and creativity which this essay will explore in *A Portrait of the Artist* and *The Odyssey*. Identity, in both, is pitched between linguistic mastery and mutilation, between the name and its declension into anonymity. Both Joyce and Homer interweave the naming and creation of the universe with the fury of the father and the son.

2

We find an Hibernian Wondjina in Joyce's story 'Grace' in *Dubliners*. But it is with somewhat less dignity than his Australian counterpart that Mr Kernan falls from a state of 'grace' or linguistic competence. Following in the slippery footsteps of no nobler antecedent than Tim Finnegan, Kernan tumbles drunkenly downstairs. He bites off a piece of his own tongue in his descent.

Linguistic impotence, however, is not confined to oral injuries. Harder to diagnose are most of the linguistic incapacities that clutter Joyce's fiction: from Dubliners like Little Chandler, Farrington, or Mr Duffy who, for their diverse reasons, fail to write, to the incriminating 'hasitense' (*F W*: 97) of HCE. For all his credentials, Stephen Dedalus also figures in the fiction as the promise of a writing (and an exile) evermore about to be. Be they the words he writes or the words he reads, language, for Stephen, punctually gives way to the primeval chaos of its elements:

> He could scarcely interpret the letters of the signboards of the shops. (*P*: 95)

... he found himself glancing from one casual word to another on his right or left in stolid wonder that they had been so silently emptied of instantaneous sense. .... (*P*: 182)

The letters of the name of Dublin lay heavily upon his mind, pushing one another surlily hither and thither with slow boorish insistence. (*P*: 115)

The edifice of language trembles, or disintegrates into a heap of empty characters. Squalid, dishevelled, insubordinate to the regime of sense, the alphabet no longer seems to be constitutive of language, but to be engaged in a guerrilla war against the word.

Why have letters become so prodigious and unmasterable? Why do all these would-be writers fail – or fall? From *The Waste Land* to *The Cantos* to *Finnegans Wake*, the modernist epic mourns or ridicules the faith that that word and world could ever coalesce – that creation could consist in the stark enunciation of the name. Instead of Adam, it offers us Wondjina, or else a Babel of competing tongues. 'Broken heaventalk', (*F W*: 261), 'the crame of the whole faustian fustian' (*F W*: 292) – these are terms by which the *Wake* describes the grammar of its own linguistic outrage. All its verbal slips, its *lapsus linguae*, re-enact the lapse or fall of man. So Faust falls, and heaven breaks: each wounded word undoes the bond between the name, the namer, and the named.

If language has no origin, no Adam, but a dumb Wondjina at its source, no author can bestill its errancy: no father can control its prodigality. For it is the fall of the father – as the writings of both Joyce and Pound betray – that precipitates the fall of language. At least, their fortunes are continuous and intervolved. They represent – to put it in Wakese – the 'lapse at the same slapse' (*F W*: 291). Even Joyce's early fiction concerns itself, however surreptitiously, with sons in search of fathers and fathers bereft of sons; fathers forgotten, absent or repudiated; impostors, usurpers, and father surrogates – foreshadowing his broken patriarchs and fallen gods.

3

'Sing, Muse, of the polytropic man. . . .' (*O*: I, 1)

The Odyssey, which fascinates the modernist epic, is as agnostic towards paternity as Joyce's writing. When Athena asks Telemachus, a counterpart of Stephen Dedalus, if he is really the son of Odysseus, his answer casts paternity into irremediable doubt:

My mother says indeed I am his. I for my part
do not know. Nobody really knows his own father. (*O*: I, 215–16)

In *Ulysses*, Stephen brings Telemachus's doubt to bear not only on
the mortal father but the question of divine paternity:

> Fatherhood, in the sense of conscious begetting, is unknown to man. It is a
> mystical estate, an apostolic succession, from only begetter to only begot-
> ten. On that mystery and not on the madonna which the cunning Italian
> intellect flung to the mob of Europe the church is founded and founded
> irremovably because founded, like the world, macro- and microcosm,
> upon the void. Upon uncertitude, upon unlikelihood. . . . Paternity may be
> a legal fiction. Who is the father of any son that any son should love him or
> he any son? (*U*: 207)

God or man, the father comes to represent at once a founding void
and a founding fiction. The 'father' stands for singular creation, for
unique authorship: 'from only begetter to only begotten'. But the
question that he introduces is prolific. By no means is this the last
time that Athena's question, explicit or implicit, will be readdressed
in Joyce.

'Where did thots come from?' demands a nameless voice in *Finnegans Wake* (597). 'Thot' is strategically misspelt, omitting the
'ugh' which haunts the modern English word like an ancestral ghost:
and the neologism confuses 'thought' with 'tot'.

The question itself may well come from Freud, as well as Homer,
among Joyce's own capricious literary patrilineage. Freud claimed
that the incessant questions children ask are variations, garbled or
sophisticated, on the single theme of 'Where do babies come from?'[3]
The critic's overwhelming question, 'Where do texts come from?'
might be seen as yet another version of the 'tot's' insatiable demand.

Dismembered of his mouth or tongue, condemned to 'hasitense' or
silence, the fallen father of the *Wake* can neither speak his thoughts
nor name his tots. No more can tots like Stephen Dedalus find out
their fathers, the authors of their strange un-Irish names. With the
fall of the father, the question of the origin of texts and babies,
thoughts or tots, becomes at once rhetorical and inexhaustible. The
word in search of a speaker – the letter in search of a scribe – the
thought in search of a thinker – the son in search of a sire: all these
orphans circulate through Joyce's writing, adrift as the itinerant
Odysseus, unappeased as fatherless Telemachus. Their wanderings
bear witness to convulsions in the order by which fathers beget sons,
authors beget thoughts, and gods beget worlds.

If Telemachus cannot be sure who his own father is, he cannot guarantee his own 'entelechy' (*U*: 190): his name, his lineage, or his substantial unity. Nor is his scepticism towards paternity the only instance where *The Odyssey* casts doubt upon identity. It may be that what attracted Joyce's writing, as it attracted Pound's, to Homer's ramifying postscript to *The Iliad*, was not so much the sanctity of its antiquity (as Eliot suggests),[4] but the questions that *The Odyssey* revolves – about the nature of the self, its history and its fictions.

For these are questions which enthrall *A Portrait of the Artist as a Young Man*. Joyce, as autobiographer, is bound to be concerned with the problem of the composition of identity. In the first part of this essay I shall put *The Odyssey* in counterpoint with Joyce's writings, to see what their encounter yields about the nature of the self and its self-portraiture. I do not mean, by this procedure, to suggest that Homer represents the 'source' of Joyce's *Portrait*. Who am I, after all, to answer the unanswerable question, 'Where did thots come from?' What intrigues me, rather, are the fortunes of identity in these two texts.

Next, I shall pursue the first Odysseus a little further. But the examples of his own pursuers should warn us that we cannot hope to hold him down. Odysseus will slip away from any reader who, like the Cyclops or the Sirens, would attempt to master, capture or enclose him, or to woo him to interpretative obedience. For the reader, as for Penelope, 'Odysseus' means wishing, waiting, hunting, missing, mourning: his name betokens that which in the text escapes a single vision, or subtler sorceries. The charms of Circe or Calypso can never tame or fix the 'polytropic man' (*O*: I, 1).

Lastly, I shall investigate, in more detail, the weaving and un-weaving (*U*: 194) of identity in Joyce's *Portrait*, concluding with a surreptitious glance at *Finnegans Wake*. By this time, we shall have begun to see two processes encroaching on the subject's mythic plenitude or unity. These I shall call 'scarification' and 'circulation' –though they really represent two movements in a single and dividual activity.

First of all, the scar, in Joyce and Homer, allies itself illicitly to nomination. It is Odysseus's scar which betrays his name to Euryc-leia: while in *A Portrait*, Stephen's name itself – as we shall see – dissolves into a scar. In a perversion of the Incarnation, the name becomes the point where word and flesh meet in a single scar.

The scar, then, represents the trace of a transaction: the conversion of the word into the flesh. This 'transaction' brings us into the domain of '*circulation*'. I suspect, however, that it would be ill-advised to speak of 'circulation' as if it were a concept or a principle. Circulation cannot really be abstracted from the text's peculiar economic policies, its own specific traffic regulations. Let it be suggested, then, in mere anticipation, that Joyce and Homer set identity adrift. Identity becomes the site of restless commerce, interchange, contagion between language and the body, word and flesh.

'Sing, Muse, of the polytropic man', invokes the *Odyssey*. Odysseus, as we shall see, turns out to be as plural in his 'tropes' as in his wanderings. In Joyce, the turnings intricate of word and flesh, the orbits of the Eucharist, digestion, or the stars, together with the most eclectic images of cyclicality, return, and repetition, constitute a 'polytropic' lexicon of circulation. As the Church, for Stephen, founds itself upon unlikelihood, and like the world revolving in the void, the subject comes to circulate around the scar that hollows out his name.

Part II

1

Odysseus eludes the reader as cunningly as he slips by the blinded Cyclops. With a kind of 'scrupulous meanness', the text withholds the father till we have made a detour through four books about the son. 'Fit out a ship with twenty oars,' urges Athena to Telemachus,

and go out to ask about your father who is so long absent,
on the chance some mortal man can tell you, who has listened to Rumour
sent by Zeus. She more than others spreads news among people (*O*: I,
280–3).

Like Telemachus, the reader is to learn about the father, not directly, but through 'Rumour', or the legends of the poets, or the stories that Odysseus invents about himself. 'A praiser of his own past' (*P*: 245), his epic consists not only of his wanderings at sea, but of his circumnavigations in the word. Uninvited to the hero's greatest wanderings, the reader weaves, instead, through the odyssey of his autobiographies.

Where do autobiographies come from? Where can we locate their subject and their source? Let us meander, for a little while, through *The Odyssey* and Joyce's writings, to see how intricately all these texts evade an answer to the question of their origin.

2

When Odysseus regales the Phæacians with the tale of his Great Wanderings, the reader also learns of his adventures retrospectively and secondhand. In addition, however, to this 'authentic' tale, he fabricates a multitude of counterfeit identities. First he fences off the questions that Athena puts to him, as to his name, his origins and genealogy, by claiming that he is a murderer from Crete, fleeing retribution for his crime (O: XIII 256–86).

Thenceforth, he tries in turn to hoodwink Eumæus, Telemachus, the suitors and Penelope with a stock of bogus autobiographies. None of these mortals can see through his fictions so swiftly as the gray-eyed goddess.

The most extravagant is the lie he tells Eumæus. He is hoping that the swineherd might lend him a mantle, disguised in which he could surprise the suitors who swarm round Penelope. But instead of asking for the disguise directly, he tells a lie about Odysseus lying to acquire a mantle for the present liar, whom Eumæus fails to recognise as Odysseus. Here fiction so enfolds itself with fact that one can scarcely disentangle them (O: XIV, 459–506).

Odysseus's lies, in general, eschew the monstrous and the supernatural so that they seem more plausible than truth. He presents himself, with variations, as a nobleman misused by fortune. Every incognito he adopts involves the leitmotif of exile: in all personae – so it seems – Odysseus must roam. The more he wanders from the 'land of his fathers', the more he multiplies in false identities. All his stories serve as answers to the question, spoken or unspoken, raised by his own strange and sudden apparition: 'Who are you and where do you come from?'[5]

Evidently, there is no one answer to the question of origination and identity. Odysseus meanders through as many memoirs as he errs among enchanted isles. His journey in the flesh, with all its waywardness, detours, and indirections, shadows forth the ruses of his autobiography.

And no more than Odysseus is the artist of *A Portrait of the Artist* to content himself with one self-portrait or self-definition. Joyce's novel only represents one version of an indefatigable autobiography. Not one portrait, but three in turn proceeded from the artist's pen: a first draft, whose rejection gave rise to *Stephen Hero* and to what we regard, teleologically, as the final text. As for this last version, the indefinite article of its title suggests that it, too, may only mark another Wordsworthian preparation to write.[6] It is *A Portrait*, not *the* portrait. From the first a repetition of the author's life, Joyce's autobiography seems henceforth destined to repeat itself.

3

> These nights are endless, and man can sleep through them,
> or he can enjoy listening to stories, and you have no need
> to go to bed before it is time. Too much sleep is only
> a bore. . . .
> . . . we two, sitting here in the shelter, eating and drinking
> shall entertain each other remembering and retelling
> our sad sorrows. (O: XV, 392–400)

We may conclude, therefore, that as far as Joyce and Homer are concerned, identity can never rest in any single definition. The autobiographer cannot escape his autobiographies. Instead, identity consists of the tales it spins about itself in the attempt to recover its own origins.

Such movements are at work in the passage from *The Cantos* we began with:

> and Rouse found they spoke of Elias
> in telling the tales of Odysseus

Guy Davenport, in 'Pound and Frobenius',[7] shows that this passage refers to the circulation of Odysseus's name in legend. The scholar W.D. Rouse repeated the itinerary of *The Odyssey*. In the Greek islands that he visited, the tales of Odysseus continued to proliferate. 'Rouse found' that the hero had been conflated with Elias, the prophet: and Pound, in turn, conflates these tales with the tales of Frobenius's pupils. Pound's is a tale of Rouse's tale of the tales he heard of Odysseus. It seems that history has itself conspired to prolong the fictive movements of *The Odyssey* – creating ever more unlikely aliases for Odysseus.

'These nights are endless,' says Eumæus to Odysseus: and it is in these endless nights they spend 'remembering and retelling' that they forge their 'sorrows' and themselves. Their presence, like

Scheherezade's, depends upon a thousand recitations of identity. When Odysseus regains his kingdom, and with it his original identity, he vanishes, with all his pseudonyms, into the silence that is Ithaca.

A *Portrait of the Artist* also takes its hero back to the land of his fathers. This return to origins takes the form of an excursion to Cork; and an attempt – if the pun can be excused – to cork identity. The journey culminates in a search for the initials which identify the father and the son: 'S.D.'. But remembering gives way to a dismemberment: these initials, rather than substantial origins, present themselves at last as living scars. What is more, another scar, or letter, or best of all, 'scarletter' (to contract Hawthorne's title, which also finds its way into *Ulysses*, in the form of the wandering 'scarlet letters' 'H.E.L.Y.S.' (*U*: 154)) – another scarletter precedes these initials in the narrative, and in a sense preempts the name that they imply. This wound, or word, is 'Fœtus'. As we shall see, its cutting letters move Stephen to a horror as extreme as it is unexplained.

So, flaunting an originary fulness of identity, these scars will not be corked, will not be stoppered. They infringe the unity and self-containment that the word identity has come to imply. It is an ironic fact, however, that the word 'identity' itself cannot be traced to any certain origin. According to the *O.E.D*, etymologists argue as to whether it derives from the Latin *idem*, meaning 'the same'; or *identidem*, which means 'over and over again, repeatedly'. It is hard to understand how the concept of a seamless unity of personality could have evolved from two such roots. 'The same over and over again' sounds much more like the repetition of the scars of Stephen Dedalus's name.

But now, in Odyssean fashion, I shall defer the recognition of these scars, and cast a last and backward glance at Homer's Ithaca. This is where Odysseus's name also reclaims its habitation in a scar. We have already seen how Odysseus cannot be fixed, but circulates among his autobiographies. The other side of 'circulation', as I suggested earlier, is 'scarification': and we have now to trace the scar's effects upon identity.

4

'*The scar's story and the story's scar*'

Having returned to Ithaca, Odysseus, in Book XIX, has entered his own house under the camouflage of yet another incognito. When his old nurse Eurycleia comes to wash his feet, she sets eyes upon the mark which indelibly and unmistakeably, and even through Athena's artifices, betrays Odysseus's true identity:

> . . . the old woman took up the shining basin
> she used for foot washing, and poured in a great deal of water, the cold
> first, and then she added the hot to it. Now Odysseus
> was sitting close to the fire, but suddenly turned to the dark side;
> for presently he thought in his heart that, as she handled him,
> she might be aware of his scar, and all his story might come out. (O: XIX,
> 386–91)

'She might be aware of his scar, and all his story might come out.' So closely joined are scar and story, under the gaze of Eurycleia, that Odysseus's story seems almost to issue, literally, from his scar.[8] Indeed, in terms of the narrative, two more stories do 'come out' or issue from the mention of his scar. The recognition of the scar produces an elision in the narrative. A long digression follows, recounting two apparently disjointed episodes from the hero's infancy and youth. This flashback occupies almost a hundred lines before the text returns to Eurycleia's recognition.

It is as if Odysseus's scar had scarred the narrative itself, which plunges into memory and self-dismemberment.[9] The two episodes which the digression treats as one concern two marks which brand the subject, word and flesh: his name and scar:

> Autolykos came once to the rich country of Ithaca,
> and found that a child there was newly born to his daughter;
> and, as he finished his evening meal, Eurykleia laid him
> upon his very knees, and spoke him a word and named him:
> 'Autolykos, now find yourself that name you will bestow
> on your own child's dear child, for you have prayed much to have him.'
>   Then Autolykos spoke to her and gave her an answer:
> 'My son-in-law and daughter, give him the name I tell you;
> since I have come to this place distasteful to many, women
> and men alike on the prospering earth, so let him be given
> the name Odysseus, that is distasteful.' (O: XIX, 399–409)

This a funny sort of name to have. 'Odysseus, that is distasteful', tells us more about the namer's irritation than it identifies the infant that it names. That the name thus represents a matrilineal bequest (for Autolycus is Odysseus's maternal grandfather) may further complicate the name, and mitigate the influence of the paternity it normally should guarantee.

Perhaps it is because of this capricious naming that the name must be reiterated in a cicatrix. For we proceed, with scarcely a caesura, from the naming to the maiming of Odysseus. As a young man, hunting with Autolycus, Odysseus receives the wound that makes his name:

> The hunters came to a wooded valley . . .
> there, inside that thick of the bush, was the lair of a great boar.
>
> . . .
>
> The thudding made by feet of men and dogs came to him
> as they closed on him in the hunt, and against them he from his woodlair
> bristled strongly his nape, and with fire from his eyes glaring
> stood up to face them close. The first of all was Odysseus,
> who swept in, holding high in his heavy hand the long spear,
> and furious to stab, but too quick for him the boar drove
> over the knee, and with his tusk gashed much of the flesh. . . . (O: XIX, 435–50)

Thus does the scar reopen, and let its story out. The mutilation and the name, in this digression, succeed the story and the scar in a further lesion of the word and flesh. Indeed, they intertwist with such complexity that it is necessary to map out the circulation of the name, the story and the scar:

The first movement (reading from the bottom left) is from the *scar* to the *story* that 'comes out' of it. This first story, as we have seen, is the story of the naming of Odysseus. And scarcely has Autolycus uttered 'Odysseus' when another *story* issues from the *name*: the story of the *scar*. Now, in flesh as yet anonymous and undismembered, the wild boar burns his indelible brand. Having slain the boar, the wounded hero returns to Ithaca in triumph. But one last *story* issues from the *scar* before the flashback ends:

and there his father and queenly mother
were glad in his homecoming, and asked about all that had happened,
and how he came by his wound, and he told well his story . . . (*O*: XIX,
462–4)

Thus the scar again must tell its story. We are unlikely ever to
encounter a more loquacious scar. The cycle ends with Eurycleia's
own repeated recognition, when she sees the scar and names it, after
the digression, as 'Odysseus'.

Now that we have traced the circulation of the scar, let us see if we
can glimpse its properties. Firstly, the scar repeats. A living scar, it
constantly resurges and reiterates itself. Secondly, the scar secretes –
and in a double sense: for while it lets the hero's story out it also
hoards it in reserve, in secret. It secretes, without distinction, in the
word and in the flesh, and sets both into fitful circulation. What is
more, the scar erupts into the narrative itself, and breaks its continuity. Linear progression suddenly gives way to cycles of remembering and dismembering.

It is the inscription of the wound upon the flesh that activates the
power in the name. By the same token, the scar depends upon the
name for its significance. It could not signify identity were it not so
inextricably engrafted in the name. This is why the term 'scarletter'
best befits Odysseus's cicatrix. The scar, effectively, is that which
writes Odysseus's name.

Why does the scar intrude into the narrative so late, when it is only
just about to close? We should expect this tale of naming and of
maiming to introduce the hero rather than to greet his last return. But
the essential feature of the scarletter that imprints identity is the
retrospective nature of its work. Because it is a letter, it demands a
reader to be recognised: and reading is a retrospective act. Only after
the event of the inscription can one read the letter that remains.
Without a reader, the scar could never tell its story: sealed in silence
on the body, it awaits a Eurycleia to discover it and read it as a name.
Only the second instance, the return, the re-cognition, can wake the
scar and make it speak.

If naming, then, involves a mutilation, the subject's unity is
threatened in the very sign by which he comes to be. The scar
dismembers that which it identifies: it fractures what it names. If it
seems to set a seal upon the subject, it also represents a seam through
which identity may constantly escape.

5

'Noman and Agnomen'

Perhaps the reason, therefore, that Odysseus so constantly escapes detection is that his name has pitched its mansion in his scar. However polytropic his identities, the name that lodges in a scar can never change. The letters of his name throb through the narrative – in contrast to his flexible persona – indelible, unaltered, unappeased. They resurge, despite his secrecies, in others' voices: they petrify his life into a legend. He confronts his name and reputation as his own self-spectre. A legislation seems to be at work: the person wanders, while the name remains.

According to Joyce, however, there is at least one exception to this rule. It does not suffice, for him, to hinge the name upon a scar: the name itself must suffer scarification.

The famous instance of this mutilation occurs when Odysseus tells the Cyclops that his name is nobody (*O*: IX, 366–7). Nobody, or 'noman', as Pound and Joyce translate it, is what the first half of 'Odys-seus' means when the second half, according to Joyce, has been lopped off.[10] The hero severs 'Zeus' from Odysseus – much as Pound severs 'Ouan' from 'Jin' – and noman – ΟΎ ΤΙΣ – is the stump that he retains.

Most Greek scholars would contest this etymology. But where do words come from? It is the very waywardness of etymologies and genealogies that Joyce and Homer's odysseys enjoy. These texts set words, as well as flesh, adrift: no word can ever quite regain its roots, its Ithaca. This derivation of Odysseus does not misfit the text's impertinence towards origins. If we suspend our disbelief towards Joyce's etymology, ΟΎ ΤΙΣ, though it conceals the name 'Odysseus', also betrays the name's true nature. ΟΎ ΤΙΣ is literally the scar of the dismembered name Odysseus.

Noman is a name that undoes nomination: it unnames what it names. What taxonomy can we ourselves attach to such a signature? The *Wake*, perhaps, suggests a classification. The second chapter of the *Wake* pretends to trace the fallen father's name back to its origins. It calls his name an 'occupational *agnomen*' (*F W*: 30; my italics). 'Noman' whispers in agnomen, and gives the name a taint of anonymity. It implies that the name of the father will not be traced to an originary fulness of identity. Rather, the further back one seeks its origins, the more the name unravels into anonymity:

First you were Nomad, next you were Namar, now you're Numah and it's soon you'll be Nomon. (*F W*: 374)

Here agnomens come thick and fast. The name itself becomes a nomad, like the errant characters it names. This series mocks the very notion of an etymology which might restore the person to his name. One cannot sift the source from its derivatives, the original name from its corrupted forms. The first name in the series no more reliably identifies the hero than the last. One agnomen leads only to another agnomen, as every story only yields another scar.

Part III

1

'What with your name and your ideas . . . Are you Irish at all?' (*P*: 206)

A Portrait of the Artist, too, as I shall try to show, conceives identity as a scar without an origin – without an author: and at last, without even a name. But I should specify, at once, that Joyce's work is not 'about' a scar. To say that the text is 'about' something is to reinstate the false dichotomy of form and content which no writing more than Joyce's has so flagrantly transgressed. The scar that lodges in the text is not a secret, to be uncovered by a probing exegesis: it is so unhidden that like Poe's purloined letter, we overlook it if we search for it too hard. Nor is it a key that will unlock the text, a final meaning into which the text's opacities dissolve: as if *A Portrait* were nothing but a euphemism for a scar. The signification of the scar consists in what it works, not what it is, for it is nothing but a principle of structure. It resurges in the epidermis of the text itself. The cuts and repetitions of the narrative rehearse the act of mutilation through which – to borrow Davin's Irishism from *A Portrait* – identity is 'disremeber[ed]' (*P*: 185) endlessly. In short, the scar becomes a form of punctuation.

Since, however, I have discussed the punctuation of the scar elsewhere,[11] I shall pursue some of its related properties. For we also know the scar by its secretion: by that which it absorbs, reserves or hoards, and that which it emits to circulate. In *A Portrait*, identity devolves into a complex circulation of the word and flesh. We may discern three major modes of traffic in the text. The first two I shall call, respectively, the economies of 'flow' and 'influence'. The last, the subtlest and the most duplicitous is that which Stephen designates as 'literature'. All the transactions that these economies encompass operate, at once, in the corporeal domain, and in the tropes which constitute the modern polytropic man.

2

'The Economy of Flows'

Let us turn first to the economy of flows. Here the subject purges or evacuates himself, and issues forth in all kinds of secretions. The aesthetic name for this economy is 'epic'. In epic form, according to Stephen,

> The personality of the artist passes into the narration itself, flowing round and round the persons and the action like a vital sea. (*P*: 219; see also 172)

Like Shem, the epic poet in this definition 'flows' or 'passes' into his own writing, disremembering his personality. 'Passing' is, in fact, the password for the economy of flows within the text (*passim*), and anything from speech to excrement can form its currency:

> His sins trickled from his lips, one by one, trickled in shameful drops from his soul festering and oozing like a sore, a squalid stream of vice. The last sins oozed forth, sluggish, filthy. (*P*: 148)

Here blood and puss and excrement have oozed into the metaphor, staining Stephen's words with flesh and flesh with words.

Rhetorically, the economy of flows corresponds to the trope of synecdoche – the part for the whole. For through these flows, the subject is fragmented and dispersed into his parts – his words, his members, his secretions – to flow into a 'vital' and undifferentiated sea.

Stephen vacillates between two states the text habitually describes as 'unrest' and 'weariness' (*passim*). These are broken by 'ejaculations', a word which spans linguistic and corporeal domains (*P*: 151). This bridge-word indicates that passion, too, must pass through language: it is through speech that flesh demands to be 'express[ed] . . . press[ed] out again' (*P*: 211; see also 173):

> Such moments passed and the wasting fires of lust sprang up again. The verses passed from his lips and the inarticulate cries and the unspoken brutal words rushed forth from his brain to force a passage. (*P*: 102)

On this occasion, the economy of flows is working pretty smoothly. If – as often happens – any of the flows are blocked, and cannot find an outlet, a devastating weariness results:

> The old restless moodiness had again filled his breast as it had done on the night of the party but had not found an outlet in verse . . . and all day the stream of gloomy tenderness within him had started forth and returned upon itself in dark courses and eddies, wearying him in the end. . . . (*P*: 79)

In this economy, verse and semen merge into a single undistinguished fluency. Nor can they protect themselves from the contamination of any other form of passing or evacuation (*P*: 142). Money 'runs' or flows through Stephen's fingers (*P*: 100); confessions 'trickle' from his lips; verses ooze, or pour, or burst orgasmically.

> A soft liquid joy like the noise of many waters flowed over his memory
> . . .
> A soft liquid joy flowed through the words where the soft long vowels hurtled noiselessly and fell away, lapping and flowing back. . . . (*P*: 230)

Poetry at last becomes as spontaneous an overflow as Wordsworth could have wished.

Many rhythms punctuate these flows, from peristalsis to the beating of the heart. The regularities of inspiration and deflation, systole and diastole or a prolonged frottage, give way to sudden climaxes and palpitations, ecstacy's crescendo and its denouement. All these, in fugue or counterpoint, provide a score for the economy of flows. Even lunar, menstrual, or 'tidal' phrasing creeps into the music of evacuation:

> The sentiment of the opening bars, their languor and supple movement, evoked the incommunicable emotion which had been the cause of all his day's unrest and of his impatient movement of a moment before. His unrest issued from him like a wave of sound: and on the tide of flowing music the ark was journeying, trailing her cable of lanterns in her wake. (*P*: 77)

These metaphors flaunt gender. They sweep aside, as quibbles or as euphemisms, all discriminations between the body's orifices. In a mischievous rhetorical imperialism, the economy of flows lays siege to all distinctions which anatomy or prudery uphold. No function can maintain its semiotic chastity. The boundaries between the genders, or sex and excrement, or word and flesh, succumb to impudent and restless violations.

According to the whim of this economy, therefore, the streams and floods which pass from Stephen's lips assume a seminal, or menstrual, or excremental guise. Breath, blood, vomit and saliva also issue from this orifice in the form of speech:

> He stretched out his arms in the street to hold fast the frail swooning form that eluded him and incited him: and the cry that he had strangled for so long in his throat *issued* from his lips. It broke from him like a wail of despair from a hell of sufferers and died in a wail of furious entreaty, a cry for an iniquitous abandonment, a cry which was but an echo of an obscene scrawl which he had read on the oozing wall of a urinal. (*P*: 102–3; my italics)

The oozing echo of an obscene scrawl, this cry is in the strictest sense a dirty word. It 'comes' orgasmically, or diarrhetically, or spurts like blood from a reopened wound.

'Issue' is another word which fascinates the text, and which besprinkles it, if anything, more lavishly than 'pass'. Its ambiguities encompass most of the perverse and polymorphous range of this economy. Books, babies, banknotes, and all the tides which ebb through Stephen's body may be 'issued', so to enter into circulation.

'Issue', then, enfolds the body with the word like the laconic image of a dream: it condenses all the 'unrest' of these flows. Like the exchequer or the mint, the subject's body 'issues' him in 'floods', or 'wakes', or 'trail[s] of foolish words' (*P*: 90).

3

'The Economy of Influence' Phase 1: 'Cuisine Minceur'

Everything that 'issues' out of Stephen must, however, first pass into him. In complicity, therefore, with his expenditures, his flows, is an economic policy of 'influence'. Food – including food for thought – participates in this economy: and transubstantial victuals particularly haunt the text (cf. *P*: 225). The sacrament converts the Word of God into a totem feast, and *A Portrait* imitates its recipe. Depending on the speaker or the cook, language can become an haute cuisine, a Eucharist or Irish stew. 'Stuff it into you,' Stephen's belly counsels him. In his greed, he gobbles words as eagerly as food (*P*: 104). He too, however, vacillates between rapacity, disgust and the discriminations of a mellowed connoisseur:

he tasted in the language of memory ambered wines, dying fallings of sweet airs. . . . (P: 237)

The text will make a meal of almost anything. Here Stephen literally eats his words. But he rarely gets the chance to sample anything so sweet as the language of his memory. Most food, or words, are old and stale: the crumbs and rotting remnants other diners, other speakers left behind:

> Mr Dedalus pushed his plate over to Stephen and bade him finish what was on it. (P: 73)

> He drained his third cup of watery tea to the dregs and set to chewing the crusts of fried bread that were scattered near him, staring into the dark pool of the jar. The yellow dripping had been scooped out like a boghole. . . . (P: 177)

Elsewhere, these scraps and dregs and pickings receive such meticulous attention that one would think the text itself were gluttonous:

> Tea was nearly over and only the last of the second watered tea remained in the bottoms of the small glassjars and jampots which did service for teacups. Discarded crusts and lumps of sugared bread, turned brown by the tea which had been poured over them, lay scattered on the table. Little wells of tea lay here and there on the board and a knife with a broken ivory handle was stuck through the pith of a ravaged turnover. (P: 167)

What goes for flesh goes for words. Language reaches Stephen half devoured:

> Old phrases, sweet only with a disinterred sweetness like the figseeds Cranly rooted out of his gleaming teeth. (P: 237)

4

'The Economy of Influence' Phase 2: 'Inspiration'

Although the process of digestion is ubiquitous, the influence of smell, in this economy, is even less resistable than food. Any orifice but Stephen's nose can regulate or 'mortify' itself:

> To mortify his smell was more difficult as he found in himself no instinctive repugnance to bad odours, whether they were the odours of the outdoor world such as those of dung and tar or the odours of his own person among which he had made many curious comparisons and experiments. (P: 154)

The words and flesh of the economy of influence converge into a single 'lunguage'. It is through pneumatic – or 'rheumatic' – means that literature disseminates its influence. The 'spirit of Ibsen', for example, blows through Stephen 'like a keen wind' (*P*: 179). Less clean and less Norwegian, unfortunately, are the verbal exhalations that besiege our hero's nose the most relentlessly:

> A smell of molten tallow came up from the dean's candlebutts and fused itself in Stephen's consciousness with the jingle of the words, bucket and lamp and lamp and bucket. (*P*: 192)

> His last phrase, soursmelling as the smoke of charcoal and dishearten- ing, excited Stephen's brain, over which its fumes seemed to brood. (*P*: 251)

Stephen's lungs provide a rendezvous for flow and influence. Here, the 'gibes and violence of speech' he breaths can 'pass . . . out . . . into his crude writings' (*P*: 80). Of all conversions in the text, evaporation is the least malodorous of ways that influence can turn back into flow:

> Conscious of his desire she was waking from odorous sleep, the temptress of his villanelle. . . . Her nakedness yielded to him, radiant, warm, odor- ous and lavishlimbed, enfolded him like a shining cloud, enfolded him like water with a liquid life: and like a cloud of vapour or like waters circumf- luent in space the liquid letters of speech . . . flowed forth over his brain. (*P*: 227)

This is how influence reverts to flow. Here the two economies are working smoothly and harmoniously: the vapours, odorous but sweet, that the 'temptress of the villanelle' lets forth, evaporate 'like a shining cloud', and issue in a rain of 'liquid letters'.

Seldom does the change from flesh to word extend such mercy to the nose. Art cannot emerge from the sluggish matter of the 'earth' (*P*: 173), nor metre rise from peristalsis, without a trace, however faint, of body odour.

Like the transformations of the Eucharist, these changes corres- pond rhetorically to metaphor, to balance the metonymies of the economy of flows. (Nor does the Eucharist escape the taint of traffic in the flesh. Any wine 'becomes water again' (*U*: 25), however blessed its origin. The 'excrementitious intelligence' of the 'Ballad of Joking Jesus' insinuates itself into *A Portrait*, too (*P*: 216.)) But Stephen's commerce with his influences tends, by contrast, to con-

clude in repetition rather than in metaphor, or in tautologies in lieu
of transsubstantiations.

For 'spontaneous' as they may be, Stephen's overflows provide an
'outlet' for his influences — which he recycles almost automatically,
scarcely staining others' words with his desires. Stephen's verses tend
to plagiarise his literary influences, or to exhale the air(s) that other
breathers left behind. Most of his attempts at verse are recorded only
paralyptically — but those few phrases which the text vouchsafes are
woven closely with quotation. Even the word 'weariness' which
issues from his crises of 'unrest' is recycled from Shelley and Ben
Jonson (P: 99; 106; 180).

If this quotation fails to come to his relief, 'the soft speeches of
Claude Melnotte' rise to his lips to 'ease . . . his unrest' (P: 102). Even
Stephen's dirty word turns out, as we have seen, to be the 'echo' of a
graffitti oozing in a urinal: where the wake of language — writing — is
stained by urine, the wake of the flesh. Almost every word that
passes, flows, or issues out of Stephen pauses first, and for a time, in
literature, until its stench conducts it to his nose, to splutter forth as
liquid speech again.

So, imperceptibly, we have transgressed the boundaries of the last,
and most mysterious economy.

5

'The Economy of Literature'

Stephen gives the name of 'literature' to this economy:

> — One difficulty, said Stephen, in esthetic discussion is to know whether
> words are being used according to the literary tradition or according to the
> tradition of the marketplace. I remember a sentence of Newman's in
> which he says of the Blessed Virgin that she was detained in the full
> company of the saints. The use of the word in the marketplace is quite
> different. *I hope I am not detaining you.*
> — Not in the least, said the dean politely.
> — No, no, said Stephen, smiling, I mean. . . .
> — Yes, yes: I see, said the dean quickly, I quite catch the point: *detain*. (P:
> 192)

The word 'detain' enters the domain of 'literature' when Stephen
forbids the English dean to let it circulate. Literature 'detains' language as the miser hoards his money, or the saints detain the virgin:

and her chastity may also represent a form of hoarding. The economy of 'literature' consists of words and flesh detained, held back, sequestered from the traffic of the marketplace.

Detained, these words become *lacunae*, dismembering the fabric of the text. Several words occulted into literature erupt into the narrative like living scars. They interrupt its fluid interchanges. The word 'Fœtus', for example, in the passage I shall presently discuss, resists all pressure to convert it from its literality. When 'literature' intrudes, however momentarily, it halts transactions in the marketplace of flow and influence – blocking 'metaphor', or the exchange of words for flesh:

> He stood still and gazed up at the sombre porch of the morgue and from that to the dark cobbled laneway at its side. He saw the word *Lotts* on the wall of the lane and breathed slowly the rank heavy air. (*P*: 89)

'Lotts' – opaque, unyielding, literal – presents itself in smelling distance of the morgue. The odour it evokes for Stephen is of 'horse piss and rotted straw' (*P*: 89). Of all the vapours, putrid or perfumed, that circulate through Stephen's nose, the most persistent and intense is the stench which emanates from 'literature'. Worse than the smell of speech is the stink of writing – dead speech stored in literature – which passes through his hospitable nose and dribbles from his lips as speech again. Fetid flesh and stagnant speech, and the aroma of mortality that circumambulates the text: all these, in the last instance, proceed from the economy of literature.

Stephen is to some extent responsible for literature's pollution of the atmosphere. He makes some contributions to the stench himself:

> The sordid details of his orgies stank under his very nostrils . . . the foul long letters he had written in the joy of guilty confession and carried secretly for days and days only to throw them under cover of night among the grass in the corner of a field or beneath some hingeless door or in some niche in the hedges where a girl might come upon them as she walked by and read them secretly. (*P*: 119)

Here Stephen has confessed to a secretion, in the double sense: for in these filthy letters he at once emits his lust and stores it in these secret niches. This double action will remind the reader of the secrets and secretions of the scarletter. Like scars, also, Stephen's littered letters administer deferred effects. Their stench is not released immediately: they must await a younger and an Irish Eurycleia to read them and let forth their flatulence.

While these letters reek of sex or excrement, the legends written in shop windows emit the 'deadly exhalations' of mortality:

> diffusing in the air around him [was] a tenuous and deadly exhalation and he found himself glancing from one casual word to another on his right or left in stolid wonder that they had been so silently emptied of instantaneous sense until every mean shop legend bound his mind like the words of a spell and his soul shrivelled up, sighing with age as he walked on in a lane among heaps of dead language. His own consciousness of language was ebbing from his brain and trickling into the very words themselves which set to band and disband themselves in wayward rhythms:
>
> > *The ivy whines upon the wall*
> > *And whines and twines upon the wall*
> > *The ivy whines upon the wall*
> > *The yellow ivy on the wall*
> > *Ivy, ivy up the wall.*
>
> Did any one ever hear such drivel? Lord Almighty! Who ever heard of ivy whining on a wall? (*P*: 182)

This is how 'dead language' smells, when words have been withdrawn from circulation, heaped up in 'mean' or miserly shop legends, and hoarded in the silence, exile and cunning of a writing always scrupulously mean. These words, like flesh, break up in loose synechdoches. Like the body's members and secretions, their letters will not stay in place, will not stand still. Stephen cannot help but breath their deadly odour, and pass it out again — as 'drivel'.

In this example, then, the three economies participate in a complete transaction. The influence of mortal odours issues in the flow of drivel, and it is the dead speech of the economy of literature that occasions both of these deferred effects. Let us now proceed to the initials I have previously mentioned that betray the father and the son: to see how Stephen's letters, his founding 'literature', reveal themselves at last as living scars.

6

The fourth section of chapter 2 involves an autobiography within an autobiography: for it describes Simon Dedalus's sentimental journey to his origins in Cork, and his struggle to remember his fugitive history. His nostalgia reaches its climax in the search for his initials, carved as deeply in a school desk as the boar's tusk tore into Odysseus's thigh.

Although the father's rehearsals of his past, and his excavation of his name, seem to repossess his lost identity, the real motive of the journey belies this sentiment. For he returns to his origins only to sell them away. He is to auction his belongings, and to dispossess himself and his resentful son (P: 90).

What is more, another scar intrudes itself into the narrative, and seems to usurp or obliterate the cutting letters of his name. Remembering reverts to disremembering.

> They passed into the anatomy theatre where Mr Dedalus, the porter aiding him, searched the desks for his initials. Stephen remained in the background, depressed more than ever by the darkness and silence of the theatre and by the air it wore of jaded and formal study. On the desk before him he read the word *Fœtus* cut several times into the dark stained wood. The sudden legend startled his blood: he seemed to feel the absent students of the college about him and to shrink from their company. A vision of their life, which his father's words had been powerless to evoke, sprang up before him out of the word cut in the desk. A broadshouldered student with a moustache was cutting in the letters with a jackknife, seriously. Other students stood or sat near him laughing at his handiwork. One jogged his elbow. The big student turned on him, frowning. He was dressed in loose grey clothes and had tan boots.
>
> Stephen's name was called. He hurried down the steps of the theatre so as to be as far away as he could be and, peering closely at his father's initials, hid his flushed face. (P: 92–3)

This passage, like the legend of the desk itself, resists the polytropic textual economies. No explanation ever comes to gloss this episode, no trope induces it to circulate. For when, in 'sudden legends' like this word or '*Lotts*', the economy of literature breaks forth, its letters function like a 'littoral': a shoreline or horizon that circumscribes the 'vital sea' of flow and influence, and severs words and flesh from circulation. As 'literature', or speech in storage, '*Fœtus*' introduces a lacuna in the tissue of the text – and the word itself remains imprisoned, strangely, in its very unequivocality. Neither Stephen, nor the reader, nor the text itself, can broach the littoral, or quite digest the literality of '*Fœtus*', which erupts so inexplicably.

If the text does not divulge the sense of this inscription, it all too palpably insists upon the act of cutting it. We can almost hear the scraping of the knives. A wound more than a word, '*Fœtus*' scores the text and flays the desk with one full cicatrix. Its sorcery arrests the narrative: the text gives way to 'tales within wheels' (F W: 247) (or better – 'weals').

For this scar, like Odysseus's has a tale to tell. But like all scars, it needs a reader to inflame it and to let its story out. Stephen, reading it, unlocks the narrative and vents the wound.

That is, he misreads it. Notice how Stephen turns the Fœtus's plurality into a singular event:

> he read the word *Fœtus cut several times* in the dark stained wood. *The sudden legend* startled his blood. . . . A broadshouldered student . . . was cutting in the letters with a jackknife. . . .

'Cut several times': this inscription is apparently prolific. Who is to say that it has fewer authors than (dis)figurations? However terrifying his hallucination, Stephen incorporates the scar into the fiction of a single author, and resurrects a father for the letter. *The student*, long ago, who slashed the desk with this uncanny *legend*, leaps back, with his accomplices, into sadistic life. This word, unlike the father's memories, can resurrect the dead.

In three ways, then, this mutilating word encroaches on the father's empire. Firstly, it breaks out where the father's name should be. Then it lets forth that vision of the dead which Simon Dedalus's words – according to his son – had been 'powerless to evoke'. Finally, its repetitions resist the fiction of a singular begetting. How can we trace a first creation in a word 'cut several times' by untold hands? Repeated, the scarletter refuses the 'Creation from nothing', 'from only begetter to only begotten', to which paternity at last refers itself and justifies itself (*U*: 43; 207). But the initials which '*Fœtus*' has pre-empted or effaced must also stand for *Stephen* Dedalus.

Psychoanalysis would invite us to diagnose castration in the cutting letters of the father's name. Indeed, the psychoanalytic critic almost yawns to find that S.D. has been turned into surgery. But why, in this account of things, should another word achieve priority, and an older wound forestall the laceration of the name? And why, of all things, does this cicatrix spell '*Fœtus*'?

Why, if not because this first scar is a navel, from which the *Fœtus* amputates itself? A navel, where the mother's namelessness engraves itself upon the flesh before the father ever carved his signature? For why should such a word, or wound, evoke such dread, if not because the phallus has surrendered to the omphalos?

The first time that the artist meets the horror of the omphalos occurs in the *Epiphanies*:

[Dublin: in the house in
Glengariff Parade: evening]

Mrs Joyce – (*crimson, trembling, appears at the
    parlour door*) . . . Jim!
Joyce – (*at the piano*) . . . Yes?
Mrs. Joyce – Do you know anything about the
    body? . . . What ought I do? . . . There's
    some matter coming away from
    the hole in Georgie's stomach . . .
    Did you ever hear of that happening?
Joyce – (*surprised*) . . . I don't know . . . .
Mrs Joyce – Ought I send for the doctor, do you
    think?
Joyce – I don't know . . . . . . What hole?
Mrs Joyce – (*impatient*) . . . The hole we all have
    . . . . . here (*points*).
Joyce – (*stands up*) [12]

'The hole we all have': the hole through which identity, like Georgie, ebbs away into the amniotic flood of its first world. 'The cords of all link back,' thinks Stephen of the navelcord in 'Proteus' (*U*: 43). This cord links all the dying generations back to Edenville and yet beyond, to disappear into a prior nameless unbegotten world. It links the '*Fœtus*' to the mother's ancient anonymity. The scarletters of '*Fœtus*' therefore unsex Stephen and unname him just as 'noman' must unman Odysseus. As a navel, '*Fœtus*' flaunts the father's name and patrilineage.

   In 'Proteus', and in 'The Oxen of the Sun', Stephen twice repudiates the notion of a 'belly without blemish': of flesh unblotted by its nameless scar (*U*: 43; 389). Just so, in Michelangelo's 'Creation' in the Sistine Chapel, Adam's navel, in mute blasphemy, foreswears the fatherhood of God. The umbilicus, which Stephen calls the 'strand-entwining cable of all flesh', belies the firstness of the father, and the originality of his creation. For rather than an origin, this blemish is the footnote of the flesh.

   In *A Portrait*, '*Fœtus*' opens up the 'hole we all have', the 'void' on which the world, the Church, the father so precariously rest. It plunges both the subject and the text toward 'agnomenity' and semiotic anarchy.

Part III

1

> 'They are disguised hands, except the letter,' Holmes said, presently, 'but there can be no question as to the authorship. See how the irrepressible Greek *e* will break out. . . .'
>
> (Conan Doyle, 'The Sign of Four')[13]

Perhaps Joyce thought of Conan Doyle when he forged his letters to Marthe Fleischmann with Greek *e*s instead of Roman *e*s in the name James Joyce.[14] In the 'Sirens' chapter of *Ulysses*, Bloom, likewise, reminds himself three times to 'write Greek ees' to Martha Clifford (*U*: 278). (By what is likely to be more than a coincidence, the Greek *e* must break forth twice and irrepressibly from 'H*e*nry Flow*e*r', as it doubles necessarily in Jam*e*s Joyc*e*.) A pseudonym – or rather, pseudo-letter – the Greek *e* works like Odysseus's agnomen: for while enabling Bloom, or Joyce, to slip out of the clutches of their Martha's, it condemns them also to Odysseus's anonymity. This letter is a 'squirtscreen' that, like Shem or Shakespeare, Bloom and Joyce have 'piled up to hide [them from themselves]' (*F W*: 186; *U* 197). The *e* by which they hide their own identity is also that which gives them irrepressibly away.

The irrepressible Greek *e* breaks out again in *Finnegans Wake*. Turned upon its side, this letter marks – as '*Fœtus*' marks for Stephen – the broken father and his broken law. ⊓ is the siglum of HCE.[15]

When HCE is dormant, the Greek *e*, too, must go to sleep. His siglum turns upside-down: ⊔ . It thus presents itself as the initial of the Wake itself: asleep and a *Wake* at the same time. That the sleeping *e* resembles female genitals only helps it to undo the father's name.

In its somnolent position, we may detect the *e* in William Shakespeare's name in 'Scylla and Charybdis'. Here Stephen speaks of Cassiopeia – whose stars dispose themselves into a W, or ⊔ – as 'the recumbent constellation which is the signature of [Shakespeare's] initial among the stars' (*U*: 210).

The *e* recurs in a headline in 'Aeolus': 'HOUSE OF KEY(E)S' where the parenthesis enables us to isolate its properties (*U*: 122). In this chapter Bloom has been commissioned to insert an advertisement in the newspaper for Alexander Keyes. This ad is to portray the sign of crossed keys which represents the Isle of Man, and also figures forth the name of the commissioner. This awkward pun is meant to cast an attractive 'innuendo of home rule' (*U*: 122). The itchy copy editor does not seem to think that anyone will catch this innuendo. No more would it be possible to catch the '(E)' that crosses 'KEY(E)S' were we confined to spoken utterance. We can't *hear* it. Inaudibility, indeed, is what distinguishes this *e* from the mob of the alphabet. The 'ees' that riddle Bloom's erotic letters, or the irrepressible Greek *e* that hides in 'KEY(E)S' — these *es* resist the blandishments of voice. They double-cross the realm of speech with the inaudible, occulted impudence of 'literature'.

The letter 'E' is set adrift from Keyes, and slips away unheard, as Odysseus slipped by the blinded Cyclops. (For Odysseus, another irrepressible Greek character, demands a *reader* to be recognised. It is eyes, not ears, that read the letter, read the scar. Only Odysseus's dog, who dwells outside the realm of literature, can recognise the hero by his voice — and die.) Under the silent ambush of the *e*, the word dismembers and unwrites itself. 'Silently emptied of instantaneous sense', its letters 'set to band and disband themselves in wayward rhythms' (*P*: 182). Rather than a 'key' that will unlock the hidden secrets of the text, the *e* dissolves the word's semantic chastity. It sets its letters swimming — to preserve the text's digestive metaphor — in alphabet soup.

Greek *es*, as we begin to see, thread through *Ulysses* like an umbilical cord. And as the siglum of the fallen father, the letter E is littered through the *Wake* as well. . . .

2

Inevitably, we return to the question we began with: 'Where did thots come from?' What haunts the *Wake* is an unspoken version of the prolific question of origination: 'Where do letters come from?' It is a question which the reader may already have begun to ask about one letter in particular: the E. In the *Wake*, we only know this question by the polytropic range of its replies: by the interminable gossip, speculation, commentary, paraphrase and exegesis that envelop the 'untitled mamafesta' of ALP (*F W*: 104). This 'mamafesta' is the unknown letter which the 'mama' plucked out of the midden, where the tribe's discarded dialects are stored.

Now in the middle of the earth, if not the midden, an anonymous initial was inscribed. It was scored into the stone that Zeus had marked to be the middle or the 'navel' of the world: the Delphic Omphalos. Plutarch wrote an essay on this ancient graffitto, which Joyce read.[16] Only Joyce could rival the abundance of its glosses, guesses, and unlikely explanations of a letter.

To give a meaning to this letter, Plutarch's 'Pythian conversation' meanders through the realms of grammar, numerology, geometry, astrology, epistemology, theology. Considered also is Apollo, who stole the Omphalos from the ancient Furies or chthonic goddesses.[17] His names and attributes and metamorphoses remind the reader ineluctably of Joyce's broken fathers, orphaned sons, dismembered artificers:

> his turning and subdivision into airs and water and earth, and the production of animals and plants, they enigmatically term 'Exile' and 'Dismemberment'. They name him 'Dionysos' and 'Zagreus' and 'Nycteleos' and 'Isodi'; they also tell of certain destructions and disappearances and diseases and new births, which are riddles and fables pertaining to the aforesaid transformations: and they sing the dithyrambic song, filled with sufferings, and allusions to some change of state that brought with it wandering about and dispersion.[18]

What, then, could be the letter that betokens all these changes amidst these wanderings, dispersions, and divisions? It is the same letter that compulsively repeats the fall of HCE in *Finnegans Wake*. The initial in the middle of this muddle – the letter carved upon the Delphic Omphalos – was none other need I say it? than the Greek E.

3

> Now, our friend Apollo appears to cure and to settle all difficulties connected with life, by giving responses to such as consult him; but of himself to inspire and suggest doubts concerning what is speculative, by implanting in the knowledge-seeking part of the human soul an appetite that draws towards the truth; as is manifest from many other things, and from the dedication of the E. For this is not likely to have been done by chance, nor yet by lot only, in settling the precedence of all the letters of the alphabet before the god, did it obtain the rank of a sacred offering and object of admiration: but either those that first speculated about the god saw in it some peculiar and extraordinary virtue of its own, or else they used it as a symbol of some important mystery. . . .
>
> (Plutarch, 'On the E at Delphi')[19]

I would not be so bold as to insist that the letter ALP recovered from the midden is so simple and so single as an E. Once again I must decline to answer the unanswerable question, 'Where did thots come from?' But the Greek E becomes a navel in the novels which succeed *A Portrait of the Artist*. It supplants the '*Fœtus*' as the letter which undoes the father's name. 'In the beginning was the letter', the *Wake*, as Joyce's Genesis, seems to declare. If this letter is, indeed, an E, or *any letter that could share its properties*, it undercuts the very notion of beginning. 'The cords of all link back,' we may remember: so even those in Edenville were not the first. Eve and Adam also had a blemish on their bellies, or an omphalos engraven with an E.

The name of the father, on the other hand, necessarily entails a first unstained creation. The patronyms of all link back to that 'creation from nothing' (represented in the 'telephone' number 'nought, nought, one') which Stephen mocks and then repudiates (*U*: 43). The scarletter on the belly tells another story, that has neither a beginning nor an end: that neither flesh nor words can ever say where they come from, or claim a unitary origin. All narratives and genealogies must end where they begin: in the middle – or the navel – or the E.

A Portrait and *The Wake* are both, in their different ways, omphalocentric. 'Gaze in your omphalos,' Stephen tells himself in 'Proteus' (*U*: 43): and his *Portrait* contemplates the navel – with all the onanistic connotations of the act. In its repeated births, its repeated exiles, the subject and the text compulsively return to the rupture and the knotting of the navelcord.

Rather than the riddle of the sphinx, with all its Oedipal and phallo-centric consequences, the *Wake* slips in the riddle of the E to supersede the central Western mystery. (The 'E', in fact, could be read into the riddle of the sphinx itself – as the creature with 'three legs (ɯ) in the evening'.) Here, narrative itself becomes omphalocen-tripetal. 'Tales within wheels' (*F W*: 247), the cycles of the *Wake*, like the revolving stories of the *Odyssey*, suggest that these texts circum-navigate the navel, and circumvent the amputation of its scar. The *Wake* begins – as it ends – in the middle, or the navel, of a sentence, as if in yearning for the navelcord's unbroken circuit. The *Odyssey* is equally umbiliform. Odysseus, like Bloom, begins in the middle – with Calypso, in the 'navel of the sea'.

4

and Rouse found they spoke of Elias
in telling the tales of Odysseus   ΟΥ̓ ΤΙΣ

ΟΥ̓ ΤΙΣ

'I am noman, my name is noman'
But Wanjina is, shall we say, Ouan Jin
or the man with an education
and whose mouth was removed by his father
because he made too many *things*
whereby cluttered the bushman's baggage
vide the expedition of Frobenius' pupils about 1938
to Auss'ralia
Ouan Jin spoke and thereby created the named
thereby making clutter.

Wanjina, now, is silent, and Odysseus has fallen into anonymity. What diagnosis whispers in this strange complicity? What violence could yoke such incongruities together – a Greek hero and an Australian god?

Some devastation has occurred in language. For all that could enweave these myths together is the common mutilation of the namer and the named. When Wanjina meets Odysseus, his own name breaks under the pressure of the agnomen, and the dismembered mouth joins the dismembered name.

In its dismembered form, 'Ouan Jin' is a French transliteration of a Chinese ideogram meaning 'man of letters', 'literary gent'.[20] The man of letters, therefore, comes to be the man without a mouth: it seems that letters, once again, must overthrow the empire of speech.

But linguistic impotence does not rely upon dismemberment. Polyphemus, his mouth intact, and howling, cannot confine Odysseus in his name. For all their rage at 'imprecision', or the semiotic vagaries of 'usury', *The Cantos* cannot seem to cure the wound which opens in the word. No more can Stephen cork the scar of his initials, or the cutting letters which precede his name. The stench escapes.

'I have tried to write Paradise,' Pound cries at *The Cantos'* end, when he has seen that all his words redouble hell.[21] Paradise, with Odyssean impudence, eludes the summons of its name. If 'heaven-talk' is 'broken', and every name a scar, not only paradise, or Odysseus, will slip away. Wanjina's silence may represent the only eloquence which really 'captures' what it means. For it may be that every word works like Odysseus's agnomen; or else succumbs to insurrections from its letters, which rebel under the banner of the *e*. And is it possible that every word which would beget the world must open up the royal road for the escape of sense, of stench, or of Odysseus?

Notes

1   Ezra Pound, *The Cantos* (London, Faber & Faber, 1975), p. 426–7.
2   My discussion of *The Odyssey* is greatly indebted to Margaret Williamson.
3   Sigmund Freud, 'On the Sexual Theories of Children' (1908), *The Complete Psychological Works*, Standard Edition, tr. James Strachey (London: Hogarth Press, 1953–74) Vol. IX, p. 212.
4   T.S. Eliot, '*Ulysses*, Order and Myth', *The Dial*, Vol. LXXV (1923), p. 480–3.
5   Cf. Richmond Lattimore, 'Introduction' to *The Odyssey*, (New York, Evanston and London: Harper, 1967), p. 11.
6   I have discussed the analogy between *A Portrait* and *The Prelude* at greater length in my article 'Disremembering Dedalus' in Robert Young, ed., *Untying the Text: A Post-Structuralist Reader* (London: Routledge & Kegan Paul, 1981), p. 189–206.
7   Guy Davenport, 'Pound and Frobenius' in *Motive and Method in The Cantos*, ed. Lewis Leary (New York and London: Columbia University Press, 1954), p. 49.
8   The Greek expression is not so explicit. But the narrative's abrupt transition from scar to story seems to justify Lattimore's translation.
9   Auerbach argues that the scar and the stories which 'come out' of it exist in a continuous present (Erich Auerbach, 'Odysseus's Scar', *Mimesis*, tr. Willard R. Trask (Princeton: Princeton University Press, 1953) pp. 3–23). I do not wish to put the case for perspectivism in *The Odyssey*, but rather to bring out the unspoken implications of Auerbach's essay. The scar, indeed, is present in the narrative – and further, active and vindictive. It manifests itself in the *cut* which interrupts the narrative; it manifests itself in *repetition*. The stories that come out of it achieve the status of a history only through the *present* act of repetition. (I discuss the scar's strange temporality at greater length in 'Disremembering Dedalus', op. cit.)
10 Cf. Richard Ellmann, *The Consciousness of Joyce* (London: Faber and Faber, 1977), p. 13.
11 Maud Ellmann, op. cit.
12 James Joyce, *Epiphanies*, no. 19 (42) in *The Workshop of Dedalus*, ed. Robert Scholes and Richard M. Kain (Evanston: Northwestern University Press, 1965), p. 29.

13 *Penguin Complete Sherlock Holmes* (Harmondsworth: Penguin, 1981), p. 96.
14 Richard Ellmann, *James Joyce* (London: Oxford University Press, 1959), p. 463.
15 Cf. Roland McHugh, *The Sigla of Finnegans Wake* (Austin: University of Texas Press, 1976).
16 Cf. Richard Ellmann, *The Consciousness of Joyce*, op. cit., p. 13.
17 Plutarch, 'On the E at Delphi' in *Plutarch's Morals: Theosophical Essays*, tr. C.W. King (London: George Bell, 1882), pp. 173–96.
18 *ibid.*, p. 183.
19 *ibid.*, p. 173–4.
20 Davenport, *op. cit.*, p. 50.
21 'I tried to make a paradiso', Ezra Pound, *op. cit.*, p. 802. Cf. my article 'Floating the Pound: The Circulation of the Subject of *The Cantos*', *Oxford Literary Review*, Vol. 3, no. 3 (Spring, 1979), pp. 16–27.

CHAPTER 5

*Exiles**

Raymond Williams

The play *Exiles* has usually proved difficult for students of Joyce, and
especially for those who are interested in the innovatory fictional
methods which are of course his major achievement. I said most of
what I thought could be said about the play in an essay written in
1947, though then as now not looking at the marginal and speculative relations between the play and Joyce's life and biography. But
there is still one point which I would like to try to take further, and I
can begin from a sentence in that earlier essay which I do not now, in
terms, agree with. I wrote then:

> The result of the words of the play is not an experience formally different
> in kind from that of Joyce's more famous work.

Read in context this can be taken as what I still believe to be true, that
the theme of *Exiles* is very close to, indeed integral with, the themes
of the major fiction. Yet though I then went on to discuss some of the
differences between dramatic and fictional writing, which I think
ought now to be our central concern, I limited this emphasis by
running the two points together: on the one hand 'the words of the
play' and 'formally different'; on the other hand 'the result of the
words of the play' and 'an experience formally different'. What I
now want to move to, in clearer terms, is a consideration of the
radical differences in formal composition. At the broadest level of
theme the earlier descriptions as 'result' and 'experience' can still, in
general, stand. But the immediate results, as I shall try to show, are
more radically different than I then began to indicate. Moreover, the
point has some wider importance in the matter of relations between
dramatic and fictional writing, and their analysis.

* This is a reconstruction of the later part of a lecture, the earlier parts of which were
based on the essay *The 'Exiles' of James Joyce*, written in 1947 and now contained in
Drama from Ibsen to Brecht (London: Chatto & Windus, 1968). An explanatory link
has been written for the present publication.

The central formal point is that in dramatic composition the writing of speech is a virtually total and explicit mode. Indications of certain actions may also be written, but as instruction for performance rather than words to be performed. Thus, speech is radically separated from anything in the nature of general narrative, analysis or commentary. But while this is necessarily true, at the most general level of dramatic composition, it is also true that the composition of words to be spoken in performance must not be reduced, as it is within the assumptions of naturalist drama, to the simple representation of speech, in the sense of words exchanged between characters in the course of represented behaviour. On the contrary, in conventions as various as the chorus of Greek drama, the messengers narrating other events in Greek and Elizabethan drama, the soliloquy over its range from local and private address to its most developed forms in the speaking of 'unspoken' or 'indirected' thought, and many other formal methods, the dramatic composition of speech includes functions which in more modern forms have been separated out as, in drama, the representation of direct speech between characters, and, in fiction, the enclosure of such representations within authorial narrative, analysis and commentary. It was of course within these conditions of separation and specialisation that Joyce was beginning to write.

We can then look back for a moment at the beginning of Joyce's idea of 'epiphanies', in *Stephen Hero*:

> By an epiphany he meant a sudden spiritual manifestation, whether in the vulgarity of speech or of gesture or in a memorable phase of the mind itself. (*S H*: 216)

'Speech or gesture', but the examples he gives are of speech. Then at once in recording them (and I think we have to say that they must have meant more to him than they now can to us) he starts writing what is in effect a fragment of text of a modern play:

> The Young Lady – (drawling discreetly) . . . O, yes . . . I was . . . at the . . . cha . . . pel. . . .
> The Young Gentleman – (inaudibly) . . . I . . . (again inaudibly) . . . I . . .
> The Young Lady – (softly) . . . O . . . but you're . . . ve . . . ry wick . . . ed. . . . (*S H*: 216).

The bracketed characterisations of tone are derived from the form of a play-text as this stabilised, under new conditions, in the nineteenth century, with some evident influence from the novel. The bracketed direction can be read, there, as an indication to actor or director, though in practice they are more often indications to the *reader*, providing a minimal further characterisation, beyond the spoken words, of a kind now familiar from fiction. Yet indeed there is already a further problem, not to say confusion, for one of Joyce's characterisations is 'inaudibly', which is across the line from any dramatic writing of speech, into the different mode of fictional representation, which can include the inaudible or the fully unspoken.

Now it is a misunderstanding of high naturalist drama, in say Ibsen or early Strindberg or Chekhov, to suppose that they repressed all functions of speech or of dramatic writing other than the representation of probable conversation between persons in everyday behaviour. Indeed one of the basic themes of this major drama is the unresolved tension between what has happened or is happening and what can be spoken about. Rejecting the conventions of theatrical speech, as these had stabilised and ossified in the dominant intrigue drama, the new dramatists entered an area of conscious tension, at one level between what needed to be said and what, within specific social limitations, could actually be said; at another level between what people wanted to say and the different objectivities of need and limitation. Thus we find the unusual and widely misunderstood phenomenon of a prolonged working within the forms of everyday speech which is at the same time a profound if unfinished critique of the state of being which these at once represent and misrepresent. From *Ghosts* and *Rosmersholm* and *The Wild Duck* to *John Gabriel Borkman* and *Little Eyolf*, Ibsen at once wrought these speech forms, in a newly concentrated intensity, and set them in tension with an only ever partly articulated dimension of otherness – other modes of being and of desire, indicated beyond the dramatic action rather than represented within it. Strindberg, from *Lady Julie* onwards, expressed a comparable tension by including forms of physical action and visual presence which more directly dramatised a destructive interaction, while in the method of 'contrapuntal' dialogue – a loosening of speech from simple fixed identity with characters, a composition of speech as both voluntary and involuntary relationship – he began to find ways of presenting rather than simply representing a flow of interactive experience. Chekhov, following Ibsen in the indication of a general dimension of otherness, from *The Seagull* to *The Cherry Orchard*, developed in his later plays what I have called the dialogue of a 'negative group': a composition of units of everyday speech into a shared failure of communication. All this is very different from what later became known as 'naturalist dialogue', in the drama of the naturalist habit, in which what is represented as said is taken as all that can or needs to be said: an unproblematic medium, through which character and action appear.

Those who are surprised by Joyce's close attention to Ibsen, through so much of his writing life, have been misled by the formulations and practice of the naturalist habit and have failed to see, beyond it, the directly connecting preoccupation with levels of being and communication and with the problems of writing them. Moreover, in Joyce as in Ibsen, there is a conscious relation between these general problems and a pervading sense of a network of illusions, self-deceptions, deceptions of others, and lies. It is in this sense, strengthened by certain structural similarities between the situations of the Norwegian and the Irish writer – an autonomy of craft and conviction within the simultaneous rejection of both the local subordinated and the wider dominant cultures – that it is no surprise to find Joyce recording 'the spirit of Ibsen' blowing 'through him like a keen wind' (*P*: 179).

But what is then really surprising is that when he came to write his play, Joyce selected a more singular mode. In effect none of the devices of disturbance, dislocation or limitation of speech, none of the indications of unarticulated modes of being and desire beyond its specific and structurally limited forms, is attempted. Of course Joyce does not then rest on the representation of everyday speech as itself. He moves, instead, in a quite different direction, to forms of mutual self-presentation, in a rhetorical and even declamatory mode. Standing right back, we can observe the cold clash of egos which such a mode sustains. We can see, clearly enough, at once the centrality of the drive to an assertion of exiled identity, and the registered consequences of this drive on others who still seek and need relationship while this deliberate distancing occurs. Thematically there is no problem: the need and the loss are very precisely defined. But then the precision of the definition is in its own way an obstacle to recognition of the substance of what is being defined. It is a linguistic mode of enclosure and presentation, not of exploration.

> ROBERT . . . There was an eternity before we were born: another will
> come after we are dead. The blinding instant of passion alone – passion,
> free, unashamed, irresistible – that is the only gate by which we can escape

from the misery of what slaves call life. Is not this the language of your
own youth that I heard so often from you in this very place where we are
sitting now? Have you changed?
RICHARD [*Passes his hand across his brow*] Yes. It is the language of my
youth. (*E*: 99)

This is, paradoxically, the language of dramatic declamation which
in their different ways Ibsen, Strindberg and Chekhov at once
rejected and complicated. It is the language of the predominant
actor-manager, 'self-exiled in upon his ego' (*FW*: 184). The major
naturalist dramatists had profoundly destabilised this kind of assurance. Such declarations were still made, but within a dramatic context which interrogated, indicated or undercut them. It is true that
the persons of *Exiles* fail to communicate, though the strict form of
this is more local, unfortunately echoing Joyce's misleading definition of drama as 'the form wherein [the artist] sets forth his image in
immediate relations to others'(*P*: 218). The assertion of singularity is
an inescapably negative form: the immediate relations are cancella-
tions and avoidances. But this persistent and central theme is
enclosed, rather than embodied, in the conscious singularity of the
language.

   This is then the point about formal difference. The play is written
as words spoken between persons in a prescribed and limited local-
ity. It excludes virtually all other forms of dramatic action and
dramatic speech. Singular characters are isolated, within their own
presumed resources, in a deliberately limited and locally represented
time and space. The disturbing indications of incompleteness, the
internal interrogations of these local assurances, which were present
in the major naturalist drama and which Joyce explored and
embodied in quite new ways in his innovatory fiction, are in *Exiles*
overridden by explication, argument and conscious exchange.

   In terms of its period, this can be made a contrast between dramatic and fictional modes of writing. It is still an open question whether
the necessary processes of interrogation and disturbance can be
adequately realised by the devices of indication, faults between
levels, internal negations and incompletenesses which major naturalist drama relied on, and which have since been erected into whole
forms, discarding the more recognisably naturalist ballast and then
often, in fact, losing the essential tension. But in fiction these modes
were more immediately accessible, in various devices of narrative,
analysis and commentary, but just as clearly, in Joyce, in specific

transformations of the conventions of speech, place and time. When we come now to analyse dramatic language we can readily observe the differences between this fictional range and what can be made to appear, as in *Exiles*, represented speech which stands alone. In the practices of a specific period this is an adequate working distinction. But more generally it is inadequate. It is not only in the most obvious examples from earlier drama, such as the storm scenes in *Lear* or the soliloquies in *Hamlet*, but also more generally in that writing of actions in which speech is a dominant mode but then speech of many kinds, with operational variations in level, direction and address, that we find, inescapably, different essential forms of the language of drama. These need to be analysed beyond the functions of representation and exchange, setting forth character and action in singular forms, to which both much modern criticism and most modern theatrical practice have tended to reduce dramatic writing. We should be especially able to go beyond this if we extend formal comparisons beyond the cases of drama and fiction, into the now major evidence of film composition, which bears very closely on just these problems and solutions.

But we shall not get there from *Exiles*, except negatively. The play effects its exchanges, defines its singularities, at a point of temporary stasis, at once after and before adequate conventions of complexity and mobility. The moment of 'epiphany' is not realised but transcribed, and is then not manifestation but exposition. The play achieves its deliberately localised effect, but it is ironic, reading or watching it, to find Joyce in temporary exile from the place he made his home: the area not of representing but of transforming practice.

CHAPTER 6

The voice of Esau:
Stephen in the Library*

Colin MacCabe

For readers of English literature, and both adjective and noun are immediately thrown into doubt, it is Joyce's texts which serve to focus and emphasise the changing attitudes to language and representation which constitute the most valuable and the most political aspects of modernism. After Joyce it should be difficult not to write differently into our future and to read differently into our past; to admit, in all its embarrassing reality, the 'heciten[t]' (F W: 119.) nature of any subjectivity, to enjoy in all its multiple aspects the 'middayevil' (F W: 423.) aspects of language that Joyce strives to ressurrect. And Joyce's unmaking of self and language, his investigation of the ways we constitute ourselves in speech is most crucially linked to questions of sexuality – its refusal to conform to any single identity, its desires which insist against and across our measured and meaningful speech. But if Joyce broke ruthlessly with the dominant orders of reading and writing, it was not for lack of trying to fit himself inside them; the attempt to write a novel within the dominant conventions of representation and identity is recorded in the fragment of *Stephen Hero* that was saved from the flames[1] and the attempt to read within the then dominant tradition of literary criticism is part of the subject matter of *Ulysses* when Stephen voices his interpretation of Shakespeare in the National Library.

Voices is here the exact verb: Stephen's whole emphasis is on speech, on a performance which will both wrest a meaning from Shakespeare and confer an identity on himself within the Irish literary movement. It is in terms of speech that, in the first chapter, Mulligan laughs off Stephen's refusal to inform Haines of the theory:

---

* In February 1977 I delivered a lecture on reading and writing in *Ulysses* as part of a circus of lectures on Joyce. Some of the material from that lecture was included in Chapter 5 of my *James Joyce and the Revolution of the Word* (London: Macmillan, 1979), particularly pp. 117–21. This essay develops the more detailed analysis of Joyce and Shakespeare which had to be omitted from the book.

'The sacred pint alone can unbind the tongue of Dedalus' (*U*: 24) and throughout the book it is the voice that holds out a guarantee of paternity and inheritance: 'You're your father's son. I know the voice' (*U*: 48). But the impossibility for the voice of holding the entire meaning of any statement is demonstrated in the very instant that the interpretation of Shakespeare is first mentioned:

> — Pooh! Buck Mulligan said. We have grown out of Wilde and para-doxes. It's quite simple. He proves by algebra that Hamlet's grandson is Shakespeare's grandfather and that *he himself* is the ghost of his own father.
> — What? Haines said, beginning to point at Stephen. He himself?
> Buck Mulligan slung his towel stolewise round his neck and, bending in loose laughter, said to Stephen's ear:
> — O, shade of Kinch the elder! Japhet in search of a father!' (*U*: 24; my italics)

Haines's confusion is caused by the ambiguity of the pronoun *he*, an ambiguity emphasised by the reflexive *himself*. In any sequence of language, the pronoun 'he' can be interpreted either anaphorically, referring back to some previous element in the text, or exophorically, referring outside the text.[2] Writing must depend on anaphor as the written text's situation is too variable for exophoric reference. But this written account of speech hesitates, like Haines, in giving too simple an identification. For it is unclear from Mulligan's words whether *he himself* is to be taken as referring back to Shakespeare, Hamlet, their respective grandfather or grandson, or the original subject of the sentence *He* which the context evidently identifies as Stephen. But this confusion of speech is also Stephen's, as in fixing an identity for both Shakespeare and Hamlet he produces one for himself, placing himself within a literary tradition which will provide him with the father he so desperately seeks. But this very search is itself the paralysis that he thinks to escape. Mulligan's reference is to Frederick Marryat's novel *Japhet in Search of a Father* (1835) which describes a foundling's quest for his father:

> . . . and if I saw a nose upon any man's face, at all resembling my own, I immediately would wonder and surmise whether that person could be my father. This constant dwelling upon the subject at last created a species of monomania, and a hundred times a day I would mutter to myself 'Who is my father?'. Indeed the very bells, when they rung a peal, seemed, as in the case of Whittington, to chime the question.[3]

It is this monomania that grips Stephen on the beach as he becomes the obsessive interpreting centre of his world. The hermetic dream of total interpretation haunts him: 'Signatures of all things I am here to read' (*U*: 42) but it is from this all-significant nightmare that he has to escape if he is to allow the 'shout in the street' (*U*: 40) to allow the liberation of a perpetual re-interpretation. Language and identity are here posed in a very specific relation: to assume an identity, to recognise and be recognised by the father, is to refuse the possibility of re-interpretation. It is to so fix oneself that interpretation is finished, brought to an end in a moment of paralysed centrality, a moment which, as we will see, is intimately linked to Stephen's reading of Shakespeare. It is in the 'Circe' chapter that Stephen's fear of the general paralysis of the insane becomes most real, as in the frenzied moments of paranoid terror when every object speaks to him, he finally almost achieves the dream of total interpretation in complete psychotic collapse.

However, by the 'Circe' chapter Joyce is using a very different form from the stream of consciousness that dominates the three opening chapters. The escape from the paralysis that threatens Stephen Dedalus is not through the production of some superior consciousness, which is one way in which we can read the aesthetic discourses that conclude *A Portrait*. Rather it is through investigating the constitution of those discourses; deepening *A Portrait's* concern with language to include the whole history and forms of the English language in which Stephen's soul 'frets' (*P*: 194). It is this formal re-writing that allows *Ulysses* to return again and again to its own events, refusing any final interpretation, liberating both subject and language in one and the same gesture. It is in the 'Circe' section that this 'return' achieves its most violent and acute form as the whole text is re-written to allow an escape from the nightmare identifications imposed by history. It is hardly surprising that Joyce had more trouble writing it than any other chapter. In a letter to Budgen dated Michaelmas 1920 he wrote that he had worked some more details into 'Circe' 'which by the way is a dreadful performance. It gets wilder and worse and more involved but I suppose it will all work out' (*Letters*, 1: 147). In the working out the key term that obsessed Joyce was *moly* – the plant that Hermes had given Odysseus and which enabled him to avoid the snares of Circe which drove men mad and turned them into pigs. In the same letter to Budgen he wrote:

Moly is a nut to crack. My latest is this. Moly is the gift of Hermes, god of public ways and is the invisible influence (prayer, chance, agility, presence of mind, power of recuperation) which saves in case of accident. This would cover immunity from syphilis ($\sigma\acute{\upsilon}\phi\iota\lambda\iota\varsigma$ = swinelove?). Hermes is the god of signposts: i.e. he is, specially for a traveller like Ulysses, the point at which roads parallel merge and roads contrary also. He is an accident of Providence. In this case the plant may be said to have many leaves, indifference due to masturbation, pessimism congenital, a sense of the ridiculous, sudden fastidiousness in some detail, experience. (*Letters*, 1: 147–8)

The letter is typical of Joyce's whole writing procedure by 1920. An interpretation is promised but immediately multiplies into an indefinite list aided by etymologies which concentrate on the material of language rather than on any historical basis. But what is important for our purposes is the emphasis within this list on chance and accident. It is this chance that confronts Stephen with Bloom, a man who does not fit into the Dublin categories of race and religion and who thus offers an escape from its paralysed grid of interpretation.

It is this chance that Stephen is so concerned to deny as he offers his interpretation of Shakespeare in the Library. He wants to centre Shakespeare's life in one moment in the fields outside Stratford when he was tumbled by Ann Hathaway, and then centre the plays on that one moment through the interpretation of *Hamlet*. For Stephen *Hamlet* must be read from the position of the ghost – from the character that he imagines Shakespeare played and from whose situation he constructs an interpretation of Shakespeare's life and works. It is important to recognise how close Stephen's method is to the then dominant literary criticism which the characters discuss as they debate the chronology of the late plays (*U*: 195–6).[4] The major source for this chapter is Georg Brandes, whose early championship of Ibsen and the fact that his study of Shakespeare was partially translated by William Archer made it an obviously important book for Joyce.[5] Brandes's study assumes a total identification of life and work and this approach is shared by Stephen. However Brandes, like Frank Harris, but unlike the scholarly Sidney Lee, simply assumes the identity of Shakespeare and Hamlet:

It cost Shakespeare no effort to transform himself into Hamlet. On the contrary, in giving expression to Hamlet's spiritual life he was enabled quite naturally to pour forth all that during the recent years had filled his heart and seethed in his brain. He could let this creation drink his inmost heart's blood; he could transfer to it the throbbing of his own pulses. Behind its forehead he could hide his melancholy; on its tongue he could lay his wit; its eyes he could cause to glow and lighten with flashes of his own spirit.[6]

But if Stephen is close to Brandes in his method, Joyce is not. Where Brandes and Stephen confront a text to extract a meaning, Joyce addresses the context of the critical act itself. At the close of the chapter the faintly ridiculous Richard Best, with his inevitable 'don't you knows' comments on what might happen to Stephen's theory: 'Are you going to write it? Mr Best asked. You ought to make it a dialogue, don't you know, like the Platonic dialogues Wilde wrote' (*U*: 213). But it is not as a Platonic dialogue that Stephen's theory sees the light of day but as an investigation of the interplay between speech and action in the Library. And what comes into focus as a result is the very act of writing, which displaces the presumed central-ity of speech. Early in the chapter John Eglinton attempts to dismiss the importance of Ann Hathaway:

> — The world believes that Shakespeare made a mistake, he said, and got out of it as quickly and as best he could.
> — Bosh! Stephen said rudely. A man of genius makes no mistakes. His errors are volitional and are the portals of discovery. (*U*: 190)

Stephen here finds himself trapped in the dilemma of interpreta-tion. Determined to leave nothing to chance, chance which might upset his view of Shakespeare's fixed identity, his own identity becomes dependent on the interpretation, fixing him in a posture of aggression. Joyce's writing, however, emphasises chance and the irony of the text begins its upsetting work as the next line continues 'Portals of discovery opened to let in the quaker librarian, softcreak-footed, bald, eared and assiduous.' As Stephen sits in the Library trying to create both Shakespeare and himself at the centre of the world, the Library doors open and close, beyond his control, produc-ing elements which constantly re-make his world. As the chapter closes Bloom and Stephen will pass through them but Stephen is still unable to accept the chance encounters which will remake him through a series of accidents. The repetition of the description of the quaker librarian which first occurred six pages earlier stresses the way in which any meaning we attach to a phrase varies with the context in which it is read. The intervening six pages have refined and transformed our interpretation of that phrase in a process which takes place time and again in *Ulysses* as words and phrases gain and lose meaning in their repetition throughout the book. The process by which time thus enters into interpretation, always present in the text's procedures, becomes one of the major structural principles in the 'Sirens' chapter.

Stephen's interpretation is a doomed attempt to make his mark within the Irish literary revival. The sequence is punctuated by unwelcome reminders that this movement will not recognise him. From Russell's collection of young poets from which he is excluded (*U*: 192) to the meeting that evening to which Mulligan is invited but he is not (*U*: 192, 214), Stephen is uncomfortably reminded of his insignificance. Most important of all is the absence of Haines, the Gaelic-speaking, culture-spotting Englishman who confers authority on the Gaelic revival. 'Are we going to be read?' asks Russell but his certainty that they are (*U*: 193) depends on an English audience. But Haines, rather than listen to Stephen's voice which he had promised to write down (*U*: 22), has gone off to Gill's to buy a copy of Hyde's *Lovesongs of Connacht* (*U*: 186). In a desperate effort to assert his centrality, Stephen identifies with the excluded Shakespeare in the effort to become the father of his own race. The failure of all the other fathers will be redeemed in an identification with the race: ' . . . he was and felt himself the father of all his race, the father of his own grandfather, the father of his unborn grandson' (*U*: 208). It is here that the notion of race comes to petrify Stephen in that final identity that Mulligan had foreshadowed in his precis of Stephen's theory.

But in the attempt to become an Irish Shakespeare (*U*: 198), to create an Irish figure which can be set against 'Saxon Shakespeare's Hamlet' (*U*: 185), Stephen encounters the problem of language. Hyde's book, which Haines is so keen to buy as an example of Irish culture denies the very language in which it is written:

> *Bound thee forth, my booklet, quick*
> *To greet the callous public.*
> *Writ, I ween, 'twas not my wish*
> *In lean unlovely English.* (*U*: 186)

The dream of Gaelic as the only language in which the Irish can find expression disturbs Stephen's claim to become the voice of Ireland. And this problem of form goes hand in hand with the problem of the race for whom he wishes to speak. Russell's claim that the peasantry

are the only repositories of truth (*U*: 186–7) threatens the urban
Stephen as the end of *A Portrait* records

> John Alphonsus Mulrennan has just returned from the west of Ireland.
> (European and Asiatic papers please copy.) He told us he met an old man
> there in a mountain cabin. Old man had red eyes and short pipe. Old man
> spoke Irish. Mulrennan spoke Irish. Then old man and Mulrennan spoke
> English. Mulrennan spoke to him about universe and stars. Old man sat,
> listened, smoked, spat. Then said:
> – Ah, there must be terrible queer creatures at the latter end of the
> world.
> I fear him. I fear his redrimmed horny eyes. It is with him I must struggle
> all through this night till day come. . . .' (*P*: 256)

This struggle all through the night which composes *Finnegans Wake*
will displace the very terms of the debate about Ireland and language
and dispel the very possibility of a simple identity for a race or a
simple meaning with which that identity can be expressed. The
impossible ideal of a father in full control of his race and his voice is
alluded to by Stephen when he reflects in the Library 'I am tired of my
voice, the voice of Esau' (*U*: 211). The voice of Esau is the voice that
cannot ensure recognition by the father. Jacob confuses the blind
Isaac into giving him his blessing by covering his skin so that it is
hairy like Esau's and Isaac confers his blessing saying 'the voice is
Jacob's voice, but the hands *are* the hands of Esau' (*Genesis* 27:22).
Even on Esau's return his voice remains powerless to force recognition from Isaac 'Hast thou but one blessing, my father? bless me,
even me also, O my father. And Esau lifted up his voice, and wept'
(*Genesis* 27: 38). The relations between voice and race are particularly clear in the case of Esau for it is clear that Esau's fault lies in his
mixing with other races:

> One who 'despised his birthright', as heir of Abraham, was not likely to
> value highly connexion with Abraham's kindred. He associated freely
> with Canaanites, who were 'strangers from the covenants of promise',
> and, at the age of 40, married two Hittite wives, Judith and Basemath, to
> the grief of his parents, who could not forget Abraham's anxiety to avoid
> such alliances.[7]

The impossibility of assuming a full voice which would confer
identity, an impossibility forced home by the very uncertainty of
national languages which runs through the section, is finally displaced by writing, by the investigation of the various forms of
language and the identities that they offer. In the 'Sirens' section this

opposition takes form in the narrative in the distance between the singing voice of Simon Dedalus which seeks to fix the listeners in a moment of identification intimately linked to a simple opposition between masculine and feminine, and Bloom's writing of his letter to Martha Clifford in the dining room of the Ormond bar which opens up a different and more ambivalent relation to desire. Joyce's writing in the Library sequence emphasises the variety of 'parody' which will become more and more dominant in the 'Cyclops' and 'Oxen of the Sun' sections. This parody is, however, to be ruthlessly distinguished from the variety of parodies offered by Buck Mulligan from his keening peasant (*U*: 199) through to his final written offering *Everyman His own Wife* (*U*: 216–17). Mulligan's parodies remain as fully understood jokes which in no way threaten his basic speaking voice, the voice of a 'servant' (*U*: 17) to the Englishman Haines. The parodies of *Ulysses* are different as their irony eats away at the very possibility of a voice which can be controlled by a consciousness held outside it. These different forms of parody can be usefully considered in the light of the distinction that Freud makes between the joke (*Witz*) and humour (*Humor*).[8] Humour is produced in the certainty of the superego that the ego is making a mistake, but that very certainty leaves the ego untouched, as Mulligan is untouched by his various parodies. But *Witz* threatens the very structure of the ego by calling attention to the ego's impossible coherence. Freud talks directly of this kind of subversive parody in *Jokes and their Relation to the Unconscious* (1905) when he tells the story of two Jews who meet at a railway station in Galicia. 'Where are you going?' asked one. 'To Cracow', was the answer. 'What a liar you are!' broke out the other. 'If you say you're going to Cracow, you want me to believe you're going to Lemberg. But I know that in fact you're going to Cracow. So why are you lying to me?'[9]

Freud comments on the story thus: 'I think that jokes of this kind are sufficiently different from the rest to be given a special position. What they are attacking is not a person or an institution but the certainty of our knowledge itself, one of our speculative possessions.'[10]

At the end of the chapter when Stephen laughs 'to free his mind from his mind's bondage' (*U*: 212), his laughter liberates him from the fixity of interpretation, from the certainty of knowledge. It is in this laugh that the sequence can begin to be written, to dramatise and set forth the theory in its relation to its audience, to the identities it seeks in Hamlet and Stephen, Shakespeare and Joyce, England and Ireland. It is usual to discuss Joyce and Shakespeare in terms of *Hamlet*[11], but, from the perspectives adopted here, *Cymbeline* is the more important play. Schutte notes 8 quotations from *Cymbeline* in the course of *Ulysses* which places it fourth in the final table that he draws up (after *Hamlet, Twelfth Night* and *Macbeth*); of these, 5 occur within the Library sequence, but there are additional references to *Cymbeline* and, arguably, one quotation that Schutte misses.[12] It is also in *Cymbeline* that we read Shakespeare's clearest statement of the problem of paternity that obsesses Stephen:

> Is there no way for men to be, but women
> Must be half-workers? We are all bastards,
> And that most venerable man, which I
> Did call my father, was I know not where
> When I was stamp'd. Some coiner with his tools
> Made me a counterfeit. (Act II, Scene iv ll.153–8)[13]

Posthumus's outburst is caused by his acceptance of Iachimo's account of Imogen's seduction, an image of female sexuality unconstrained by law which contrasts with his own memory:

> Me of my lawful pleasure she restrain'd,
> And pray'd me oft forbearance: did it with
> A pudency so rosy, the sweet view on't
> Might well have warm'd old Saturn; that I thought her
> As chaste as unsunn'd snow. (Act II, Scene iv, ll 161–5)[14]

Cymbeline turns around the question of lawful inheritance and the passage from father to son. This question is interwoven with the identity of the nation, or, to be more precise, of Britain. It is the change from England to Britain that makes *Cymbeline* so important a re-statement of the themes of the earlier history plays, and which rendered it so significant for Joyce. Shakespeare's use of sources in this play is particularly interesting in the context of the concerns that circulate in the National Library in Dublin. *Cymbeline* runs together a story of unfounded sexual jealousy current in Renaissance literature but most notably in Boccaccio (*The Decameron*, Day 2, Nov. 9) and a patchwork of references from Holinshed with the story of the abduction of the king's two sons which has a possible source in a play entitled *The Rare Triumphs of Love and Fortune* but which is, in any case, recognisably and unmistakably a folk tale.[15] These elements bring together questions of identity and sexuality, nation and race in a particular configuration. Unlike any of Shakespeare's earlier history plays, the nation that must be constituted in the play is Britain and not England. The word *Britain* and its cognates occur no less than 47 times in *Cymbeline*, a startling fact when one realises that in no other play, except for the similarly late *Henry VIII*, does it occur more than once.[16] This change from England (emphasised by the fact that neither *England* or *English* occurs once within the play, and in this *Cymbeline* differs from *Henry VIII*) finds an evident cause in the changed status of the realm after the accession of James VI of Scotland to the throne of England. But this plain political fact is given symbolic gloss within *Cymbeline*.

In Shakespeare's second tetralogy of plays, Henry's claim to rule the political realm is underlined by his mastery of communication. Hal's claim to Poins 'I am so good a proficient in one quarter of an hour that I can drink with any tinker in his own language during my life' (*Henry IV Part 1*, Act II, Scene iv, ll 17–19) indicates his ability to master all the languages that circulate in the realm and allow him, in *Henry V*, to become the king of England and the heir of France, able to talk to both his soldiers and Princess Katherine. This mastery of communication is contrasted with the situation of the pretender Mortimer, in the earlier play, who cannot understand or speak to his Welsh wife, Glendower's daughter.[17] Indeed the enemy camp is defined through the disjuncture of language and reality. Glendower's mastery of language is exposed as an empty sham by Hotspur:

> *Glendower:* I can call spirits from the vasty deep.
> *Hotspur:* Why, so can I, or so can any man,
>   But will they come when you do call for them?
>   (*Henry IV Part 1*, Act III, Scene i, ll. 50–2)

But in *Cymbeline* there is no such confusion. Wales is not the site of meaningless signifiers and misconstrued speech acts but a place of simple communication in which the king's sons can be reared, where body and language are in direct relation:

>   this story
> The world may read in me: my body's mark'd
> With Roman swords. (Act III, Scene iii, ll. 55–7)

And the narrative includes Scotland within this United Kingdom of transparent language. The moment when

Two boys, an old man twice a boy, a lane,
Preserv'd the Britons, was the Romans' bane
(Act V, Scene iii, ll. 57–8)

is taken from Holinshed's *The Description and Historie of Scotland* (1587).[18]

This transparency of language and nation, this evidence of identities, becomes apparent at the conclusion of the play when, after the host of false reports and misdirected communications, Imogen is revealed in the legal position of wife, a position untainted by desire. It is the transformation of word into flesh, sound into identity, which the soothsayer accomplishes as he interprets the riddle left by Posthumus's family:

The piece of tender air, thy virtuous daughter,
Which we call *mollis aer*; and *mollis aer*
We term it *mulier*: which *mulier* I divine
Is this most constant wife. (Act V, Scene v, ll. 447–50)

The constant demands to speak which run through the play and which produce nothing but desire and violence are finally answered when Iachimo and Belarius are able to speak all. The threat posed by speech, articulated so violently by Imogen to Pisanio,

Talk thy tongue weary, speak:
I have heard I am a strumpet, and mine ear,
Therein false struck, can take no greater wound,
Nor tent, to bottom that. But speak. (Act III, Scene iv, ll. 114–17),

is allayed when, in a passage entirely dominated by a consideration of the constraints on speech, Cymbeline begs Iachimo to 'strive, man, and speak' (V, v, l.152). It is Iachimo's ability to speak one half of the narrative and Belarius's confidence in mastering 'a dangerous speech' (l.313) to convey the other which produces a situation in which both sexual difference and political revolt become equally unimportant (identified with the body of the dead queen lying offstage). The king becomes both mother and father, ruler and subject:

O, what am I?
A mother to the birth of three? Ne'er mother
Rejoic'd deliverance more. . . . (ll.369–71)

Well,
My peace we will begin: and Caius Lucius,
Although the victor, we submit to Caesar,
And to the Roman empire. (ll. 459–62)

The 'wicked queen' (1.464) in her feminine opacity – 'Who is't can read a woman?' rhetorically laments Cymbeline (1.48) – and the headless Cloten are all that are left to remind us of other possibilities. For Shakespeare, *Cymbeline* offers a final national totalisation which, ignoring the actual political divisions within the British Isles and Europe, produces an imaginary unity which embraces everyone from the Druid priests to the Roman Emperor. For Joyce, who did not see 'what good it does to fulminate against the English tyranny while the Roman tyranny occupies the palace of the soul' (*C W*: 173), *Cymbeline* makes clear the distance between Shakespeare's situation and his own. The final lines of Cymbeline, which close the chapter in the Library, produce an imperial peace, an identification which joins the Celts to the English and the English to Rome, against which Joyce is to spend the rest of his life writing.

The key to such writing is the renouncing of speech, the 'silence' with which Stephen Dedalus will initiate his exile and his cunning. Whereas the king had ordered the effort of speech – 'strive, man, and speak' – Stephen thinks at the end of the chapter that he must 'cease to strive' (*U*: 218). This abandonment of speech is signalled earlier in the chapter by some Latin interpolations. It is tempting to say that these interpolations are simply Stephen's thoughts but, in fact, notably from the 'Aeolus' section and indeed before, it is never a simple matter to allocate many of the words of the text either to an authorial narrative voice or to any single character's consciousness.[19] It is this difficulty which makes it necessary to consider the relation between Stephen and Joyce in terms of writing – as Joyce remakes the images of his youth so he remakes himself writing – and impossible to consider that relation in terms of representation – a Joyce finally sure of his identity representing a finally identified earlier self. The interpolations occur on page 205:

> – Prove that he was a jew, John Eglinton dared, expectantly. Your dean of studies holds he was a holy Roman.
> *Sufflaminandus sum.*
> – He was made in Germany, Stephen replied, as the champion French polisher of Italian scandals.
> – A myriadminded man, Mr Best reminded. Coleridge called him myriadminded.
> *Amplius. In societate humana hoc est maxime necessarium ut sit amicitia inter multos.*

The first Latin quotation '*sufflaminandus sum*' is perhaps best translated as 'I ought to be repressed'. The reference is to Ben Jonson and through him to Augustus and the *Pax Romana*. In writing of Shakespeare Jonson comments that '. . . hee flow'd with that facility, that sometime it was necessary he should be stop'd: *Sufflaminandus erat*; as *Augustus* said of *Haterius*.'[20] Augustus's comments about a particularly fluent Roman senator which Jonson applied to Shakespeare, are now applied by the text to Stephen. His desire to speak must be – the gerundive indicates obligation – 'stop't' or repressed. The dream of speaking everything will lead to the paralytic fixity of psychotic collapse. It is this paralysis which confronts Stephen and Bloom when they gaze in the mirror during the Circe episode:

> (*Stephen and Bloom gaze in the mirror. The face of William Shakespeare, beardless, appears there, rigid in facial paralysis, crowned by the reflection of the reindeer antlered hatrack in the hall.*) (U: 508)

Stephen's dream of speaking everything, of adding Bloom to himself to become the all-knowing artistic consciousness, is doomed to paralytic failure, crowned, as this search for identity is, by the determination to fix woman's desire in an allotted masculine space. It is in the splitting of the subject, in the movement from Stephen to Bloom, that a writing can begin which, freed from the demands of identification, is also freed from the compulsion to fix woman's desire in its lawful place. And this writing re-articulates the criticism that Stephen utters. Freed from the concern with identity, Stephen's and Shakespeare's, the theory is no longer imposed by force of speech. The content of the theory (which constantly works against Stephen's attempts to define his own and his nation's identity – in answer to the demand to produce Shakespeare as a Jew or a Catholic, Stephen produces him as a series of displacements: German/French/Italian) can become form as the logic of these displacements works into the writing of the chapter to unmake Stephen's fixation as it unmakes those of Best, Eglinton and Mulligan. And with this 'unmaking' the reading of Shakespeare no longer becomes an aggressive weapon which isolates Stephen. The second sentence in the longer Latin quotation in the passage quoted above can be translated thus: 'In human society it is of the utmost importance that there be amicable relations among as many as possible.' It is by repressing his desire to speak a truth so final that it will freeze speaker and audience in their place that Stephen can prepare the way for a writing which will promote amicability in the multitudinous possibilities that it opens up.

In the light of this dramatisation of theory, this writing of criticism, it is pertinent to question the status of the critical discourse of this very essay. Does it not fall into that fixity which Joyce's writing seeks to unmake, the aggression that grips Stephen in the library? There is a certain force to this contradiction, but what distinguishes this criticism from Stephen's is its concern to bring Joyce's text into dialogue with a specific set of questions, in this case questions of politics and sexuality, language and race, which cannot be simply reduced to a literary discourse. It is in such a heterogenous dialogue that the misleading universality of literary interpretation can be evaded.

In conclusion one can consider in some further detail the questions of national identity which have informed this reading. Most immediately at stake is that image of Ireland, produced by the Celtic revival and sanctified by the Easter Rising, whose force and potency has not been notably diminished in the course of the century. For Joyce the notion of a Gaelic culture and a Gaelic nation was fatally constituted as a mirror-image of an English or Saxon culture understood as irremediably alien. Between two such imaginary identities the reality of modern Ireland passed unnoticed. Nowhere is the fatal fixity of Pearse's ideology delineated more clearly than in the monstrous final stanza of Yeats's 'The Statues' (1938):

> When Pearse summoned Cuchulain to his side,
> What stalked through the Post Office? What intellect,
> What calculation, number, measurement, replied?
> We Irish, born into that ancient sect
> But thrown upon the filthy modern tide
> And by its formless spawning fury wrecked,
> Climb to our proper dark. . . .[21]

That 'proper dark' still paralyses many Irish imaginations, but in *Finnegans Wake*, finally published the year after Yeats's poem was written, the 'filthy modern' Joyce produced an improper dark in which the notion of any pure racial identity becomes an impossibility confronted with the realities of desire and language in which 'miscegenations on miscegenations' (*F W*: 18) is the only lineage we can trace. Finn, not Cuchulain, becomes the ever-changing image of the 'father of all his race':

> All the features which distinguish the Celtic hero are discernible in the
> Cú Chulainn story and all tribal heroes must have followed this pattern to
> a greater or lesser extent. Cú Chulainn, however, was a hero within the

tribe, fighting for his people. Beyond the minutely ordered social life of the tribe existed another hero-figure best typified by Finn. Finn shared the more important of the personal qualities of Cú Chulainn but he and his peers were conceived of as extra-tribal heroes.[22]

For Joyce, Finn in his aspect as the fair-haired result of the Norwegian invaders becomes the archetype of the miscegenated Irish race on which he lectured to a Triestine audience in 1907:

> Recently, when an Irish member of parliament was making a speech to the voters on the night before an election, he boasted that he was one of the ancient race and rebuked his opponent for being the descendant of a Cromwellian settler. His rebuke provoked a general laugh in the press, for, to tell the truth, to exclude from the present nation all who are descended from foreign families would be impossible, and to deny the name of patriot to all those who are not of Irish stock would be to deny it to almost all the heroes of the modern movement. . . .
>
> Our civilisation is a vast fabric, in which the most diverse elements are mingled, in which nordic aggressiveness and Roman law, the new bourgeois conventions and the remnant of a Syriac religion are reconciled. In such a fabric, it is useless to look for a thread that may have remained pure and virgin without having undergone the influence of a neighbouring thread. What race, or what language (if we except the few whom a playful will seems to have preserved in ice, like the people of Iceland) can boast of being pure today? And no race has less right to utter such a boast than the race now living in Ireland. Nationality (if it really is not a convenient fiction like so many others to which the scalpels of present-day scientists have given the coup de grâce) must find its reason for being rooted in something that surpasses and transcends and informs changing things like blood and the human word. The mystic theologian who assumed the pseudonym of Dionysius, the pseudo-Areopagite, says somewhere, 'God has disposed the limits of nations according to his angels', and this probably is not a purely mystical concept. Do we not see that in Ireland the Danes, the Firbolgs, the Milesians from Spain, the Norman invaders, and the Anglo-Saxon settlers have united to form a new entity, one might say under the influence of a local deity? (*C W*: 161–6)

Joyce consistently, in all his writings, opposes a notion of a plural race to that of a single nation and this opposition may be of vital importance to our own understanding of Shakespeare and the unity of Britain under an English tongue. To pursue such investigations, pressing as their necessity is, will involve a return to considerations of both life and work, a conjunction so long considered jejune or simply tasteless in so many of the dominant critical schools. But such a return will not be to the spurious and coherent biographies of a Harris or a Brandes; it will involve the fragmentation of both body and text to delineate those moments, historical and symbolic, in which fictional forms produce the language and identity of a nation; those moments of terrible repression to which *Cymbeline* bears such magnificent witness.[23]

Notes

1   See Colin MacCabe, *James Joyce and the Revolution of the Word* (London: Macmillan, 1979), p. 52–65.

2   For an account of the relations between anaphoric, exophoric and cataphoric relations in a text see M.A.K. Halliday and Ruqaiya Hasan, *Cohesion in English* (London: Longman, 1976), p. 14–19.

3   Quoted in Weldon Thornton, *Allusions in Ulysses* (Chapel Hill: The University of North Carolina Press, 1968), p. 22–3.

4   Two of the three critics discussed there had already published books: Sidney Lee, *A Life of William Shakespeare* (London: Smith, Elder & Co., 1898); Georg Brandes, *William Shakespeare: A Critical Study*, translated by William Archer, Mary Morison and Diana White (London: William Heinemann, 1898), 2 vols. Frank Harris's articles in the *Saturday Review* formed the basis for a subsequent book, *The Man Shakespeare and His Tragic Life Story* (London; Frank Palmer, 1909). William M. Schutte's *Joyce and Shakespeare; a Study in the Meaning of Ulysses* (New Haven: Yale University Press, 1957) gives a detailed account of the relation between this chapter and these sources. Although this account brings out the fact that Brandes is the major source, Schutte does not recognise the full importance of this. It is important that Brandes's book is the only one of the three in Joyce's Trieste library, cf. Richard Ellmann, *The Consciousness of Joyce* (London: Faber & Faber, 1977), p. 103. Brandes was also quoted by Joyce in the lectures he gave on Shakespeare in Trieste in 1912–13 of which only a newspaper account remains, *ibid.* p. 51.

5   For Joyce's relations with Archer see Richard Ellmann, *James Joyce* (New York: Oxford University Press, 1959), particularly p. 76–7.

6   Brandes, *op. cit.*, vol. 2 p. 26. It should be noted that metaphors of light and dark pervade Brandes's account of Shakespeare as they do Stephen's.

7   *A Dictionary of the Bible*, ed. James Hastings (Edinburgh: T. and T. Clark, 1898), Vol. 1, p. 734.

8   For the distinction between *Witz* and *Humor* see the article 'Humour' (1927) in *The Complete Psychological Works of Sigmund Freud* (London: The Hogarth Press, 1953–74), Vol. XXI, p. 161–6.

9   Freud, *op. cit.*, Vol. VIII, p. 115.

10 *Ibid.*

11   E.g. Schutte, *op. cit.* and Ellmann, *The Consciousness of Joyce, op. cit.*

12   For the further references to *Cymbeline*, see Thornton, *op. cit.* and Don Gifford with Robert J. Seidman, *Notes for Joyce* (New York: Dutton, 1974). Thornton argues for an additional quotation in Stephen's thought 'Cease to strive' (*U*: 218): 'Nowhere does Shakespeare use this exact phrase, but in *Cymbeline*, V, v (which is alluded to [shortly after]), Cymbeline, wanting to know about his daughter, urges Iachimo "Strive, man, and speak" (l.152)' (p. 219–20). The argument of this paper would certainly support Thornton's hypothesis. A further possible reference to *Cymbeline*, not noted by either Gifford or Thornton, occurs when Mr Best remarks '– That's very interesting because that brother motive, don't you know, we find also in the old Irish myths. Just what you say. The three brothers Shakespeare. In Grimm too, don't you know, the fairytales. The third brother that marries the sleeping beauty and wins the best prize' (*U*: 210). There are two sets of three brothers in *Cymbeline*: Guiderius, Arviragus, and Fidele (Imogen); Posthumus and his two dead brothers who visit him in V, iv. Posthumus does marry Imogen who spends part of the play as a sleeping beauty. What is important is not to decide whether there is direct reference to *Cymbeline* in this quotation but to recognise how familiar Joyce was with the structure of the folk-tales that Shakespeare uses in *Cymbeline*.

13   *Cymbeline*, ed. J.M. Nosworthy (London: Methuen, 1969). All further quotations from Shakespeare are taken from the Arden edition. One might note that the juxtaposition of doubts about paternity with the metaphor of forging brings the elements in Posthumus's speech into even more direct alignment with Joyce's concerns.

14   The quotation continues:

> O, all the devils!
> This *yellow* Iachimo, in an hour, was't not? (my italics)

My own suspicion that *Cymbeline* was one of the plays that Joyce had not read in 1904 must remain a personal surmise. What is certain is that the events of 1909 when he believed Cosgrave's claim to have seduced Nora (cf. Ellmann, *James Joyce*, p. 288–90) must have made *Cymbeline* a much more immediately personal play. It may be significant in this context that Lynch, the Cosgrave character in *A Portrait*, continually uses the adjective *yellow*.

15   In 1887 R.W. Boodle suggested that Shakespeare was indebted to an anonymous play, *The Rare Triumphs of Love and Fortune*, in *Notes and Queries*, VII, iv (19 Nov. 1887), p. 404–5. None of Joyce's three major sources seem aware of this theory and there is nothing in his Trieste library to suggest that he had read Boodle or the play. What is important for the argument of this essay, as already suggested in note 12, is Joyce's recognition of the way in which *Cymbeline* directly incorporates and transforms folk-tale material. Anyone in doubt of the

importance of the folk-tale for *Cymbeline* should consult D.S. Brewer's *Symbolic Stories* (Cambridge: D.S. Brewer, 1980), pp. 133–46.

16   When it does occur more than once, it occurs with the meaning of Brittany. See Marvin Spevack, *The Harvard Concordance to Shakespeare* (Cambridge: Harvard University Press, 1973). For earlier considerations of the British element in *Cymbeline* and its place as an historical drama see J.P. Brockbank, 'History and Histrionics in *Cymbeline*', *Shakespeare Survey*, ed. Allardyce Nicoll (Cambridge: Cambridge University Press, 1958), p. 42–9 and Emrys Jones, 'Stuart Cymbeline', *Essays in Criticism*, vol. 11, No. 1, p. 84–99.

17   The worst example of linguistic opacity in this scene is, of course, Irish: '*Hotspur*: I had rather hear Lady my brach howl in Irish' (l.230). The citizen's dog in Ulysses would seem to answer Hotspur's wish and to provide yet another example of the dominance of an English audience to the production of an Irish tongue (*U*: 309–10). My understanding of the importance of language in Shakespeare's second tetralogy of history plays is indebted to an unpublished student paper by Henry Davis (an auditor, though sleeping, of the original lecture) entitled 'Shakespeare's Histories: A Game with Plays'.

18   *Narrative and Dramatic Sources of Shakespeare*, ed. Geoffrey Bullough (London: Routledge & Kegan Paul, 1975), Vol. VIII, p. 48.

19   For further comments on the relation between Stephen Dedalus and James Joyce see C. MacCabe, 'Language, Linguistics and the Study of Literature', *Oxford Literary Review*, Vol. 4 no. 3, p. 73.

20   Ben Jonson, *Collected Works*, ed. Herford and Simpson (Oxford: Clarendon Press, 1925–52), Vol. VIII, p. 584.

21   W.B. Yeats, *Collected Poems* (London: Macmillan, 1950), pp. 375–6. I am indebted to Seamus Deane for indicating the importance of this stanza.

22   *Larousse Encyclopedia of Mythology*, ed. Félix Guirand (London: Batchworth Press, 1959), p. 242.

23   Other than Joyce's own writing, the two most fruitful approaches to Shakespeare along the lines suggested here are Edward Bond's *Bingo* (London: Eyre Methuen, 1974), and Ted Hughes's afterword to *A Choice of Shakespeare's Verse* (London: Faber & Faber, 1971).

CHAPTER 7

Joyce in Language*

Stephen Heath

Joyce in Language. An eye and an ear for *Finnegans Wake* – the
'aural eyeness' (*F W*: 623) with which we are called upon to address
its writing – will have noted already in that title a whole programme
in a nutshell: joy, sin, language (language and sin, 'sinse' (*F W*:
239)), time (time since language and the time of this joy-sinse-
language book itself, 'Not a salutary sellable sound is since' (*F W*:
598)) plus the name slipping out of identity, Joyce to joysin, Joyce in
language. In the shifting movement of the *Wake*, 'Acomedy of letters!' (*F W*: 425), 'Joyce' as name never appears; only a succession of
transformations, so many *drifts* – 'joyicity' (*F W*: 414), for example
– that are never brought to any final stasis, to the 'proper name':
'since in this scherzarade of one's thousand one nightinesses that
sword of certainty which would indentifide the body never falls' (*F
W*: 51).

One such drift appealed particularly to Joyce and will land us at once
in the problem of language: from Joyce to Jousse.
   'In the beginning was the gest he jousstly says' (*F W*: 468). Thus is
the Abbé Marcel Jousse mentioned in *Finnegans Wake* in connection
with that theme of his teaching which held the interest of Joyce and
which could be readily conjoined with similar ideas to be found in
Vico, Joyce's great imaginative source. Beckett describing the writing of *Finnegans Wake* does so with Vico in mind but in a way that
makes clear the fascination that Jousse would have: 'This writing
that you find so obscure is a quintessential extraction of language
and painting and gesture, with all the inevitable clarity of the old
inarticulation. Here is the savage economy of hieroglyphics.'[1] Jousse,

* This essay reproduces as nearly as is compatible with its transposition into written
form the lecture given in the Cambridge English Faculty in connection with the special
paper on Joyce; additional matter is to a large extent limited to the notes at the end.
For more extended development of the material suggested here, see S. Heath,
'Ambiviolences', *Tel Quel* no. 50 (Summer 1972), p. 22–43 and no. 51 (Autumn
1972), p. 64–76; 'Trames de lecture', *Tel Quel* no. 54 (Summer 1973), p. 4–15.

a priest and a linguist concerned with the nature of language and its origins, lectured in Paris at the same time that Joyce was there writing the *Wake*. Joyce attended at least one of the Abbé's lectures and was highly enthusiastic. The best account is given by Mary Colum, a friend of that period:

> At that time the Abbé Jousse was lecturing in Paris. He was a noted propounder of a theory that Joyce gave adherence to, that language has its origin in gesture – 'In the beginning was the rhythmic gesture,' Joyce often said. . . . If the Abbé's lecture did not interest me as much as it interested Joyce, still it interested me a great deal, and that largely because of its original method of presentation. It took the form of a little play, based on the Gospels. Around the lecturer was a group of girls, who addressed him as 'Rabbi Jesus'. The words spoken – one of the parables, I think, – were, I gathered, in Aramaic, and what was shown was that the word was shaped by the gesture. Joyce was full of the subject. . . .[2]

For Jousse gesture was the foundation of language, the very basis of the possibility of any human communication, and the development of language could be traced in relation to the strength of this gestural presence. Like Vico, Jousse postulates three main stages of development, which he calls *style manuel, style oral* and *style écrit*: the first is that of living gesticulation, language as depiction of meaning; the second is that of utterance miming gesture, shaped and supported by its accompanying presence; the third is that of alphabetism in which utterance is recorded in the medium of a language of conventional signs. This last stage is the moment of a possible loss of the reality of gesture which needs to be permanently reactivated under the surface of language if any vital communication is to take place. Alphabetic writing, the argument runs, loses all contact with gestural life and falls into a dead conventionalism, a kind of empty passivity of meaning. Hence Jousse's plea for a new active form of response to language, of reading, in his *Mimisme humain et psychologie de la lecture* published in Paris in 1935 and something of what such an active response was to be can be glimpsed in the description given by Colum of the lecture attended by Joyce. That lecture was one of the demonstrations staged by Jousse under the title of 'L'École de Rabbi Iéshoua': an attempt to recreate the gestural reality of the teaching of Jesus, to refind what a collaborator called 'intacte et vivante, sous l'envelope grecque, la parole vivante de "Rabbi Iéshoua" '.[3] Speaking Aramaic, a group of girls arranged around him, the Abbé would mime the word of Christ, a whole rhythm and depiction of his teaching. Joyce could hardly but be 'full of the subject'; just as *Finnegans Wake* itself was to be, even down to its echoing repetitions of lecturer and girls, notably in the chapter concerned with Shaun's address to the St Bride's Academy 'galaxy girls' (*F W*: 432; this is the chapter in which the main reference to Jousse occurs).

In insisting on the primacy of gesture ('In the beginning was the gest'), Jousse, like Vico before him, insists at the same time on the primacy of 'hieroglyphic' (Vico's term) or 'mimographic' (Jousse's) writing as being directly related to gestural presentation.[4] When Beckett talks of 'the inevitable clarity of the old inarticulation . . . the savage economy of hieroglyphics' in connection with *Finnegans Wake*, the phrases equally describe the ideas of an original vital state of language in Vico and Jousse: the loss of that inevitable clarity in alphabetic writing and increasingly in speech conditioned by the 'literacy' such a writing brings with it can only be remedied by getting back to the basic underlying gestuality (refinding what Stephen Dedalus calls the 'structural rhythm', *U*: 427).[5] For Jousse, again much like Vico, etymology is a key procedure here, going back through the history of language, returning through words to origins in gesture: 'Or, je crois que la nécessité – une fois sentie – de mieux comprendre notre propre langue, nous obligerait à retourner aux sources gréco-latines, aux mots originels, aux racines indo-européennes toujours concrètes et, par suite, aux gestes mimiques sous-jacents, identiques aux nôtres.'[6] The final aim is then, in fact, to throw off the envelope of language, to move from the conventions of letters to *the* letter, the living word, the original intention of meaning. At the close of *Mimisme humain et psychologie de la lecture* Jousse specifically distinguishes his project from Mallarmé's modernist attachment to writing, to the enclosure of the world as book: 'Contrairement à ce qu'affirmait Mallarmé, le monde n'existe pas pour aboutir à un livre, mais pour se transformer par le livre ou mieux sans le livre, en une pensée vivante et créatrice.'[7] But at this point Jousse separates equally from Joyce and Beckett's phrases, apt enough for the former, are both right and wrong for the latter. Joyce is full of Jousse, emphasises gesture and goes in for origins and the search for the letter in the whole narrative-thematic organisation of the *Wake*; but then, first and last, the *Wake* remains writing, goes on with the interminable play of language, comes back to no origin, knows no break between world and book, the world always already writing, 'is, was and will be writing its own wrunes for ever' (*F W*: 19). 'In the beginning was the gest he jousstly says' but also 'In the buginning is the woid' (*F W*: 378), the void of language, the 'ginnandgo gap' (*F W*: 14) in which the letter disappeared and the comedy of letters began, before which we cannot return, cannot *be*. Words and things move together in the ceaseless production of 'the world', the 'fictionable world' (*F W*: 345) that the writing of *Finnegans Wake* describes and explores and creates again and again. The end comes round and round to the beginning anew, 'a long the riverrun, past Eve and Adam's' (*F W*: 628–3). *That* is Joyce's return.

We can put it this way: for Joyce and for Jousse language, the activity of language, is a *memory*, but not the same. Jousse, etymologically, wants to get back up language, go deep beneath the surface unfolding successive layers and expose – re-expose – the living kernel of meaning, which can thus be remembered in and through language. Joyce, anti-etymologically (the *Wake* as a gigantic derision of etymology, 'wordloosed over seven seas crowdblast in celtelleneteutoslavzendlatinsoundscript', *F W*: 219), extends language, pulls out more and more 'any way words all in one soluble' (*F W*: 299), finds not a simple history but a network of fictions in a perpetual process of stories in words, a kind of infinitely expanding and regressing surface of language – 'There are sordidly tales within tales, you clearly understand that?' (*F W*: 522). We can say, summarising, that, in every sense, *Finnegans Wake tells tales on language*. And yet, at the same time, something of the *getting-back-up* desire is always there, a theme and a movement of the book, the constant obsession of the question of the origin.

With regard to language and memory and origins, let us consider for a moment that section of *Ulysses* which is so often left aside or regarded as a self-indulgent joke, a *tour de force* of gratuitous cleverness: the 'Oxen of the Sun' chapter, in which Bloom visits the Holles Street Hospital where Mina Purefoy is in labour and in which Joyce gives a series of parodies of stages in the development of English prose. 'Although the writing of this chapter was doubtless great fun for Joyce, it must be admitted that it is an ostentatious display of literary finesse calculated to mystify as much as to entertain.'[8]

Joyce drew a diagram for the writing of the 'Oxen of the Sun' chapter, two versions of which are extant: nine concentric rings, moving out from the base from the first to the ninth, something of the aspect of a cross-section through an onion; the nine rings correspond to the months of the gestation of the foetus in the womb and in all but one of the rings Joyce made a few embryological notations (thus for the seventh ring or mouth: 'fore fontanelle smaller/old face/testicles in groin/breastbone/heelbones/ 40 cm 1500 g').[9] In the elaborate system of correspondences according to which *Ulysses* is organised, this chapter is naturally the chapter of the womb, 'Matrice Utero', as Joyce noted in the 'Linati schema',[10] and the diagram can also stand as a representation of the female sex, a hidden premonition of the diagram of ALP's sex revealed to the children in the middle of *Finnegans Wake* (F W: 293).

Looking at the *Ulysses* diagram, thinking of its function for Joyce during the writing of the chapter and as an image of the chapter and its writing, one can see that it is also and importantly a memory system, a 'memory theatre' very much like those that Frances Yates describes in her well-known study *The Art of Memory* (and her examples include, centrally, systems developed by Giordano Bruno, another of Joyce's key imaginative sources): elaborate mnemic techniques by which knowledge is stored for recall in the 'places' of some diagrammatic pictorial representation – the spheres of the universe, for instance, projected as a memory system, concentric rings moving outwards with tag headings for each sphere.[11] The resemblance of such memory-system representations to Joyce's 'Oxen of the Sun' diagram is striking and *Ulysses* itself is written and works anyway as a gigantic memory theatre, with its encyclopedism, its chapter by chapter correspondence (each with its organ, art, technic, symbol, colour and so on), everything that Pound refers to as the result of Joyce's 'mediaevalism'.[12]

Yet the 'Oxen of the Sun' diagram is also significant in its difference in that resemblance, its new inflection: not the spheres of the universe projected as a memory system but the stages of the cycle of gestation in the womb. *Ulysses* has everything of the fascination with assembling and stocking knowledges and at the same time memory is now turned on to other scenes, memory of the human individual's original growth and birth and memory of language – and remembering the two together, each as the other, in a kind of simultaneity of writing. For that is the point of the 'Oxen of the Sun' chapter. The imitative history of language and prose from Anglo-Saxon to the present is not gratuitous, simply 'clever'; it goes along with the history of the development of the foetus. And if 'goes along with' is vague, it catches nevertheless exactly what is at stake: a simultaneity that is not some acquired theoretical position about the development of language and its parallel or reflection in the development of the human individual but that is no more – no less – than a desire to remember, to return, to get back into memory of birth and language, the question of origins again. The 'Oxen of the Sun' chapter is an instance of that desire which becomes all the writing of *Finnegans Wake* and it insists clearly enough on the *return*, the desire *from the present*. One is always 'sinse', since any origin, any beginning, and fallen into language, caught up in meanings, identities, the whole mesh of fictions. It is that that Joyce finds and stresses as the memory of 'Oxen of the Sun': the account of the development of the foetus is not 'scientific' or in any way close up with the foetus, it is compiled out of bits and pieces of knowledge and folklore and gossip, from contemporary embryology manuals to ideas derived from classical medical authorities (such as Hippocrates's belief that male children are produced by fertilisation of the right ovaries) and from there to popular stories and reports (so many superstitions, abnormalities, monstrosities); the account of the development of English prose works from the current representation of that development, Joyce using the existing memory as his source, books such as George Saintsbury's *History of English Prose Rhythm* (1912) and W. Peacock's *English Prose; Mandeville to Ruskin* (1903), going back from them.[13] The 'Oxen of the Sun' chapter, in other words, deals in memory, desire in its terms, with all its gaps and fragments and excesses and wanderings and forgetfulness.

Birth, language. . . . Absent from the 'Oxen of the Sun' chapter is the woman, off-stage, in labour, giving birth while the men debate and carouse in the hospital common-room, a mass of words and notions and jests finding a memory of life in the womb. 'In the beginning was the gest he jousstly says, for the end is with woman, flesh-without-word' (*F W*: 468).

Ulysses, indeed, ends with woman, Molly's inner monologue; as too does *Finnegans Wake*, Anna Livia flowing out into the ocean. Molly looks back over, remembering, the day and the book, her life and the themes and motifs and actions that make up the novel we have read. 'Flesh-without-word': in the system of correspondences, the organ of this 'Penelope' chapter is flesh, fat, 'grasso'; to which word is now given, for the end and as though by magic – we might, wrote Arnold Bennett, be reading 'the magical record of inmost thoughts thought by a woman that existed'.[14] The chapter enters literary history as the unsurpassable expression of 'feminine psychology' (Bennett again: 'Talk about understanding "feminine psychology" '),[15] a judgment which is quite correct: the unsurpassable expression of *the woman*, an imaginary of the female 'flesh-without-word', the other who is assigned to that otherness, flesh, mystery, the inexpressible outside of the law and speech of men, and is then asked to confirm, magically to say her reality as that. The action of *Ulysses* over, the day drawn to its close, the men asleep, the woman has her place, is added to complete the picture, the nighttime flow, the universal female: 'the force of this long, unpunctuated meditation, in which a drowsy woman's vagrant thoughts are transferred in all their naked candour of self-revelation on to the written record, lies precisely in its universality.'[16]

The position of the expression of the woman at the close of the book, the over-eager chorus of male praises for its brilliance of understanding and the determined insistence on its universality are indicative. The 'Penelope' chapter contains but also says the other; Molly's monologue stands out from the book it concludes, a necessary addition or coda that brings with it the pressure of that necessity which inevitably returns in *Finnegans Wake*. The end of the *Wake* remembers the end of *Ulysses*, another woman monologue picking up Molly's according to that spiral movement of rewriting and displacement so characteristic of the relations of each of Joyce's texts with those which precede it. The perspective of identity – Molly's monologue is continually reinserted into patterns of identity, *attitudes* – slips away in the flow of Anna Livia and with it the imaginary of the woman, the simple representation, the held position. That Anna Livia's flow occupies the same structural place as Molly's monologue, at the end of the book, underlines the force of the pressure in evidence in the latter but also shows up the difference from the one to the other, exactly the rewriting and displacement. With Anna Livia, we are in the whole question of the writing of the *Wake*, where syntax – the logic of subject-predicate – is overtaken by 'sintalks' (*F W*: 269), the constant transgressive underrunning of accepted orders, rules of stability, the laws of language and identity – 'the farmer, his son and their homely codes' (*F W*: 614). Anna Livia's ending of the *Wake* is an epitomising moment of this transgression general to its writing, brought to a head again and again in the theme of incest: Anna Livia rushes indefinitely into her father's arms, the river running out and losing itself in the vast ocean, a fearfully ecstatic loss of self: 'I go back to you, my cold father, my cold mad father, my cold mad feary father, till the near sight of the mere size of him, the moyles and moyles of it, moananoaning, makes me seasilt saltsick and I rush, my only, into your arms. I see them rising! Save me from those therrble prongs!' (*F W*: 628).

Finnegans Wake was to be to *Ulysses* for Joyce as night to day, a 'nightynovel' (*F W*: 54): 'Mon livre . . . n'a rien de commun avec *Ulysse*. C'est le jour et la nuit!'[17] Its writing is situated before – in hesitation of – waking reason: 'In writing of the night, I really could not, I felt I could not, use words in their ordinary connections. Used that way, they do not express how things are in the night, in the different stages – conscious, then semi-conscious, then unconscious. I found that it could not be done with words in their ordinary relations and connections.'[18] It is as though the material of the 'Oxen of the Sun' chapter of *Ulysses* has become the overall impulse and procedure and aim of Joyce's writing: language and origins, all the 'sinse' of the book. Anna Livia's flow says that movement and theme of memory, from recollection of the paradise peace of pre-birth ('as I was sweet when I came down out of me mother. My great blue bedroom, the air so quiet, scarce a cloud. In peace and silence. I could have stayed up there for always only. It's something fails us. First we feel. Then we fall.' (*F W*: 627)) to the future return to heavenly childhood bliss ('Carry me along, taddy, like you done through the toy fair! If I seen him bearing down on me now under whitespread wings like he'd come from Arkangels, I sink I'd die down over his feet, humbly dumbly, only to washup.' (*F W*: 628)). 'Mememormee' (*F W*: 628): *Finnegans Wake* is no longer so much memory theatre as memory production, a massive attempt to work in memory, the remembering of a past of which what can be said except that it is night to day, the other side, another scene? In other words, *Finnegans Wake* places itself not on the grounds of the memory of some coherent subjectivity or centre of knowledge but through and across the forgetfulness on which any such coherence is constructed. Hence the imaginary of the woman that assures the subjectivity of *Ulysses*, completes the picture, here no longer holds, no longer fits into place; the writing displaces, the book now as a long 'letter selfpenned to one's other' (*F W*: 489). From 'the steady monologuy of the interiors'

(*F W*: 119) we move into the 'drama parapolylogic' (*F W*: 474) of the very process of subjectivity which can then be called 'feminine' from a perverse assumption of the imaginary of the woman which Joyce repeats and for which he is praised at the end of *Ulysses*. The woman is the other, thus to write to one's other, to drop from an established coherence of the self – oneself, the self as one – to the heterogeneous production of a subject of which that coherence is simply an identifying and stabilising version, a fiction of unity, is to write 'feminine' (so HCE, central figure of the *Wake*, is simultaneously identity and process, 'feminisible name of multitude' (*F W*: 73)). The steady monologue of the guy gives way to the disruptive polylogic of a writing which from 'Oxen of the Sun' through 'Penelope' has come to a total recasting of the position of the novel, to a radical questioning of the how and from where and on what basis of position, of all the novelistic of character and plot and the representation of reality. Hence its activity of 'mememormee', its rememoration: me and more than me and the memory of me in that more than me – the question of what is involved in the construction, the process, of me, trying to remember.

Memory flow, *Finnegans Wake* is full of people trying to remember – mulling over documents, asking questions, conducting interviews, having trials, theatrical performances, listening to the radio, watching films, ceaselessly: 'And so they went on, the fourbottle men, the analists, unguam and nunguam and lunguam again, their anschluss about her whosebefore and his whereafters and how she was lost away away in the fern and how he was founded deap on deep in anear' (*F W*: 95). The book itself appeals to story after story in a gesture of permanent explication: 'We are told how in the beginning it came to pass' (*F W*: 30), 'as the aftertale hath it' (*F W*: 38). What really happened? Tell us. 'Now tell me, tell me, tell me then! What was it? A. . . . .! ?. . . . . . . .O!' (*F W*: 94).

What was it? What happened? Well, language for a start, alpha to omega, man 'put out his langwedge and quite quit the paleologic scene' (*F W*: 72–3). And sin, of course: the whole thing starts with the river running 'past Eve and Adam's' (*F W*: 3); then too, like any other good myth, the Bible tells us that at the beginning there is incest, father and wife-daughter born from his side, which is where *Finnegans Wake* ends as it begins again, Anna Livia in her father's embrace as the river runs back. Language and sin, the question of

'sinse'; 'What then agentlike brought about that tragoady thunders-
day this municipal sin business?' (*F W*: 5). We can see what kind of
memory the *Wake* is. It wants to find out, get back to the beginning,
know origins. But there are only origins *since*, in projection from the
present back, only through language which confronts us at every
turn – hence, interminably, the writing of *Finnegans Wake*.

In this context, let us look at something of that writing – how it
functions, how and what it moves – by considering the last section of
Finnegans Wake (*F W*: 593–628), an important section that brings
together in a highly condensed form the organising meanings – the
pressure points – of the text.

   The section gathers up a mass of myths and sacred stories: Christian (the two main narrative actions are the coming of St Kevin with
the purificatory rites he accomplishes and the arrival of St Patrick
and the establishment of Christianity, these surrounded by a host of
references to Christ and the resurrection, Moses, Noah's Ark, and
any number of other figures and themes), Irish (the whole story of
Finn, plus references to Nuada, Lug, the goddess Anu – an evident
avatar of Anna Livia – and so on) Oriental (multiplication of allusions to Hindu thought, for example). Behind these, as something of
a mirroring backdrop, appears a constant suggestion of paradise
lost: 'Peredos Last' or 'paladays last' (*F W*: 610; 615), which is also
the sun city Heliopolis ('Heliotropolis, the castellated, the enchanting', *F W*: 594)) whose Egyptian name was Anu, and also Balbek
('Bullbeck' (*F W*: 609) the Phoenician city itself equally known under
the name of Heliopolis, as well as the Balbec of the youth of the
narrator of *A la recherche du temps perdu*, magical site of the 'jeunes
filles en fleurs' who enter this section corolling and carolling, 'A
family, a band, a school, a clanagirls', (*F W*: 601)), and Atlantis (the
fabulous continent described by Plato and supposed to have sunk
under the ocean and which is here confounded with the lost Breton
city of Is: 'the citye of Is is issuant (atlanst!) . . . froms umber under
wasseres of Erie' (*F W*: 601), and the other world of Celtic literature,
tir tairngire, country of joy and promise ('Tirtangel' (*F W*: 594)).

   At work here, as always, the question of origins, the origin.
Moving through these myths and stories and references, the writing
looks not for some metaphysical unity but for something like a
ground on which such a question might be displayed, from which it
might be *produced*: 'the first and last rittlerattle of the anniverse' (*F*

W: 607). The riddle, that of the Sphinx to Oedipus for example, turns on man, his identity: 'the first riddle of the universe: asking, when is a man not a man?' (*F W*: 170). Answer: *before* (he is 'sinse'), when he was in the night of the womb or the flow of the river, a fluidity pre-form, pre-individual. ALP, Anna Livia Plurabelle, is, of course, the writing's imagination of this, river and mother (in Turkish, for example, *ana* means precisely 'mother'), source and site of the generation of life as the children's diagram reveals ('A is for Anna like L is for liv' (*F W*: 293)).

The question of origins, getting back. Suppose we try to imagine finding the unknown source of a great river. ALP carries with her the Alpheus, the sacred river of Arcadia, described by Plutarch as deriving from the sun, and no doubt all rivers too but most especially the Nile, supremely invested with religion and myth, beginnings. Alpheus and Nile: the movement from the one to the other is made with the help of Coleridge's 'Kubla Khan', one of the most important texts for the writing of *Finnegans Wake*, giving both the 'riverrun' of the first page – 'Where Alph, the sacred river, ran' – and the drop into the cold ocean of the last – 'down to a sunless sea'. The famous study of the poem by Livingston Lowes which appeared in 1927, *The Road to Xanadu*, demonstrated with the help of writings by such classical authorities as Pausanius, Strabo and Seneca that the Alph of 'Kubla Khan' also brought with it for Coleridge a reference to the Nile: the undiscovered and so mysterious source of the Nile could be explained as arising from the underground course of the sacred Alpheus.[19] And it is this problem of the source that is the concern of this last section of the *Wake*, which incorporates in its writing stories of explorers trying to discover the source of the Nile: 'Nuctumbulumbumus wanderwards the Nil. Victorias neanzas. Alberths neantas. It was a long, very long, a dark, very dark, an allburt unend, scarce endurable, and we could add mostly quite various and somewhat stumbletumbling night' (*F W*: 598). Up the Nile, towards the zero point, Victoria, Albert, source and nothingness (*néant*), dark night, all but unending birth (-*burt*).

Mother, river *and writing*: ALP, Alpheus and alphabet. 'Kubla Khan' is again present here, the possibility of a brief signal memory that this Khan had a hand in the introduction of a new script for the Chinese and Mongolian languages, the passepa script:[20]

> Polycarp pool, the pool of Innalavia, Saras the saft as, of meadewy marge, atween Deltas Piscium and Sagittariastrion, whereinn once we lave

'tis alve and vale, minnyhahing here from hiarwather, a poddlebridges in a passabed, the river of lives, the regenerations of the incarnations of the emanations of the apparentations of Funn and Nin in Cleethabala, the kongdomain of the Alieni, an accorsaired race, infester of Libnud Ocean, Moylamore, let it be!' (*F W*: 600)[21]

Alphabet — passepa — passabed: the 'passabed, river of lives' is what elsewhere the text produces as the 'allaphabed' (*F W*: 18) or 'amphybed' (*F W*: 619), the bed of ALP, of the alphabet, body of the inscription of the first letters, riverbed, source of life, ebb and flow. 'Whereinn once we lave 'tis alve and vale . . .': the descent from out of the mother (*where in once we leave*), the river from beginning to end, from hallo (*salve*) to goodbye (*vale*), the whole of the vale of life, the whole *matter* of the 'alve' — at once *alveus*, cavity, bath, bed of a river, and *alvus*, belly, excremental contents or movement of bowels, womb.

The section plunges into matter (it might be noted here that already in 'Oxen of the Sun' Joyce had wanted to link the development of the foetus to the stages of 'faunal evolution').[22] Mud is everywhere and the desire to dig into the earth, the riverbed, 'mudden research' (*F W*: 595), always after the source, the origin, the buried letter that could explain everything, give the answer. Primitive substances and forms of vegetable life abound, 'A spathe of calyptrous glume . . . fungoalgaceous muscafilicial graminopalmular planteon' (*F W*: 613), and mix up with silt and slime, 'seasilt saltsick' (*F W*: 628), which turns into excretory fantasies of food: 'So an inedible yellowmeat turns out the invasable blackth', 'primilibatory solicates of limon sodias will be absorbable', 'one-gugulp down of the nauseous forere brarkfarsts oboboomaround . . . wreathe the bowl to rid the bowel; no runcure, no rank heat, sir; amess in amullium; chlorid cup' (*F W*: 594; 604; 613). All of which gives a fever of matter, transformation, procreation, brought to a head of meaning in what is one of the most charged passages of the project of the writing of the *Wake*:

Lok! A shaft of shivery in the act, anilancinant. Cold's sleuth! Vayuns! Where did thots come from? It is infinitesimally fevers, resty fever, risy fever, a coranto of aria, sleeper awakening, in the smalls of one's back presentiment, gip, and again, geip, a flash from a future of maybe mahamayability through the windr of a wondr in a wildr is a weltr as a wirbl of a warbl is a world. (*F W*: 597)

A children's game, 'cowboys and indians', and the primal scene, copulation. The ejaculation of the arrow-penis, the 'shaft of shivery in the act', is doubled with the palpitations of feverish matter, pushing out in the small of the back, a presentiment of birth. Here then *the* question can be posed: 'Where did thots come from?' Where do they come from, thought (*thoughts*), gods (*Thot* and all the others, and Thot, we should note, was the god of *writing*),[23] the sexes, male and female (*that* referring back to the penis moving into Anna Livia, 'analancinant'; *toth*, Irish for 'female organs'), and children (*tots*)?

The question in its final form is the very one that Freud in the *Three Essays on the Theory of Sexuality* of 1905 takes as the original manifestation of 'the instinct for knowledge or research': 'the first problem with which [the instinct] deals is not the question of the distinction between the sexes but the riddle of where babies come from.'[24] So that that is effectively 'the first and last rittlerattle of the anniverse', the riddle of the Sphinx: 'This, in a distorted form which can easily be rectified, is the same riddle that was propounded by the Theban Sphinx.'[25] Freud and *Finnegans Wake* then meet further in their emphasis on the importance of excremental theories of birth: the earliest researches into where babies come from 'fell a victim to repression long since, but all their findings were of a uniform nature: people get babies by eating some particular thing (as they do in fairy tales) and babies are born through the bowel like a discharge of faeces.'[26] Moving back along and through that 'since' is the time and the project of *Finnegans Wake* and some of the infantile elements of question and answer which it produces have already been cited, from the 'nuctumbulumbumus' birth felt in the small of the back to the excretory fantasies of the transformation of matter. The writing of the *Wake* throughout is underpinned by a layer of children's language – nursery rhymes, comptines, singing and guessing games, and so on – which provides the basis for the explicitation of the 'researches': 'the vialact coloured milk train on the fartykket plan run with its endless gallaxion of rotatorattlers and the smooltroon our elderens rememberem as the scream of the service, Strubry Bess' (*F W*: 604) – playing trains, another journey, parents ('elderens', *Eltern*), an endless movement and shaking, violet, the milky way, milk, ice cream, strawberries, digestion and excrement (*rot*, fart, the 'smooltroon' stool-*étron*). The host of references to pantomimes and fairy stories (over fifty in seven or eight pages (*F W*: 619–26)) works in the same context, comes back to the riddle, the instinct for knowledge: 'the gist of the pantomime, from cannibal king to the property horse, being, slumply and slopely, to remind us how, in this drury world of ours, Father Times and Mother Spacies boil their kettle with their crutch. Which every lad and lass in the lane knows' (*F W*: 599–600). The gist of the pantomime is at once the deformed knowledge of the sexual act (mother and father boil their kettle with their crutch) and the continual question of birth and origins, time, space and species – where do we begin?

Joyce's writing career (from the piece on Ibsen's *When We Dead Awaken* in the *Fortnightly Review* in 1900 to the publication of *Finnegans Wake* in 1939) is exactly contemporary with Freud's psychoanalytic work (from *The Interpretation of Dreams* of 1900 to, say, *Moses and Monotheism* of 1934–8, the last of Freud's works to appear during his lifetime and another great exploration of origins). Psychoanalysis furnishes an object for mocking fascination, so many appearances of 'we grisly old Sykos who have done our unsmiling bit on 'alices, when they were yung and easily freudened, in the penumbra of the procuring room' (*F W*: 115); the writing holds all the terms in ironic play: 'You have homosexual catheis of empathy between narcissism of the expert and steatopygic invertedness. Get yourself psychoanolised!' (*F W*: 522).

The mockery and irony of the relationship with psychoanalysis, however, must not be allowed to hide the fact of the relationship nevertheless. Freudian 'intrepidation of our dreams' (*F W*: 338) is hardly alien to this 'nightynovel' full of dreams and itself drawing to a close when 'all-a-dreams perhapsing under lucksloop at last are through' (*F W*: 597). It may be that 'I can psoakoonaloose myself anytime I want . . . without your interferences or any other pigeon-stealer' (*F W*: 522) but then this 'letter selfpenned to one's other' is exactly caught up in psychoanalysis, making much of the same gesture of investigation and research. What is finally interesting is not the question of immediate influence (references to Freud and Freudian terms and ideas, though these abound) but the way in which Joyce's practice of writing in the *Wake* finds the same concerns and occupies the same terrain as psychoanalysis, cuts across and displaces 'by itself' analytic concepts.

The many stories of *Finnegans Wake* are one story, always the same; are so many versions of a kind of ur-narrative, permutations of a handful of agents and actions: 'Yet is it but an old story, the tale of a

Treestone with one Ysold, of a Mons held by tentpegs and his pal
whatholoosed on the run, what Cadman could but Badman
wouldn't, any Genoaman against any Venis, and why Kate takes
charge of the waxworks' (*F W*: 113). Or again: 'One's apurr apuss a
story about brid and breakfedes and parricombating and coush-
couch but others is of tholes and oubworn buyings, dolings and
chafferings in heat, contest and enmity' (*F W*: 597). That is the story,
'which everabody you ever anywhere at all doze' (*F W*: 597); the
versions are as clear as they are obscure, you can get the gist, the main
elements, and the writing will go over and over them, man and
woman, mother and father and sons and daughters, a whole family
history. Which is where, of course, psychoanalysis comes in, that is
its terrain, it too tells a single story, that of the oedipal structure of
human being and its history.

Both Joyce and Freud go in for mythology, religion, history from
the beginning; *Moses and Monotheism, Totem and Taboo* have
much in common with *Finnegans Wake*. For both, however, that
development is a transposition and extension from the central concern, the fact of the individual – how do we find ourselves here, what
is our identity, where do I come from? Psychoanalysis is the investigation and theory of that, grasping the individual in a history – the
major events of which take place in the first five or so years of life –
that is ever present: my identity depends on it, it is the structure of my
individuality, the past is held in that structure and psychoanalysis
can help to bring out and understand its unconscious presence and
action. The writing of *Finnegans Wake* works with – or in – the same
history, finds the same elements; hence the fascination and overlap
and repetition with Freud's work. The *Wake*'s 'old story' comes
down to the family and the production of the individual subject from
birth to 'I', identity in language. It is in this process of production
that the writing tries to move, from nought to one – 'boony noughty',
'Funn and Nin', 'Niluna' (*F W*: 597; 600; 627). Going back up,
looking for the source of the Nile, is also finding the nil, the nothingness, the non-one out of and over against which the one is defined.
My 'I', me as one, is a limit, exists by virtue of repression, forgetfulness of the other, the other scene on which I am produced; selfpenning a letter to one's other is knowing that limitation, breaking down
the mastery, the givenness, the whole coherence of 'I'. Thus *Finnegans Wake* as radical experience of language; thus, indeed, the
very 'wake' of the title, playing between life and death, the waking of

identity and the mourning its loss, and adding the interminable since, the shifting and perpetual motion of forms, like the wake of a ship tracing endless patterns over the ocean, 'noughty times ∞ ' (*F W*: 284).

'I yam as I yam' (*F W*: 604); on the one hand, the statement of the subject individual equal to himself, absolutely one, who can as he can, may as he may; on the other, the recognition of the limits of that subject one, one only by a fiction of mastery, in denial of the process that 'one' is, that is in excess of the declared assurance of self – *yam* is a Sanskrit verb meaning master, subjugate, retain: by retention I am. That Sanskrit should slip in to undermine the certainty of the 'cogito' is no more than another indication of the demonstration of the other scene at which the writing works. What is at stake is to change language in language, to pass from English to 'unglish' (*F W*: 609) and, in that experience, from one to other, the heterogeneity of process, nought, non-identity: 'Now let the centuple celves of my egourge . . . by the coincidance of their contraries reamalgamerge in that identity of undiscernables' (*F W*: 49–50). The major thematic elements with which the writing proceeds are so many thematic expressions of 'contraries', dramas of one and other: West and East, adult and child, man and woman, erection and flow. Using them, the writing comes back to heavy cultural stereotypes (woman as flow, man as the subject in command of language, bringing order, fixing the 'I': 'For newmanmaun set a marge to the merge of unnotions' (*F W*: 614)) at the same time that it derides and overturns them, switching them into an exploration of identity simultaneously male and female, adult and child, subject in intention of meaning and play of the letters and sounds and relations of languages. *Finnegans Wake*? 'It is a sot of swigswag, systomy dystomy, which everabody you everanywhere at all doze. Why? Such me!' (*F W*: 597). Search me, suck me, such is me, such am I! That's what it's all about.

But that too is then the problem of this gigantic and astonishing book. Such is me, but what is this me? Exploring, analysing, selfpenning a letter, *writing*, Joyce produces a history but which is transposed and set in terms of history *tout court*, given as universal – 'everabody you everanywhere'. Once again the closeness to psychoanalysis can be noted, psychoanalysis notoriously prone to an 'anthropological history' in which findings in respect of individuals in particular social groups and contexts are pulled out into a general account of the development of mankind (think of *Totem and Taboo* with its description of the origin of the Oedipus complex) and, corollary to this, notoriously unable to deal with the actual historical – material, social, cultural – status of the particular realisations of subjectivity it confronts. *Finnegans Wake* with its themes and mythological panorama and its kaleidoscoping history is not far from this, save only – but this is its crucial distinction – for the fact of its writing. Joyce in language: the writing of the *Wake* is an experience of the subject in process, the unconscious (compare psychoanalytic case studies from Freud on, written in the terms and style of the nineteenth-century novel). 'Such me' is the risk taken against the universalising meta-psychology of psychoanalysis: from Joyce to reader, the *Wake* is the letter of language that cannot but be particular – we are all of us bound to the cross of our 'own cruelfiction' (*F W*: 192) – but which can be offered as a mode of radical understanding, a book of interminable analysis in which we can be caught up through the attention to language, the displacement of our orders and conventions of reading – hence the emphasis on the permanent, never-finished nature of the book, 'sentenced to be nuzzled over a full trillion times for ever and a night till his noddle sink or swim by that ideal reader suffering from an ideal insomnia' (*F W*: 120). With *Finnegans Wake* Joyce wrote the book of himself and his time, filled it with the contemporary concerns and with the current theories and ideas of language and subjectivity, and then also, in the writing, the activity in language, said more than the expression of those concerns and those theories and ideas, put them into matter, gave the experience: 'His writing'; wrote Beckett in his contribution to *Our Exagmination Round His Factification For Incamination of Work in Progress,* 'is not *about* something; *it is that something itself*'.[27]

Notes

1   Samuel Beckett, 'Dante . . . Bruno . Vico . . Joyce', in *Our Exagmination Round His Factification For Incamination of Work in Progress* (Paris: Shakespeare & Co., 1929), p. 15.

2   Mary Colum, in Padraic and Mary Colum, *Our Friend James Joyce* (London: Gollancz, 1959), p. 130–1. Cf. Mary Colum, *Life and the Dream* (London: Macmillan, 1947), p. 394 and Richard Ellmann,

James Joyce (New York: Oxford University Press, 1959), p. 647. The date of this lecture is placed by Colum as early 1931 but the recorded dates for the 'Rabbi Iéshoua' demonstrations are – as far as I can ascertain – 1928–9 (at the Théâtre des Champs-Élysées and the Sorbonne) and 1933–5 (at the Société de Géographie and the Faculté de théologie protestante). It is not impossible that Colum has confused the date. The only public lecture of which I have been able to find trace in early 1931 was entitled 'Méthodologie de la Psychologie du Geste' and given in the first half of May (cf. *Revue des cours et des conférences*, 15 May 1931, p. 201–18); this lecture bears no formal relation to the one described by Colum.

3   Gabrielle Baron, *Marcel Jousse: Introduction à sa vie et à son oeuvre* (Paris and Tournai: Casterman, 1965), p. 104.

4   Jousse influenced research in this area; see, for example, the thesis by Tchang Tcheng Ming, *L'Écriture chinoise et le geste humain* (Sorbonne, 1937).

5   'So that gesture, not music, not odours, would be a universal language, the gift of tongues rendering visible not the lay sense but the first entelechy, the structural rhythm' (*U*: 427).

6   Marcel Jousse, *Mimisme humain et psychologie de la lecture* (Paris: Geuthner, 1935), p. 4.

7   *Ibid*., p. 18.

8   Phillip F. Herring, *Joyce's 'Ulysses' Notesheets in the British Museum* (Charlottesville, Virginia: University Press of Virginia, 1972), p. 31. Joyce himself ended an exuberant description of the chapter in a letter of 13 March 1920 to Frank Budgen with the cry of 'How's that for High?' (*Letters*, I: 139). This certainly indicates a feeling of 'fun' and bears witness to a degree of ostentation when writing to friends; it is no evidence, however, for any calculated wish to mystify.

9   This follows the transcription given by J.S. Atherton in his essay 'The Oxen of the Sun' in *James Joyce's 'Ulysses': Critical Essays*, ed. by Clive Hart and David Hayman (Berkeley, Los Angeles and London: University of California Press, 1974), p. 338, which corrects that given by Herring, *op. cit*., p. 164. The British Museum Notesheets version of the diagram is reproduced between p. 162–3 of Herring's edition. The other version, apparently a copy, is held by Cornell University Library; see Robert E. Scholes, *The Cornell Joyce Collection* (Ithaca, NY: Cornell University Press, 1961), item 58, p. 26.

10   The 'Linati schema', the first known schema for *Ulysses*, is so called because it was sent by Joyce to Carl Linati in a letter of 21 September 1920. The manuscript is in the Library of the State University of New York at Buffalo and is reproduced as the front and back endpapers of Richard Ellmann, *Ulysses on the Liffey* (London: Faber & Faber, 1972) which also includes a tipped-in transcription and English translation.

11   Frances A. Yates, *The Art of Memory* (London: Routledge & Kegan Paul, 1966). For reproductions of 'spheres of the universe' memory-system diagrams, see p. 111, 116.

12   'These correspondences are part of Joyce's mediaevalism and are

chiefly his own affair, a scaffold, a means of construction. . . .' Ezra Pound, 'Paris Letter', *The Dial*, Vol. LXXII no. 6 (June 1922), reprinted in *Pound/Joyce*: 197. Pound's stress falls on the organisation of *Ulysses* through a number of systems which provide different levels and orders of places for the writing to work along and fill out. Joyce could talk equally in this way of such major elements as Vico's cyclical history (' "Of course," Joyce told me, "I don't take Vico's speculations literally; I use his cycles as a trellis" ', Padraic Colum, in *Our Friend James Joyce*, p. 123) and Homer's *Odyssey* ('È il mio sistema di lavoro', cit. Italo Svevo, *Saggi e pagine sparse* (Verona: Mondadori, 1954), p. 217).

13 For details of Joyce's use of Saintsbury and Peacock, see Atherton, *op. cit.*, p.315–33, and Herring, *op. cit.*, p.32–3, 165. Atherton, who was the first to draw attention to the importance of Peacock's anthology for 'Oxen of the Sun', shows how Joyce's prose imitations are based on the contemporary availability of the different writers rather than on direct reference to the original works (Joyce imitates Peacock's rewritten and repunctuated Pepys, for example) and how they pick up present linguistic difficulties and interesting words signalled by the anthology's notes.

14 Arnold Bennett, review in *The Outlook* (29 April 1922), reprinted in *James Joyce: The Critical Heritage*, edited by Robert H. Deming, Vol. I (London: Routledge & Kegan Paul, 1970), p. 221.

15 *Ibid.* No doubt the supreme accolade came from Jung who commented at the close of a somewhat tortuous apology for his misgivings concerning *Ulysses*: 'The 40 pages of non stop run in the end is a string of veritable psychological peaches. I suppose the devil's grandmother knows so much about the real psychology of a woman, I didn't.', letter to Joyce of 27 September 1932, cit. Ellmann, *James Joyce*, p.642. To which Joyce's wife Nora is reported by Beckett to have replied: 'He [Joyce] knows nothing at all about women', cit. Ellmann, *ibid*.

16 Stuart Gilbert, *James Joyce's 'Ulysses'* (1930) (Harmondsworth: Penguin, 1963), p. 328.

17 Remark by Joyce reported by Louis Gillet, *Stèle pour James Joyce* (Paris: Sagittaire, 1941), p. 74.

18 Remark by Joyce reported by Max Eastman, *The Literary Mind* (New York: Scribner's, 1931), p. 101.

19 J.L. Lowes, *The Road to Xanadu* (London: Constable, 1927), p. 393–6.

20 'A famous Grand Lama of Sa-skya (. . . known as P'a-sse-p'a or 'Phags-pa (1234–1279), invited to China by Qubilay Khan) played a great part in the conversion to Buddhism of the Mongolian imperial court, and adapted the Tibetan square script to the Chinese and Mongolian languages, replacing the Uighur alphabet. . . . Under Chinese influence, this script, commonly called Passepa, was written in vertical columns, downwards, although unlike Chinese, the columns read from left to right. This character, officially adopted in 1272, was only sparsely used owing to the convenience of the Uighur script, and did not last long, but it lingered on at the imperial Chancery under the Yüan dynasty, particularly in the official seals.' David Diringer, *The*

Alphabet: A Key to the History of Mankind (London: Hutchinson, 1951), p. 355.

21 The passage suggests several references to Coleridge: 'Cleethabala' remembers the poem 'Christabel' (cf. later 'The old Marino Tale' (*F W*: 607), for 'The Rime of the Ancient Mariner'); 'Libnud Ocean' quotes the 'lifeless ocean' of 'Kubla Khan'; 'Saras' brings with it Coleridge's 'beloved sister' Sara; these being accompanied by references to other Romantic poets — Longfellow ('minnyhahing', 'hiarwather' — 'Hiawatha'), Byron ('accorsaired' 'The Corsair'), etc. The importance of 'Kubla Khan' for the writing of the *Wake* is confirmed by the number of allusions to it in the book: e.g. 'kingable khan' (*F W*: 32), 'Khubadah' (*F W*: 609), 'Karmalite Kane; a sunless map' (*F W*: 211; Kubla Khan + the 'sunless sea' of the poem), 'Alpyssinia' (*F W*: 318; the poem's 'Abyssinian maid', cf. in the passage cited 'Del*tas Piscium*'), 'One time you told you'd been burnt in ice' (*F W*: 621; in the poem, 'A sunny pleasure-dome with caves of ice'), 'Heliotropolis, the castellated, the enchanting' (*F W*: 594; in the poem, 'as holy and enchanted'), 'Annah the Allmaziful' (*F W*: 104; the poem's 'meandering with a mazy motion . . . the sacred river ran'), 'cublic hatches endnot' (*F W*: 604; Kubla plus the HCE monogram already visible in the poem, 'a cedarn cover!/A savage place! as holy and enchanted . . .').

22 Joyce's expression in the letter to Budgen referred to in note 8 above: 'This procession [of English prose] is also linked back at each part subtly with some foregoing episode of the day and, besides this, with the natural stages of development in the embryo and the periods of faunal evolution in general' (*Letters* I: 139).

23 'Thoth, the god of writers, writing with a reed upon a tablet and bearing on his narrow ibis head the cusped moon' (*P*: 229). Socrates refers to Thot's invention of writing in Plato's *Phaedrus*, in a passage that has been given a lengthy commentary by Jacques Derrida in an essay, 'La pharmacie de Platon', itself announced as 'nothing other than a reading of *Finnegans Wake*'; in *La Dissémination* (Paris: Seuil, 1972), p. 99. On Derrida and Joyce, see S. Heath, 'L'Écriture spiralée', *Le Discours social* no. 3–4 (1973), p. 9–21.

24 Sigmund Freud, *Three Essays on the Theory of Sexuality* (1905), *The Complete Psychological Works*, Standard Edition tr. James Strachey (London: Hogarth Press, 1953–74), Vol. VII, p.194–5.

25 *Ibid.*

26 *Ibid.*, p.196.

27 Beckett, *op. cit.*, p.14.

CONTEXTS

CHAPTER 8

The Strange Necessity: James Joyce's Rejection in England (1914–30)

Patrick Parrinder

Biologists recognise that the study of immunology, or the body's resistance to alien tissues, bears intimately on the question of identity. The way in which a host organism responds to other organisms can tell us what its identity is. Yet that response may also be viewed as a learning process, in which it is facing up, for the first time, to a challenge not previously met with. The outcome will depend on a contest, a trial of strength between conflicting impulses. To speak of Joyce's rejection in England between 1914 and 1930 may sound tendentious. After all, he began this period as a literary unknown and ended as one of the most famous (or should we say notorious?) writers of his time. 'Rejection', however, is in certain ways more adequate than the conventional cliché 'reception' to describe this process. If Joyce's name was well known in the England of 1930, it was as a writer widely regarded as unreadable, whose masterpiece – thanks to the operations of the censor – could not be lawfully read.

The alien tissues of our immunological metaphor were those of modernist writing. During the 1920s the innovations of T.S. Eliot and Virginia Woolf were, so to speak, digested by the English literary mind. Those of Joyce, Pound and Wyndham Lewis on the whole were not. Joyce in particular seemed not only exotic but also offensive and threatening. Even the most sympathetic critics found it difficult to welcome his books without making some concessions to the majority view of them as incomprehensible and obscene. The reservations, the reluctance to fully engage with Joyce expressed by people regarded as the embodiments of liberal and enlightened taste are, in fact, far more revealing than the outright Philistine denunciations of his work. To recall 'Who Said What About Whom, When' in such a case is to sketch an immunological process whose effects – in the general reaction against experimental fiction as well as the complacent neglect of Joyce's later work – were to last into the 1960s and 1970s.

At Joyce's funeral in 1941, the British consul in Zürich spoke of him as not only a great Irishman but a great Englishman. (The Irish consul did not bother to attend.) Ezra Pound, one suspects, was not alone in seeing the irony of this (*Pound/Joyce*: 270). A young man born in nineteenth-century Dublin was, indeed, technically British. Yet few of our great writers (even Irish ones) have been less 'English'. When he left University College, the young Joyce headed not for London but for Paris and then Trieste. In Paris he used to meet with an ageing Fenian, Joseph Casey. Casey appears in *Ulysses* as Kevin Egan of the 'gunpowder cigarettes', who tried (Stephen recalls) to 'yoke me as his yokefellow, our crimes our common cause' (*U*: 48). It was not lost on some of his acquaintances that Joyce, too, filled to perfection the role of the conspiratorial Irishman – the lone revolutionary dedicating his life to silence, exile and cunning. He himself may have thought so too:

> [Scene: draughty little stone-flagged room, chest of drawers to left, on which are the remains of lunch, in the centre, a small table on which are *writing materials* (*He* never forgot them) and a saltcellar: in the background, small-sized bed. A young man with snivelling nose sits at the little table: on the bed sit a madonna and plaintive infant. It is a January day.] Title of above: *The Anarchist*. (*Letters*, II: 206)

The quotation is from a 1907 letter to Stanislaus. Joyce, struggling with family cares in Rome, might be excused this outbreak of savage humour. ('I shall never be a model bank clerk', he lamented in the same letter.) Yet here he is as remembered by Arthur Power, an Irish friend who came to know him fifteen years later, on the eve of the publication of Ulysses:

> Indeed I realized that there was much of the Fenian about him – his dark suiting, his wide hat, his light carriage, and his intense expression – a literary conspirator, who was determined to destroy the oppressive and respectable cultural structures under which we had been reared, and which were then crumbling. Indeed, I remember his saying to me once: – You know that there are people who would refuse to sit in the same room as me.[1]

What Power had glimpsed here was the fanatical *artist* Joyce, the man who would talk of the genius of Gogol and van Gogh and then declare that 'the reasonable man achieves nothing'.[2] While not a Fenian in the literal sense, he preferred to reach the public by his own brand of shock tactics than to listen to the advice of 'reasonable men'. Initially he inherited this attitude from the aesthetes and decadents of the late nineteenth century with their desire to *épater le bourgeois*. Thus his letter offering *Dubliners* to the English publisher Grant Richards in 1905 ends on a note of self-conscious Wildean audacity, with the thought that 'people might be willing to pay for the special odour of corruption which, I hope, floats over my stories' (*Letters*, II: 123). Passed from publisher to publisher, and delayed on one pretext after another, *Dubliners* did not appear until 1914. Meanwhile Joyce was writing *A Portrait of the Artist*, in which the symbolist-naturalist dialectic of the 1890s is transcended by a new stage of artistic development: the birth of modernist writing. The exasperating and humiliating delay over the publication of *Dubliners* at least had the advantage of consolidating Joyce's sense of determinate absence from – and, potentially, his explosive presence in – English letters. *Dubliners* was objected to on the grounds of immorality, of libellous indiscretion (in its naming of actual Dublin shopkeepers) and of disrespect towards Royalty. 'Gas from a Burner', the satirical broadside that Joyce wrote in 1912 on the back of the contract that his Dublin publisher had refused to honour, shows him extracting a sort of savage joy from the affair. The speaker is George Roberts, manager of Maunsel & Co.:

Who was it said: Resist not evil?
I'll burn that book, so help me devil.
I'll sing a psalm as I watch it burn
And the ashes I'll keep in a one-handled urn.
I'll penance do with farts and groans
Kneeling upon my marrowbones.
This very next lent I will unbare
My penitent buttocks to the air
And sobbing beside my printing press
My awful sin I will confess.
My Irish foreman from Bannockburn
Shall dip his right hand in the urn
And sign crisscross with reverent thumb
Memento homo upon my bum.[3]

Joyce stands accused of 'black and sinister arts', but in fact it is Roberts who has defiled the name of Ireland –

> O lovely land where the shamrock grows!
> (Allow me, ladies, to blow my nose)

— and, as a communicant in the Black Mass, has ended up helping the
Protestant enemy. After Maunsel & Co. had rejected his books it was
his English rather than his Irish reception that would be important to
Joyce.

Joyce's literary career falls roughly into three stages: the early phase
of 'silence, exile, and cunning' in Trieste, culminating in the publication of *Dubliners* in 1914; the decade after 1914, in which he moved
to Zürich and then to Paris and came to the forefront of the modern
movement in the arts; and finally the years of *Work in Progress*,
when he was largely abandoned by his fellow 'men of 1914', and
found himself instead the focus of a much more marginal literary
group whose organ was the review *transition*.

During his 'modernist' years Joyce was regarded as a revolutionary writer whose work presented an immediate cultural challenge
or threat. Where he had shown the way, other writers must surely
follow. His 'stream-of-consciousness' method was imitated by
novelists of the calibre of William Faulkner in *The Sound and the
Fury* and Virginia Woolf in *Mrs Dalloway*. After a time, however,
the novelty of his presence wore off. While still recognised as a
powerful creative force, it was as if the threat posed by his work to
established cultural modes and conventions had been contained and
neutralised. English culture was now confident of repelling the
invader. Particularly significant was the role of the Bloomsbury
writers and critics, who at this time reached their greatest ascen-
dancy in London literary circles.

Joyce's first real critic, and in some ways his most influential one,
was Ezra Pound. Pound had written at Yeats's instigation in
December 1913 to ask Joyce for contributions to the various little
magazines with which he was connected. Less than six months later
he was reviewing *Dubliners* in the *Egoist*, the small radical paper of
which he was literary editor, and beginning his review with the
forthright declaration that 'Mr Joyce's book of short stories is prose
free from sloppiness.'[4] Later *A Portrait of the Artist* was serialised by
the *Egoist* and published in book form by the Egoist Press. The
impact of Pound's sponsorship on Joyce himself cannot be over-
stated. To be taken up by Pound was to become one of the 'men of
1914' who were revolutionising English art and literature, and it was

also to acquire the services of the man Joyce later called a 'wonder-worker', a most dedicated and effective literary publicist. Joyce in Pound's hands was first published in the *Imagist Anthology*, and then, as Pound moved from Imagism to Vorticism, he became a sort of honorary Vorticist. His name was coupled with those of Wyndham Lewis, T.S. Eliot, and Henri Gaudier-Brzeska in Pound's memoir *Gaudier-Brzeska* (1916) – one of the key manifestoes of English modernism. Pound's championship launched Joyce as a name to be watched and a leader of the avant-garde. By introducing Joyce's work to such people as John Quinn and Harriet Shaw Weaver, he transformed the Irish writer's financial position. But, we must now ask, how deeply did he in fact understand and sympathise with what Joyce was doing? How much authority can we allow his outspoken assessments of the Irish writer's merits and defects?

Pound's 'movement' was certainly not as cohesive as Hugh Kenner, in his epic work of literary myth-making *The Pound Era*, has made it appear. No close-knit artistic movement has ever embraced five geniuses of the calibre and independence of Eliot, Gaudier, Lewis, Pound and Joyce, and it would seem that the only evidence of really close collaboration and mutual understanding between them is that between Pound and Eliot, above all in Pound's editing of the drafts of *The Waste Land*. Pound's excitement at discovering Joyce's work, and his determination to boost him and claim him for the 'movement', sprang from opportune recognition rather than from any profound similarity of aims and outlook. Nor, despite the vivacity of response which makes the Pound-Joyce letters so readable, did he show much sign of Joycean influence during the years of their association.

Pound, as he wrote to Joyce in 1914, was 'not supposed to know much about prose' (*Pound/Joyce*: 24). He wrote a number of critical articles on Joyce over the years, but his position does not diverge appreciably from his initial perceptions of 1914. There were two main grounds on which he welcomed Joyce into the modern movement, both of them implicit in that opening phrase of his review of *Dubliners* – 'prose free from sloppiness'. Joyce, he saw, was a writer dedicated to an ideal of totally disciplined creation, however forbidding and unpopular this might make him. Pound was deeply concerned with the historical ancestry of the modernist movement. He saw the men of 1914 as heirs of the late nineteenth-century aesthetes who had championed the artist's integrity against the Philistine public. From his gallery of nineteenth-century heroes – Whistler, the Goncourt brothers, Gautier, Stendhal – he chose Flaubert as Joyce's lineal ancestor. Much later, when he had become thoroughly disenchanted with Joyce in the 1930s, he would claim that the Irish writer had never done any more than to repeat Flaubert's prescriptions. Flaubert had invented a kind of 'specific for literary diabetes', and Joyce had 'got some of the real stuff, full strength' (*Pound/Joyce*: 252). The medicine Pound had in mind was the studied clarity of Flaubert's prose and his scrupulous respect for fact. These were the 'prose virtues' of clarity and hardness which Pound advocated for poetry in many of his early essay.[5] He believed that such poetry would appeal to an intelligent, tough-minded and anti-Georgian public and that it could have measurable social and political effects, 'purifying the dialect of the tribe' in Mallarmé's words. His conviction as to the impact of a clear diagnosis of social reality led him in 1917 to commit himself to the remarkable statement that 'If more people had read *The Portrait* and certain stories in Mr Joyce's *Dubliners* there might have been less recent trouble in Ireland' (Pound/Joyce: 90).

In addition to championing Joyce's work in his own articles, Pound in these early years did all he could to promote Joyce's cause with editors, publishers, patrons and reviewers. Early in 1917 he approached H.G. Wells through Rebecca West (who had written for the *Egoist* in its former guise as the *New Freewoman*). Wells, then at the height of his fame, reviewed the *Portrait of the Artist* by the almost unknown Joyce in an article syndicated both in the London Liberal weekly the *Nation* and in the *New Republic*. Its repercussions were to continue for much longer than he can ever have anticipated. Wells's praise of the *Portrait* as a unique social document, 'by far the most living and convincing picture of an Irish Catholic upbringing', was still being quoted on Penguin book-covers more than fifty years later. But Wells also coined a phrase which stuck to Joyce himself for the rest of his life. Like Swift and 'another living Irish writer',[6] he pronounced, 'Mr Joyce has a cloacal obsession'.[7] Reference to the dictionary gives the Latin word *cloaca* meaning a sewer, excremental cavity, or 'gathering-place of moral evil'. Joyce's own 'odour of corruption' had now been named in criticism for the first time. Pound, presumably in response to this, wrote to Joyce that '[Wells] IS a bloody damn fool, but a full page from him ought to do a good deal of good to your sales' (*Pound/Joyce*: 94). But very soon after this he too came to be deeply troubled by the cloacal aspects of *Ulysses*, then being written for serial publication (again through Pound's good offices) in the American *Little Review*.

The 'Calypso' episode, in which Bloom eats his breakfast and then defecates, made Pound a little uneasy. 'You overdo the matter: leave the stool to Geo. Robey', he wrote (*Pound/Joyce*: 131), implying that the natural functions were a more suitable subject for music-hall comedy than for *avant-garde* realism. When the 'Sirens' episode arrived, with its sound-effects ranging from the twanging of a barmaid's garter to Bloom's passing of wind, Pound reacted with what must be one of the most bizarre pieces of epistolary prose ever written. It begins like this:

> O gloire et decor de la langue Irso-Anglais:
>   The peri-o-perip-o-periodico-parapatetico-periodopathetico –
> Idont-off-the markgetical structure of yr. first or peremier
> para-petitec graph – will cause all but your most pig-o-
> peripatec-headed readers to think you have gone marteau-
> dingo-maboule –

(this last phrase being glossed by Forrest Read as 'got knocked on the head or bit by a wild dog and gone dotty' (*Pound/Joyce*: 157)) Space forbids further quotation – the letter should be read as a whole – but as it progresses it becomes clear that Pound's worries are centred on the link between Joyce's experimental writing and his physiological explicitness, which he sees as a turning loose of 'obsessions arseoreial, cloacal' – echoing the phrase that Wells had used. The public effect of the 'Sirens' episode may be disastrous, he suggests. After all, 'Mass effect of any work depends on conviction of author's sanity' (*Pound/Joyce*: 158). Pound was right up to a point about the 'mass effect'. Soon the *Little Review* containing the 'Nausicaa' episode was banned, making *Ulysses* into an underground masterpiece which could only be published in Paris. But Pound's uncomprehending reaction to the 'Sirens', coming at such a crucial point in the unfolding of *Ulysses*, must have been a bitter blow to its author, who never again felt full confidence in his friend's critical judgment.

In his autobiography *Blasting and Bombardiering* (1937) Wyndham Lewis looked back on the period of *Blast*, *Ulysses*, and *The Waste Land*, which now appeared an 'island of incomprehensible bliss, dwelt in by strange shapes labelled "Pound", "Joyce", "Weaver", "Hulme" ':

As people look back at them, out of a very humdrum, cautious, disillusioned society . . . the critics of that future day will rub their eyes. They will look, to them, so hopelessly *avant-garde*! so almost madly up-and-coming!

What energy! – what impossibly Spartan standards men will exclaim! . . . *We are the first men of a Future that has not materialised*.[8]

I wonder if any writer has satisfactorily explained *why* the artistic future visible in 1914 failed to materialise. The usual explanation, which holds simply that the War was to blame, cannot be more than a half-truth. After the War, the 'movement' broke up into rival sects under the strain of the different artistic and political affiliations of its members. At the same time, the London literary world came to be dominated by the Bloomsbury Group and its allies, who opposed any extension of modernism beyond the point that they themselves had reached.

Let us consider the disintegration of the modernist movement first. Pound was already claiming in 1917 that the *Portrait* ought to have had a political effect. As the years went by, he took less and less interest in a novelist who was ignorant of the theories of Social Credit and had no love for Mussolini. Pound was surely referring to his former friend's political backwardness when he wrote in 1934 that 'Joyce knows very little of life as it has been in the large since he finished *Ulysses*' (*Pound/Joyce*: 256). Later on he became still more brusque and scatological on the subject of Joyce, referring to the 'diarrhoea of consciousness', '*transition* crap', and 'Jheezus in progress' (*Pound/Joyce*: 257).

Of the other modernists who survived the War, Eliot is notable for his somewhat ambivalent sponsorship of Joyce's work in England, while Lewis became one of its most outspoken antagonists. Eliot's sponsorship began with his essay 'Ulysses, Order and Myth' (1923), which – to my mind misleadingly – describes Joyce as abandoning the narrative method for the 'mythical method', which Eliot saw as 'the most important expression which the present age has found'.[8a] The practical effects of Eliot's enthusiasm are still to be seen in the list of Joyce titles (the earliest was *Anna Livia Plurabelle* in 1930) published by Faber and Faber. The *Criterion*, however, preserved a studied neutrality – printing first 'Anna Livia Plurabelle' and then an essay by Sean O'Faolain prompted, in the author's words, by Joyce's 'maltreatment of language'.[9] In *After Strange Gods* (1934), Joyce received the doubtful blessing of Eliot's theological imprimatur. He was the 'most ethically orthodox of the more eminent writers of my time', Eliot pronounced; his work was 'penetrated with Christian feeling'.[10] Eliot had no interest in Ireland, except as an offshoot of Catholic Europe, and his view was that Joyce's 'orthodoxy', like Baudelaire's, was merely confirmed by his blasphemous rejection of the religion of his childhood. Whether or not he altered his opinion on this in later years, he did not hesitate to express his rather negative reaction to *Work in Progress* and, later, *Finnegans Wake*. *Work in Progress*, he predicted in 1936, would prove 'a blind alley for the future development of the language'.[11] Twenty years later he said of *Finnegans Wake* that 'one book like this is enough'.[12]

What was enough for T.S. Eliot was too much for Wyndham Lewis. Though he became a friend and sincere admirer of Joyce, Lewis was never one to let friendship or admiration stand in the way of artistic and ideological conviction. He had, perhaps understandably, rejected some of Joyce's stories which Pound submitted to *Blast* early in 1914 (*Pound/Joyce*: 26). In 1926 Joyce was again expecting Lewis to publish some of his work in the new review that he was starting, and again he was disappointed.[13] Instead, the first number of *The Enemy* contained the explosive 'Analysis of the Mind of James Joyce', which was to form the centrepiece of Lewis's *Time and Western Man* (1927).

Lewis chooses his ground in this essay carefully. He is concerned almost entirely with *Ulysses* – he has a low opinion of the rest of Joyce – and yet he starts out by dismissing some of the more commonplace contemporary objections to the book. Joyce, he argues, is a comic artist, 'the amiable author of *Ulysses*' – a poet of shabby-gentility rather than any sort of Swiftian misanthrope. His supposed obscenity is another red herring. Joyce's mind is 'more chaste than most'.[14] Nor is he as original as his admirers, or as eccentric as his detractors, would like to believe. He epitomises the type that Lewis names the 'revolutionary simpleton'. Like Pound, Lewis reads Joyce's art largely as an exercise in naturalism. Oddly enough, since he rejects the idea that Joyce is an obscene writer, his discussion of of the naturalism of *Ulysses* is riddled with cloacal metaphors. The book is an accumulation of objects, bric-à-brac – the facts of pre-war Dublin stored away in Joyce's mind – resulting in 'an immense *nature-morte*' (p. 107). The modernist revolution in artistic methods had enabled Joyce to discharge all this stored-up material:

So rich was its delivery, its pent-up outpouring so vehement, that it will remain, eternally cathartic, a monument like a record diarrhoea. (p. 109)

Lewis makes fun of the commonplace situations and stock types — the Englishman (Haines), the Irishman (Mulligan) and the Jew — which he discerns beneath Joyce's formidable technical skills. Joyce is a *'craftsman*, pure and simple' (p. 106), not a philosophical or reflective intelligence. This makes him the involuntary tool of the 'masked ideologies' around him. Lewis unmasks *Ulysses* as a 'time-book', the product of the dominant (Bergsonian and Einsteinian) world-view which it is the object of *Time and Western Man* to dislodge. Despite his condescending account of Joyce the man and his brutally reductive view of his art, he does not despair of making him an ideological convert. For all the pedantry, 'apeishness', and mental confusion that Lewis detects in him, Joyce — the reader is assured — would make a 'very valuable adherent' to the *Enemy's* cause.

Lewis's essay gave rise to a polemical exchange with Joyce's Parisian admirers. In 'First Aid to the Enemy' (December 1927), the editors of *transition* accused Lewis of political and artistic reaction, and faulted him, moreover, for sticking to the comparatively safe ground of *Ulysses* instead of passing judgment on *Work in Progress*.[15] Lewis responded by accusing Joyce in his later work of ' "philological" pretentiousness' and 'mirthless formal verbal acrobatics'.[16] Looking back on the whole episode, he would later vehemently deny Harry Levin's assertion that he had been motivated by personal malice towards Joyce.[17] Yet Joyce was both puzzled and hurt, and he also responded with distaste to the political direction in which Lewis, Eliot and Pound were all now turning. As he wrote to Harriet Weaver in 1929, 'the more I hear of the political, philosophical, ethical zeal and labours of the brilliant members of Pound's big brass band the more I wonder why I was ever let into it "with my magic flute" '.[18] For the uncommitted and yet democratically inclined Irish artist it was a dramatic reversal of the climate of 1914.

The second cause of the disintegration of modernism in England was the resistance put up by the literary establishment. What took place, more exactly, was the assimilation of those elements of the modernist movement which could be reconciled with the dominant image of English cultural identity. The rest were rejected. We need not be concerned here with the reaction of tradionalist critics to

Joyce's innovations, for that can be taken as read.[19] We should look instead at figures like Clive Bell, a leading member of the Bloomsbury circle and propagandist for post-Impressionist art, who in 1921 dismissed Joyce as an untalented mediocrity; at Desmond MacCarthy, who found *Work in Progress* a 'physical impossibility to read'; at Richard Aldington, co-author of Pound's Imagist manifesto in 1913, who described *Ulysses* as 'a tremendous libel on humanity'; at E.M. Forster, who misread *Ulysses* in *Aspects of the Novel* (1924) as a 'dogged attempt to cover the universe with mud'; at John Middleton Murry, who spoke of Joyce's 'inspissated obscurities'; and, above all, we should look at Virginia Woolf.[20]

Virginia Woolf was influenced by Joyce, for whose work she nevertheless felt a strong dislike. She gave him a leading position in her essay 'Modern Fiction' (1919), in which she contrasted the 'materialism' of the Edwardian novelists, Wells, Bennett and Galsworthy, with the superior spirituality of the moderns. Joyce was a modern, but was he really as spiritual as a novelist ought to be? As soon as her essay asks this question, Woolf's reservations about Joyce's achievement start to appear. He may be the best of the moderns, but he is not in her view as great as Hardy or Conrad. The episode of Paddy Dignam's funeral fails, she says, 'because of the comparative poverty of the writer's mind – we might say simply and have done.' Joyce's supposed mental poverty is connected with another matter – a failure in taste. This is something that Woolf alludes to with more delicacy than Wells, with far more delicacy than vulgar, unbuttoned Ezra Pound, but the reference to an insalubrious 'obsession' is nevertheless unmistakable. 'Does the emphasis', she writes, 'laid, perhaps didactically, upon indecency, contribute to the effect of something angular and isolated?'[21] In the privacy of her diary she was a good deal less circumspect than this. *Ulysses*, she noted, was the 'underbred' book of a 'self-taught working man', or perhaps of a 'queasy undergraduate scratching his pimples'.[22]

Poor Joyce; once again his obscenity had been found reprehensible, not by a spokesman for conventional morality, but by a leading avant-garde artist – though admittedly this epithet seems a bit strong when Woolf is put beside Pound or Lewis. Woolf was unwilling for the Hogarth Press to try the experiment of publishing *Ulysses*,[23] but she did borrow many of Joyce's procedures, such as the stream-of-consciousness monologue, the use of city streets as a setting, and the 'day in the life' of a number of characters, when writing *Mrs Dallo-*

way (1925). The diluted and anglicised modernism of *Mrs Dalloway* in its turn seems to have influenced one of the most telling of all English responses to Joyce, the long title-essay of Rebecca West's book *The Strange Necessity* (1928). Rebecca West owed none of her position in the literary world to Bloomsbury, and had first made her name as a critic in the 'advanced' and left-wing press before 1914. 'The Strange Necessity', however, shows her rejecting international modernism for Bloomsbury values, in a whimsical, stream-of-consciousness meditation which, like so many of its critical predecessors, tries to explain Joyce by focussing on his predilection for obscenity.

'The Strange Necessity' recounts a day in the life of an English literary lady on a visit to Paris. Naturally she calls on her dressmaker and milliner, where she purchases three new hats. She goes to the bank and has half-an-hour's talk with a lawyer about her investments. All the time, however, she is brooding over her early-morning visit to Sylvia Beach's bookshop, where she purchased Joyce's latest book, which happened to be *Pomes Penyeach*. Her mind is in turmoil because of her conflicting feelings about this 'great writer' who is all the rage in Europe but is banned in England. As the day goes on, however, her view of Joyce begins to fall into place. Her stream of discourse leads via Proust and Pavlov's work on conditioned reflexes (both recently published in English) to the aesthetic process as defined by Roger Fry and Clive Bell – a process to which the spirit of Joyce's work, she concludes, is utterly alien. West accuses Joyce of writing didactically, in order to shock his readers, and then declares that his desire to shock is a form of sentimentality. Obscenity in fiction is sentimental because it appeals purely at the level of infantile gratification, and so is 'altogether outside the aesthetic process'.[24] Joyce, indeed, is guilty of writing much as Pavlov's dogs salivate, and his much-vaunted technique is no more than a 'tin can tied to the tail of the dog of his genius' (p. 57). Unlike those 'Fortnum & Mason authors' – her teasing description of Woolf and Fry (p. 119) – he has no inkling of the secret that matters (the secret of art) and the secrets he knows are, on the whole, too unpleasant to contemplate. If Joyce still has to be granted the title of 'genius', it is done in precisely the spirit of which D.H. Lawrence once complained: 'They were always telling me I had got genius, as if to console me for not having their own incomparable advantages.'[25]

Joyce, then is 'a great man who is entirely without taste' (p. 15).

Naturally West backs up this verdict with some reasoned arguments, about Joyce's inveterate naturalism – she suggests that *Ulysses* is a work of the same order as Frith's 'Derby Day' – and about his mawkishness as a poet. But what is most noticeable is the degree of relief and satisfaction that her verdict affords her. Because he has no taste – because, when it comes down to it, he is not a cosmopolitan *rentier* intellectual, one capable of admiring 'the old Madame Tussaud's Exhibition, Amelia Bingham's house on Riverside Drive, and the furniture of the modern Palace at Seville' (p. 71) – he does not need to be taken seriously. Joyce's mind, she asserts, 'is furnished like a room in a Westland Row tenement in which there are a bedstead and a broken chair, on which there sits a great scholar and genius who falls over the bedstead whenever he gets up' (p. 56). This is an astonishing passage, which entirely bears out Wyndham Lewis's strictures in *Men Without Art* (1934) on the Bloomsbury world and its hostility to 'any vigorous manifestation in the arts': 'anything above the *salon* scale is what this sort of person most dislikes and is at some pains to stifle'.[26] For who, Rebecca West seems to say, given access to Fortnum & Mason's and to the drawing-rooms of Riverside Drive, needs a genius with a mind like a Westland Row tenement?

To argue that the English 'reception' of Joyce culminates in 'The Strange Necessity' is, no doubt, one-sided. There were certain artists and critics (though, I would claim, less eloquent and less influential than those cited here) who did respond to the magnitude of Joyce's achievement. For example, there is Charles Duff, whose fine essay *James Joyce and the Plain Reader* (1932) makes the point that Joyce's popularity completely bypasses those usually entrusted with the nurturing of literary reputations. ('A writer of distinction whom I know recently denounced *Anna Livia Plurabelle* to me as sheer nonsense and declared *Ulysses* to be inexplicable and boring', he unsurprisingly records.[27]) Yet it is clear both that the critics cited above articulated a deeply 'English' reaction, and that they made a considerable impression on Joyce himself and his Parisian circle. The Englishness of their reaction is seen in the haste with which they were inclined to fall back on criteria of class snobbery and 'taste'. What was allowable in England was the genteel, respectable modernism represented by T.S. Eliot in his clerical suit, by Forster's *Aspects of the Novel* with its discreet deprecation of traditional story-telling, and by the cults of pre-revolutionary Russian fiction and of Proust.

In addition, the English critics responded to Joyce's 'cloacal obses-sion' with their own kind of sanitising obsession. The alien tissues of his work were diagnosed as a contamination and dealt with accord-ingly. As Joyce himself once retorted – and I believe we must apply this metaphorically as well as literally – 'Cloacal obsession! Why, it's Wells's countrymen who build water-closets wherever they go.'[28]

Joyce, it need hardly be said, enjoyed being in the centre of con-troversy. He would not necessarily have resented all the comments quoted in the previous section. Some he unquestionably took pride in. Yet I would argue that his rejection in England had a cumulative effect on the writer himself, as well as on his posthumous reputation. The evidence lies in *Finnegans Wake* with its obsessive references to Eliot, to Lewis and to Rebecca West with her 'forty bonnets'.[29] It lies in the protectiveness of his Parisian circle, such as the editors of *transition* who claimed in 1928 that publication of *Work in Progress* had been met with 'almost nothing but infantile ridicule and abuse'. (Nevertheless, they assured their readers, 'The world's greatest living writer is in solitude, harrassed by the spite of his former friends, but working patiently, prodigiously, continuously.')[30] More evidence lies in the strange mixture of definitive criticism, hagiographical praise of the master and sneers at the opposition to be found in that remarkable book *Our Exagmination Round his Factification for Incamination of Work in Progress* (1929) by Samuel Beckett and thirteen others. Does the title capture a whiff of crankiness that surrounds the whole venture? Do the contributors show a suspect degree of unanimity which is not dispelled by the self-conscious inclusion of the 'litters of protest'? All this may be so: but for all its coterie atmosphere it is to *Our Exagmination*, and not to the London critics, that we must go for the first real clarification of what Joyce in his later years was about. The final essay in the volume is by William Carlos Williams, and includes this declaration:

> What Joyce is saying is a literary thing. It is a literary value he is forward-ing. He is a writer. Will this never be understood? Perhaps he is fixed in his material and cannot change. It is of no consequence. The writing is, however, changing, the writing is active. It is in the writing that the power exists. Joyce is a literary man writing as he may – with as much affection from his material, his Freudian category as – Esop from his hump or Scarron from his nerves. It is stupid, it is narrow British to think to use that against him. . . . They are *literary* critics. That's what gets me.[31]

Williams' essay, a deliberate reply to Rebecca West, is entitled 'A Point for American Criticism'. The story traced in the present sketch is in part the story of how Joyce was let drop by the English and passed into American hands. English magazines would not print his work. Edgell Rickword wanted to publish part of *Work in Progress* in the *Calendar of Modern Letters*, but the printers refused to set it up in type.[32] After 1925, when part of *Anna Livia* appeared in the *Criterion*, there was to be no further periodical publication of *Work in Progress* in England (though Faber and Faber did, of course, produce it in pamphlet form), with one tiny exception. Three pages of the 'Museyroom' sequence appeared in the final (Spring 1931) number of *Experiment*, a Cambridge undergraduate magazine edited by William Empson. Thirty pages of material from *Experiment* had earlier been reprinted, under the heading 'A Manifesto of Young England', in *transition*.[33] Like Joyce's own work, this was itself an exception to the rule that *transition* was a magazine for visiting and expatriate Americans, including not only the editorial group but Malcolm Cowley, Ernest Hemingway, Archibald MacLeish, Katharine Anne Porter, Laura Riding, Gertrude Stein and Yvor Winters as well as Williams.

With Empson's short-lived *Experiment* we are on the verge of a different history, into which this essay cannot enter. The rejection of Joyce's 'obscenity' and of his experimentalism by the London literary intelligentsia was, in effect, a refusal to accept any writing which could not be translated into, or judged in accordance with, the familiar terms of English cultural debate, Joyce, it was frequently argued, did violence to the very essence of language; thus Rebecca West claims that where he writes down 'strings of words', real human beings think in 'sentences' (p. 32). So culture-bound was the English notion of literary language that forty years after 'The Strange Necessity', and thirty years after the legalisation of *Ulysses*, it would still be a radical gesture in England to assert the legitimacy of Joyce's experiments in *Finnegans Wake*. In the meantime, the writings proscribed by modernists, Bloomsburyites, and later by Leavisites in England had become the subject of a whole scholarly industry in New-Critical America. What was once a point for American criticism had now become a melancholy tale for English cultural historians.

Notes

1   Arthur Power, *Conversations with James Joyce*, ed. Clive Hart (London: Millington, 1974), p. 69.

2   *Ibid.*, p. 60.

3   Joyce, *Pomes Penyeach* (London: Faber & Faber, 1966), p. 46–7.

4   Reprinted in Ezra Pound, *Literary Essays*, ed. T.S. Eliot (London: Faber & Faber, 1954), p. 399.

5   See Eric Homberger, 'Pound, Ford and "Prose": The Making of a Modern Poet', *American Studies*, 5 (1971), p. 281ff.

6   The other living writer was probably George Moore.

7   Reprinted in *H.G. Wells's Literary Criticism*, ed. Patrick Parrinder and Robert M. Philmus (Brighton: Harvester, 1980), p. 171–5.

8   W. Lewis, *Blasting and Bombardiering* (London: Eyre & Spottiswoode, 1937), p. 256–8.

8a Reprinted in *James Joyce: Two Decades of Criticism*, ed. Seon Givens (New York: Vanguard, 1963), p. 198–202.

9   Sean O'Faolain, 'Style and the Limitations of Speech', *Criterion*, 8 (September 1928), p. 83.

10 Eliot, *After Strange Gods* (London: Faber & Faber, 1934), p. 38, 48.

11 Eliot, *On Poetry and Poets* (London: Faber & Faber, 1957), p. 143.

12 *Ibid*; p. 108.

13 See Timothy Materer, *Vortex: Pound, Eliot, and Lewis* (Ithaca: Cornell University Press, 1979), p. 164–5. Materer's chapter on 'James Joyce and the Vortex of History', which came to hand as the final draft of this essay was being prepared, is the fullest treatment to date of Joyce's relations with Eliot and Lewis, and should be read as a whole.

14 W. Lewis, *Time and Western Man* (London: Chatto & Windus, 1927), p. 110. Page references in the text are to this edition.

15 *transition*, 9 (December 1927), p. 165, 169–70.

16 W. Lewis, *The Diabolical Principle and The Dithyrambic Spectator* (London: Chatto & Windus, 1931), p. 73.

17 W. Lewis, *Rude Assignment* (London: Hutchinson, 1950), p. 54–6.

18 Quoted by Richard Ellmann, *James Joyce* (New York: Oxford University Press, 1959), p. 621–2.

19 See *James Joyce: The Critical Heritage*, ed. Robert H. Deming, 2 vols (London: Routledge & Kegan Paul, 1970), for a broad selection of contemporary critical responses to Joyce.

20 See *James Joyce: The Critical Heritage*, 1, p. 183 (for Bell); p. 376 (for MacCarthy); p. 197 (for Murry); and p. 188 (for Aldington). Aldington's comment is especially disingenuous. He introduced his best-selling 'jazz novel' *Death of a Hero* (1929) with a note recording his 'astonishment' at being told by his publisher that 'certain words, phrases, sentences and even passages' of his manuscript were taboo in England. Faced with the alternative of revising his text or merely consenting to deletions, he let *Death of a Hero* be published as, possibly, the original novel-subsiding-into-asterisks. There is no evidence

(though he was living in Paris at the time) that he ever considered the Joycean alternative of not allowing publication of a mutilated text in any form. For Forster, see *Aspects of the Novel* (Harmondsworth: Penguin, 1962), p. 125.

21 Virginia Woolf, 'Modern Fiction', in *The Common Reader: First Series* (London: Hogarth Press, 1925), p. 190–2.

22 Virginia Woolf, *A Writer's Diary*, ed. Leonard Woolf (London: Hogarth Press, 1953), p. 47.

23 Leon Edel, *Bloomsbury: A House of Lions* (London: Hogarth Press, 1979), p. 247.

24 Rebecca West, *The Strange Necessity* (London: Cape, 1928), p. 21. Page references in the text are to this edition.

25 D.H. Lawrence, 'Autobiographical Sketch', in *Assorted Articles* (London: Secker & Warburg, 1930), p. 150.

26 W. Lewis, *Enemy Salvoes*, ed. C.J. Fox (London: Vision, 1975), p. 94–5.

27 Charles Duff, *James Joyce and the Plain Reader* (London: Desmond Harmsworth, 1932), p. 20.

28 Frank Budgen, *James Joyce and the Making of 'Ulysses' and Other Writings* (London: Oxford University Press, 1972), p. 108.

29 For *Wake* references to Rebecca West, see Mary and Padraic Colum, *Our Friend James Joyce* (London: Gollancz, 1959), p. 125.

30 *transition*, 12 (March 1928), p. 145.

31 Samuel Beckett and Others, *Our Exagmination Round his Factification for Incamination of Work in Progress* (Paris: Shakespeare & Co., 1929), p. 179–80.

32 Private communication from Alan Munton, to whose comments on an earlier draft of this essay I am greatly indebted.

33 *transition*, 19–20 (June 1930), p. 105–38.

CHAPTER 9

Joyce and Nationalism

Seamus Deane

It is well known that Joyce, like Stephen Dedalus, considered himself to be the slave of two masters, one British and one Roman. It is equally well known that he repudiated the Irish literary revival, going so far as to call 'Gogarty and Yeats and Colm (sic) the black-legs of literature' (*Letters*, II; 187). Repudiating British and Roman imperialisms and rejecting Irish nationalism and Irish literature which seemed to be in service to that cause, he turned away from his early commitment to socialism and devoted himself instead to a highly apolitical and wonderfully arcane practice of writing. Such, in brief, is the received wisdom about Joyce and his relationship to the major political issues of his time. Although some revision of this estimate has recently begun,[1] it remains as one of the more secure assumptions about his life and work.

It is, however, seriously misleading to view Joyce in this way. His very real disaffection with politics, Irish or international, enhanced his sense of isolation and was translated into his creed of artistic freedom. Since history could not yield a politics, it was compelled to yield an aesthetic. In this process, disaffection became disdain, political reality dissolved into fiction, fiction realised itself purely in terms of its own medium, language. As a consequence, the finite nature of historical fact was supplanted by the infinite, or near infinite, possibilities of language. Language was cast into a form which would extend the range of possible signification to an ultimate degree of openness, thereby setting itself against the closed world of limited and limiting historical fact. Stephen Dedalus, in the course of his history lesson, wonders about the brute facts of the deaths of Pyrrhus and Caesar:

> They are not to be thought away. Time has branded them and fettered they are lodged in the room of the infinite possibilities they have ousted. But can those have been possible seeing that they never were? Or was that only possibly which came to pass? (*U*: 31)

The finite has replaced the infinite. Minor modifications are, of course, possible. In *Ulysses*, we learn that Bloom perhaps 'gave the idea for Sinn Fein to Griffith' (*U*: 334) or that he may have picked up Parnell's fallen hat and returned it to him after a fracas. (*U*: 575). But this is harmless embroidery. Parnell's downfall and death is a brute fact that Joyce found it more difficult to counter. He took it from the world of history and re-established it in the world of fiction by unfettering it from actual circumstances and making of it a maieutic image which helped him to understand what he already knew – that in Ireland possibility would always be humiliated into squalid fact. The more squalid the fact, the more finite it seems. Joyce's Dublin was, after all, a carefully composed image of squalor and the 'naturalism' of his rendering of the city claims our assent because it is so unflinching in the face of all that is mean and unpleasant.[2]

History, then, must be countered by fiction. But the fiction, to perform its necessary function, must have broken its traditional affiliations with history. Plot and theme, those elements which produce the story, are to be subdued, even abolished, and replaced by language. Even though language will inevitably carry the traces of these story patterns, it will not allow them to dominate. The last six sections of *Ulysses* upset many of the expectations raised by the preceding twelve because they abort the story element in order to redeem the status of language. Even the story of Stephen's or of Bloom's consciousness is a kind of internal history. We are deprived of that too. In *Ulysses*, and more so in *Finnegans Wake*, Joyce manages to achieve inter-relationships between the various elements in the novels which cannot be effectively demonstrated in a summary of the story of the works. Mere story ousts too many possibilities which language retains.

A history as calamitous as Ireland's could certainly do with some countering, but Joyce was by no means the first Irish writer to feel this. In 1907, he spoke of Ireland's claim, articulated in the nineteenth century, to a renewed cultural identity:

> . . . the Irish nation's insistence on developing its own culture by itself is not so much the demand of a young nation that wants to make good in the European concert as the demand of a very old nation to renew under new forms the glories of a past civilisation. (*C W*: 157)

Among his contemporaries, Yeats and Pearse were the most articulate of the cultural nationalists, systematically rereading the past in order to supply a model for future development. The differences which separate them are less important than the similarities they share. Both sanctified Ireland as a legendary and revolutionary place which was again about to take her place among the nations.

Nationalism, as preached by Yeats or by Pearse, was a crusade for decontamination. The Irish essence was to be freed of the infecting Anglicising virus and thus restored to its primal purity and vigour. The Gaelic League pointed one way towards this restoration – the recovery of the Irish language and the displacement, partial or total, of English. Pearse concentrated on the educational system, the famous Murder Machine as he called it, and its replacement by one known to the Gael of Celtic times, nobler, more liberal, more suited to the national temperament. Yeats and Synge looked to the emergence of a new literature in English vivified by the linguistic energies of an Irish civilisation not yet blighted by the inanities of 'parliamentary speeches and the gutter press'.[3] The presiding opposition between a 'spiritual' Ireland and a 'mechanical' England lent itself to an immense number of subsidiary variations – sexual purity as opposed to sexual squalor, ancestral faith as opposed to rootless urban alienation, just rebellion against imperial coercion, enduring faith as against shallow modernism, imaginative vitality as against dehydrated utilitarianism. History too could be realised in a new form. Pearse's line of heroes – Tone, Emmet, Davis, Lalor, Mitchell – and Yeats's line – Berkeley, Swift, Burke, Goldsmith – both had their justification in their essential contact with the spirit of Irishness which was retained by the mass of the people.

It would be inaccurate, however, to claim too close a kinship between Pearse, Yeats and Joyce in this respect, even though all three do visibly share in the heroicising spirit which informed the whole Irish Literary Revival. In 1914, in a speech delivered in New York, Pearse spoke of patriotism in terms which are precisely those rejected by Stephen Dedalus in his *non serviam*:

> For patriotism is at once a faith and a service . . . a faith which is of the same nature as religious faith and is one of the eternal witnesses in the heart of man to the truth that we are of divine kindred . . . So that patriotism needs service as the condition of its authenticity, and it is not sufficient to say 'I believe' unless one can say also 'I serve'.[4]

Such belief and such service as Pearse demands repelled Yeats as much as it did Joyce. It refused freedom to the mind. It had, in Yeats's words, pedantry not 'culture' as its distinguishing mark and for him 'Culture is the sanctity of the intellect'.[5] In his Journal, for 12 March, 1909, he wrote,

> There is a sinking away of national feeling which is very simple in its origin. You cannot keep the idea of a nation alive where there are no national institutions to reverence, no national success to admire, without a model of it in the mind of the people. You can call it 'Kathleen-ni-Houlihan' or the 'Shan Van Vocht' in a mood of simple feeling, and love that image, but for the general purposes of life you must have a complex mass of images, making up a model like an architect's model. The Young Ireland poets created this with certain images rather simple in their conception that filled the mind of the young – Wolfe Tone, King Brian, Emmet, Owen Roe, Sarsfield, the Fisherman of Kinsale. It answered the traditional slanders on Irish character too, and started an apologetic habit, but its most powerful work was this creation of sensible images for the affections, vivid enough to follow men on to the scaffold. As was necessary, the ethical ideas involved were very simple, needing neither study nor unusual gifts for the understanding of them. Our own movement began by trying to do the same thing in a more profound and enduring way.[6]

But, Yeats goes on to say, in a famous passage, that the appearance of Synge's work persuaded him that the revival must be content to express the individual.

> The Irish people were not educated enough to accept as an image of Ireland anything more profound, more true of human nature as a whole, than the schoolboy thought of Young Ireland.[7]

All of this appears in the midst of Yeats's attack on the journalistic spirit which had infected the Gaelic League and the national movement as a whole, degrading it to little more than an exercise in chauvinism.

Despite the differences which separate them, Yeats and Joyce repudiate the more pronounced forms of political nationalism – those associated with Pearse and with the journalism of newspapers like D.P. Moran's *The Leader* – on the same grounds. It is, in effect, too crude, too schoolboyish, too eager to demand a spirit of solidarity and service that has more in common with propaganda than it has with art. But whereas Yeats did indeed give up, to some extent, 'the deliberate creation of a kind of Holy City in the imagination' and replace it with images of enduring heroism and not so durable authority, Joyce remained faithful to the original conception of the Revival. His Dublin became the Holy City of which Yeats had despaired.

Joyce had been as fascinated by the career and achievement of James Clarence Mangan as Yeats had been by William Carleton. For Yeats these writers were premonitions of what was yet to come. But for Joyce, Mangan was in fact the finished product, the figure in whom 'an hysterical nationalism receives its final justification' (C W: 186). His two lectures on Mangan (1902 and 1907) are highly ambivalent, for he is sympathetic to this 'poète maudit' insofar as he portrays the plight of the artist in Ireland, and unsympathetic to him insofar as Mangan remained subject to those environing forces which he, Joyce, must elude. Joyce is as willing as is Pearse to speak of Ireland's soul, to speak of the nation as a spiritual entity, and to conceive of her plight as one in which something ethereal has been overwhelmed by something base. In his review of Lady Gregory's *Poets and Dreamers*, published in 1903 under the title 'The Soul of Ireland', he wrote of Ireland's 'one belief – a belief in the incurable ignobility of the forces that have overcome her' (C W: 105) although the same article characteristically reveals his acid contempt for the Gregorian old men with 'red eyes and short pipe' (P: 256). Joyce, in other words, believes in Ireland and the sorry tale of her doomed spirit through the ages. His conception of history is dominated by the idea of the noble spirit debased by ignoble domination and demeaning circumstance. Like Pearse, he assumed that there was a necessary connection between belief and service. The question was, then, to what should the service be given – Church, Nation, State? Refusing all of these, left him with the idea of service to Art.

Still, while the service is to Art, Art is itself in service to the Soul of Ireland. This soul is still uncreated. It is the function of true art to create it – a function all the more necessary since all other forms of Irish activity had failed by producing a debased version of that spiritual reality. Whether it was in Mangan or in Lady Gregory, in the Citizen or in Buck Mulligan, in Arthur Griffith or in John Redmond, Ireland found herself travestied. The new day that threatened to dawn was always an Ivy Day, or a Day of the Rabblement, and its light would always break on a committee room or a theatre shadowed by betrayal. Until, that is, the fictive day of 16 June 1904. Joyce, in other words, put his art in service to something which would be created only by that act of service. The absence of Ireland would be overcome in his art; there it would achieve presence. But the presence is itself dependent on the conviction that, before Joyce, there was nothing. The desire of nationalism pales in comparison with this desire. An act of writing which will replace all earlier acts; which will replace all politics; which will make the ignoble, noble; which will make history into culture by making it the material of consciousness – this extraordinary ambition is at the heart of Joyce's enterprise. Yeats had it and gave it up for the theme of individuality, despairing of Ireland's incompleteness. But for Joyce, that incompletion was the very ground of his art. The unfinished and the uncreated culture provided the opportunity for the most comprehensive, the most finished, the most boundlessly possible art. The colonial culture produced imperial art. A culture which had never known the idea of totality was to have it embodied in art. Further, it could produce such art precisely because it was so bereft. Only a minority culture could seek an articulation of itself as a total culture. Pearse and Yeats knew this. In that respect they were nationalists. But such articulation had to be achieved by a process of repudiation, the rejection of all previous abortive attempts, the incorporation of them as imperfect paradigms and the extension of the ironic conception of the paradigm and the harbinger into a principle of structure. Yeats and Joyce knew this and in that respect they went beyond nationalism into a universalism for which history, myth and legend supplied the imagery merely. The supreme action was writing.

Therefore in Joyce we can never forget the primacy of writing as action. Its early 'scrupulous meanness' in *Dubliners*, the delicate fission in *Portrait* between the narrative and the narrated voice of Stephen, the interior monologues and parodies of *Ulysses*, the multilingual voices of *Finnegans Wake*, all coerce the reader into accepting the text as writing which is calling attention to its written nature. Even the plots of these books, insofar as they can be said to have plots, are so designed that their interconnections are aggressively verbal, insisting on the linkages of words rather than on the illusion of events. Joyce dismantles the agreed relation between author and reader whereby fiction was allowed autonomy as story. Instead, he insists upon the dependence of the story and of the very idea of fiction upon language. Given that, he can then make language constitutive of reality, not merely regulative of it. Irish nationalism was one of the forces which enabled him to do this, largely because it had been trying to do so itself for over half a century before Joyce wrote.

Since the last decade of the eighteenth century, Ireland had learned to believe in the relationship between literature and rebellion as a natural one. Burke had pointed to the influence of men of letters on the French Revolution, blaming them for the introduction into European politics of an element of abstract ideological fury which had never existed before. Nineteenth-century Ireland tended to follow the remedy promoted by Coleridge in his completion of Burke's thought – the establishment of an intellectual clerisy as an integral part of the structure of the State, safeguarding the historical continuity and cultural complexity of the nation's heritage. In Ireland, this led to the foundation of the *Dublin University Magazine* and the attempt by Sir Samuel Ferguson to create a cultural identity for all the factions of Irish society, past and present, by conjoining a conservative Tory politics with a cultural nationalism. But since the Irish situation was a semi-colonial one, the aspiration towards cultural identity could not be indulged without involving itself in the aspiration towards political identity. Thomas Moore's sentimental songs helped to create that atmosphere of misty nostalgia in which the ballad, especially the political ballad, became a more effective stimulator of national consciousness than the essay, poem or novel. But poetry did tend towards the ballad form as the only one in which the two impulses, political and cultural, were effectively fused. Otherwise, poetry ran the risk of becoming 'literary', out of touch with the deepest aspirations of the people. The myth of Mangan takes its origin from this complex of factors, all the more enhanced by the Young Ireland movement's disagreement with O'Connell and its consequent tendency to move towards violent rebellion and away from constitutional agitation. Thus, the Irish intelligentsia was split into two factions – one, led by Ferguson which was pro-Union, politically conservative, and romantic nationalist in the cultural sense; the other, anti-Union, politically separatist and also romantically nationalist. Yeats brought these two streams together in his life and work. Joyce repudiated both.

This is not to say he was not interested. Joyce recognised the importance of Arthur Griffith's Sinn Fein movement and how formidable 'this last phase of Fenianism' was in having 'once more remodelled the character of the Irish people' (*C W*: 191). Parnell and O'Leary, the constitutional and the physical force movements, and their interaction on one another under the pressure of Westminster and the Vatican, absorbed a good deal of his attention. The Ireland that sought to remodel herself while 'serving both God and Mammon, letting herself be milked by England and yet increasing Peter's pence' was, nevertheless, politically vibrant, not at all like the Yeatsian version of an Ireland that turned its attentions to art following its disillusion with politics after Parnell. But if Yeats's Ireland was one in which the Celtic past was to be embraced, Joyce's Ireland was one in which spiritual reality did not yet exist. Stephen Dedalus's diary records;

> Michael Robartes remembers forgotten beauty and, when his arms wrap her round, he presses in his arms the loveliness which has long faded from the world. Not this. Not at all. I desire to press in my arms the loveliness which has not yet come into the world. (*P*: 255)

The relationship between literature and politics was not, for Joyce, mediated through a movement, a party, a combination or a sect. For him, the act of writing became an act of rebellion; rebellion was the act of writing. Its aim was to bring into the world a loveliness that still did not exist. Such writing therefore achieves its aspiration by coming into existence. It serves only what it is. Between the idea of service and the idea of the thing served, the distance has disappeared. In pursuing this conception of the artist and art, Joyce was presenting himself, via Stephen Dedalus, with a specifically Irish problem which had wider implications. How was he to create as literature something which would otherwise have no existence and yet was believed to exist already? The idea of Ireland still uncreated, awaited its realisation. The minority culture desired total embodiment.

But its embodiment in literature inevitably meant its embodiment in the English language. This was a central paradox. For English literature supplied Ireland with no serviceable models for imitation. Irish experience, different from English and anxious to assert that difference to the ultimate extent, needed a new form of realisation which would not only differentiate itself in formal terms from its English counterpart, but would also have to do so while fretting in the shadow of the coloniser's language. In accepting these challenges, formal and linguistic, in accepting the unique role of the artist in whom a minority culture, characterised by incompleteness and fracture, would achieve completeness and coherence, Joyce necessarily became a rebel against all that preceded him.

His rebellion took three forms, corresponding to the three forces from which he had to extricate himself. The Roman imperium he overcame by inversion, taking the idea of priesthood and dedicated vocation and applying it to a secular art. The British imperium was overcome by parody, taking the tradition of literature as it had expressed itself in the novel, and scrutinising its silent assumptions. The Irish imperium he overcame by exile, refusing the various forms of commitment and renewal which it preached and preferring instead isolation. But these three forms of rebellion – exile, parody, vocation – were strategies of displacement, not radical amputations. The Church, the English literary tradition and Ireland all remained as forces in his imagination. They operated under the aegis of irony, but the irony depended on their presence. Joyce was always to be the Irish writer who refused the limitations of being Irish; the writer of English who refused the limitations of being an English writer; the priest who refused the limitations of the conventional priesthood. His loyalty to himself was measured by the disloyalty he displayed towards the forces which had moulded him. It is not, therefore, surprising that he should have been obsessed by the notion of betrayal. Betrayal for the sake of integrity is his form of displacement and also lies at the source of his ironic method. Stephen betrays his mother and becomes superbly ironical at the expense of those who, like Buck Mulligan, wish to confront him with this fact. For Mulligan does not see the integrity which Stephen seeks through this betrayal. Instead, Mulligan reveals himself to be treacherous, for he is blind to the existence of integrity as a possibility. Ill-formed, he has no part in that loveliness which still does not exist, although its presence is often sentimentally invoked. Mulligan's Hellenism, the Citizen's Celticism, are twins. They indicate the existence of an ideal which they fail to embody. Bloom, the victim of so many betrayals, by father and by wife, embodies integrity without knowing what it is. Stephen, the sponsor of so many betrayals, knows what it is without embodying it. Each is the fulfilment of the other's desire.

Yet *Ulysses* is not primarily concerned with the alienation of these two men from their native culture. Although they are both in a minority – each is indeed a minority of one – they are not provincial as the other Dubliners are. To be excluded from parents, lovers, ideologies, and yet to be in some way respected as out of the ordinary, is the fate of the universal man in the local culture. They are concerned with the mystery of being, not with the mystery of being Dubliners or of being Irish. The relationship between parent and child is one which they understand as part of an ever-present identity and anxiety. For others, it is an historical relationship. Historical relationships are determined by the fidelity shown towards them. Whether it is the history of the Fenians, or the development of English prose, the history of Dublin, Church dogma, one's own family, the idea of sequence demands that one should conform to the pattern of the past so that, in doing so, the pattern becomes extended or fulfilled in oneself. Stephen and Bloom, however, try to avoid sequence and to replace it with simultaneity. For them, history is not a record of facts but the material of their consciousness. The act of reflection constantly moulds the past into the present. Their present determines the past. Their history is always the present. The interior monologue or stream-of-consciousness method is appropriate to them. For in it, the kaleidoscope of past and present can be constantly shaken to form transient patterns which are not essentially historical but psychological. The apparently uncensored reflections of Stephen and Bloom allow for the emergence of ostensibly inconsequential or random associations, all the more attractive because they are, so to speak, 'unofficial' versions of history (Bloom's vision of the Middle East, Stephen's version of Shakespeare and *Hamlet*) but also cryptic because they seem to be so arbitrary. It would be possible to speculate upon Joyce's increasing interest in the liberty bestowed upon an author by the exploration of these uncensored states of consciousness. Below the threshold of complete wakefulness, there is a universe of associative patterns which, in their unofficial way, might be more real or universal or simply more interesting than those the world of recorded fact can provide. But Joyce is not simply opening a Pandora's box. Whatever emerges has to be named, organised, 'placed' in some context of relation. The mode of Stephen's thought, or of Shem's, might reveal something of that character's personality, type or bias. But it is most remarkable for the way in which it establishes itself as only one mode among others in a larger discourse which is meaningful to the reader in a way not available to the putative character. The loss of censorship in relation to a single consciousness demands the articulation of a final, all-encompassing orderliness in which the uncensored reflections finally lose their cryptic, arbitrary status. In getting rid of the 'author' at one level, Joyce re-establishes him more emphatically at another. His chaos is local; his order is universal.

Although a dreamer like HCE is both narrator and narrated, the very scope of his consciousness, which embraces world history, indicates his universal status. Yet his universality, precisely because it avoids the stable identifications which are possible in the local Irish context – that of Irish nationalism – produces a form of consciousness which is essentially esoteric. The universal hero, in other words, can only be read by a specialised audience. He does not produce a universal language. Instead we are given a language in which the desire for universality expresses itself, paradoxically, in the most arcane form imaginable. In breaking away from the restrictions of a local nationality and from the kinds of identity conferred upon him by tradition, Joyce achieved a language which, by the sheer number of its polyglot associations, appears to be all-inclusive and yet which, by the sheer complexity of its narrative orders, manages to be almost wilfully exclusive. A text like *Finnegans Wake* is characterised by a dispute between the anarchic possibilities of its vocabulary and the despotic demands of its various structuring paradigms. On occasion, we can perceive that the male voices seem to adhere to a form of discourse which is seeking to achieve discrimination and pattern, while the female voices tend towards an undifferentiated mode of discourse in which discriminations are blurred and in which the very process of language being formed is revealed to us. This is also, to a lesser extent, true of *Ulysses*, in which Molly's coda to the novel restores us to the surging principle of existence itself, free from the helpless orderings to which Stephen and Bloom have tried to subject it. Of course, in each work, the sexual differentiation is important, since it is aligned with the opposition between ordered discourse and discourse which attempts to elude order. Nevertheless, the central problem remains insolubly there. The difficulty of these texts is an indication of Joyce's failure to discover for universal man a language comparable in its serviceability to the language for local man which had been developed by writers like Pearse. The 'schoolboy thought' of Young Ireland was replaced by the language and thought of a specialised researcher. In that sense, Joyce's politics, although it contains the idea of solidarity, also retains with that the idea of a privileged isolation – the isolation of the extraordinary individual.

In many ways it is appropriate that, in the twentieth century, a work of imagination should also be a work of research and that the burden of research should be imposed upon the reader as well as upon the author. Yet all the important Irish writers of the period between 1880 and 1940 were engaged in a kind of research which produced discourses which had very specific relationships to the

Irish nationalist movement. The language of Synge and of O'Casey, of George Moore (at least in *The Lake, The Untilled Field* and in *Hail and Farewell*) and of Yeats is, in many important respects, quoted language. That is to say, it is offered to us as a sample of a larger discourse which enfolds and is characteristic of a nation or a group. Nationalism is one of these larger discourses. It is not simply a way of speaking, but a way of speaking directed towards a specific goal – the goal of vitality, re-awakening, recovery. The highly stylised writing associated with all these authors, the fascination with heroism, the extraordinary individual, the willingness of all of them to subvert that heroism even while sponsoring it, gives them, when we look at these characteristics more closely, a striking family resemblance to Joyce. The absence of such a resemblance would be even more surprising than its existence, but Joyce did succeed in making the separation between his work and that of his contemporaries appear more complete than in fact it is. In *Portrait*, Stephen Dedalus is, so to speak, quoted into existence by nursery rhymes, political squabbles, church doctrine, literature. Then he responds by quoting on his own initiative – Aquinas, the villanelle, the diary. Possessed by language, he comes to possess it. Pateresque cadences and the vocabulary of Irish nationalism and of Irish Catholicism combine to form a new pattern, Stephen's, not reducible to these component parts, yet certainly including them. Stephen endows his existence with a figurative meaning which might seem to be far in excess of the resources of his own life to sustain. But his social and political experience has been of such figurative crises – Ireland and its uncrowned king, Catholicism and its hell of endless torment. In his culture, imagination figured powerfully *as true* what fact could not provide. The crowned king of Ireland, Edward VII, is a sorry figure beside the uncrowned king, Parnell. Even the points of similarity, their sexual escapades and the different reactions to them, for instance, ironically enhance the contrast.

There are many historical parallels in *Ulysses* and in *Finnegans Wake* which become a source of frustration if taken straightforwardly and yet which have definite ordering functions in the economy of these narratives. The parallel between the Jews and the Irish in *Ulysses* is one well-known instance, ratified by various analogies between Moses and Parnell, the fondness of Irish Home Rulers for this sort of comparison, the extension from that of the Hebraic and Hellenistic contrast, with the Hebraic related to politics, the Hellenistic to art. Yet no matter how urgently we pursue this parallel we can come to no satisfactory conclusion about the bearing it has on the relationship between Stephen and Bloom, or on any other relationship between people in the novel. Equally, while noting its recurrence, and the manner in which it thereby establishes certain patterns throughout the novel, it is impossible to specify for it any particular function other than the sheer function of being there as a possible but not as a necessary system or ordering. It has to compete with many others – Bloom's bar of soap, for instance – and it seems to be in the end as arbitrarily introduced as they are. In the same way, Homer's epic is probably less useful to a reader of *Ulysses* than a knowledge of *Hamlet*. A knowledge of Vico's theories, or of Croce's rediscovery of Vico, is helpful for understanding certain important formal aspects of *Finnegans Wake*. But is this knowledge of the same order as that which John Garvin supplies when he tells us about the background to the Maamtrasna murders of August 1882, an incident which also supplies a recurrent motif-phrase to the novel?[8] The switching back and forth from one order or kind of knowledge to another, and the discovery that the knowledge is useful only to a limited and formal degree, never in a substantial, historical sense, leaves the reader in the curious position of realising that the kind of research which these books demand is itself parodied by the way in which its discoveries are shown to lead nowhere.

Ezra Pound's view of Joyce, although obviously dominated by the development of his own political ideas, is persuasive. In 1922, he wrote that

> Joyce has set out to do an inferno, and he has done an inferno.
>
>   He has presented Ireland under British domination, a picture so veridic that a ninth rate coward like Shaw (Geo. B.) dare not even look it in the face. By extension he has presented the whole occident under the domination of capital. (*Pound/Joyce*: 198)

But in 1933, he 'can not see that Mr Joyce's later work concerns more than a few specialists' (*Pound/Joyce*: 251) and claims that Anthony Trollope would have been more alert to the main historical forces of the present than is the Joyce of *Work in Progress*. A more subdued and sustained version of this point is made by Alick West[9] and by Gÿorgy Lukács in his essays on Thomas Mann.[10] It is curious to see the right- and left-wing combine to accuse Joyce of passivity, indifference to the historical realities of the present, absorption in language as a form of boredom, indifference, as a symptom of the decadence of the imperialist era in which subjectivity has become the principle and not the theme of modern literature. Yet the assumption upon which these views rest is the very one which Joyce would have most fiercely challenged – namely the assumption that his fiction stood over against a reality by which it could be tested. Instead, his fiction was creating a reality which otherwise would have no existence and in which the external reality, used so often as a criterion in so-called realistic fiction, would be only one ingredient among others. He had learned from Irish nationalism the power of a vocabulary in bringing to existence that which otherwise had none except in the theatre of words. Joyce, we may say, discovered the fictive nature of politics. His work is, in consequence, an examination of the nature of the fictive – how it is created, how words operate within and without patterns of formal symmetry, how history can be magnified or reduced to archetype, how dream becomes speech and sounds become words, accident becomes design.

Therefore, to attempt to understand Joyce's relationship to politics or to language in terms of simple oppositions – nationalism outfaced by socialism, socialism outfaced by an apolitical stance, sequence supplanted by simultaneity, design replaced by accident, stream of consciousness by ventriloquism or parody – is misleading. No simple opposition and no version of a dialectical tension between these and other principles or attitudes is sufficient to do justice to his fundamental concerns. He belonged to a culture in which there was no congruence between established structures and political or social rhetoric. The various efforts to establish such a congruence were all failures. No group had its ambitions realised. Home Rulers, republicans, unionists, Anglo-Irish, socialists, Irish-language enthusiasts, were all disappointed by what finally emerged in the 1920s and 1930s. Joyce was not directly concerned with these failures, as such. He was more concerned with what they indicated about the relation between structure and language. Rather than consign his fiction to any single structure or set of structures, he investigated the activity of structuration itself as it was revealed through the exploration of language, discovering always that there is something excessive in language, something which is of its nature beyond the reach of any structuring principle that can be articulated and yet is within the reach of a structuring activity. For language is itself that structuring activity. Many of the coincidences that surround Joyce's work seem entirely accidental. Much that is discovered is *ben trovato*, not designed. Yet that in itself ratifies the nature of Joyce's enterprise. Language is both arbitrary and systematic. The two features seem to exist in ratio to one another.

So it is with his politics. He repudiated Irish nationalism, socialism, Irish history. He invented the figure of treachery as a way of reading Ireland when he wished to make the repudiation emphatic; a figure of contamination when he wished to make his sympathy with Ireland predominate; a figure of subservience and slavishness when he wished to mix his sympathy with his repudiation. But this is merely a selection of possible figures. Many others are used. Rather than seek one which predominates over the others, we do better to note their variety, the inexhaustibility of the figures, the endlessness of language in creating the very thing to which it apparently refers. Out of Shem's body and biography, world history flows in a continuous unfolding, the very same Shem whom Shaun had berated for having 'kuskykorked himself up tight in his inkbattle house' (*F W*: 176) during the War of Independence. Exiled from Ireland's turmoil, ensnared in *Ulysses*,

> this Esuan Menschavik and the first till last alcshemist wrote over every square inch of the only foolscap available, his own body, till by its corrosive sublimation one continuous present tense integument slowly unfolded all marryvoising moodmoulded cyclewheeling history (thereby, he said, reflecting from his own individual person life unlivable, transaccidentated through the slow fires of consciousness into a dividual chaos, perilous, potent, common to allflesh, human only, mortal) but with each word that would not pass away the squidself which he had squirtscreened from the crystalline world waned chagreengold and doriangrayer in its dudhud. This exists that isits after having been said we know. (*F W*: 185–6)

That which exists depends for its existence on having been said. Even the Ireland of *Ulysses* is included with the Ireland of the War of Independence and the later Ireland of De Valera, after 1932, into the Ireland of *Finnegans Wake*. Ireland, in such a world of words, is a protean sound. Reality is not conferred upon it by Eccles Street or De Valera. Nothing in history, not even the readers of this English, could confine it within any conventional structure of knowledge or understanding. It was and is not fettered or lodged 'in the room of the infinite possibilities they have ousted.'

You brag of your brass castle or your tyled house in ballyfermont? Niggs,

niggs and niggs again. For this was a stinksome inkenstink, quite puzzonal
to the wrottel. Smatterafact, Angles aftanon browsing there thought no
Edam reeked more rare. (*F W*: 183)

Indeed nothing reeked more rare. Ireland as an entity, cultural or
political, was incorporated in all its mutations within Joyce's work
as a model of the world and, more importantly, as a model of the
fictive. In revealing the essentially fictive nature of political imagin-
ing, Joyce did not repudiate Irish nationalism. Instead he understood
it as a potent example of a rhetoric which imagined as true, structures that did not and were never to exist outside language. Thus, as a
model, it served him as it served Yeats and others. It enabled them to
apprehend the nature of fiction, the process whereby the imagination
is brought to bear upon the reality which it creates.

Notes

1   See Colin MacCabe, *James Joyce And The Revolution of The Word*
    (London: Macmillan, 1979) and Dominic Manganiello *Joyce's Poli-
    tics* (London: Routledge & Kegan Paul, 1980).
2   See J.C.C. Mays, 'Some Comments on the Dublin of "Ulysses" ' in
    *Ulysses: Cinquante Ans Après, témoignages franco-anglais sur le chef
    d'oeuvre de James Joyce*, compiled by L. Bonnerot, with J. Aubert and
    C. Jacquet (Paris: Didier, 1974) pp. 83–98.
3   W.B. Yeats, *Explorations*, selected by Mrs W.B. Yeats (London: Mac-
    millan, 1962), p. 42.
4   *Collected Works of Padraic H. Pearse: Political Writings and Speeches*
    (Dublin: Maunsell & Roberts, 1922), p. 65.
5   W.B. Yeats, *Memoirs*, ed. Denis Donoghue (London: Macmillan,
    1972), p. 179
6   *Ibid.*, p. 183–4.
7   *Ibid*, p. 184.
8   John Garvin, *James Joyce's Disunited Kingdom and the Irish Dimen-
    sion* (London: Macmillan, 1976), p. 159–69.
9   Alick West, *Crisis and Criticism and Selected Literary Essays* (London:
    Lawrence & Wishart, 1975), p. 104–27.
10 György Lukács, *Essays on Thomas Mann* trans. Stanley Mitchell,
    (London: Merlin Press, 1964), p. 104–5.

CHAPTER 10

The Joyce I knew and the Women around him*

Maria Jolas

'Throughout my life women have been my most active helpers.'[1]
(Joyce, to Carola Giedion-Welcker)

La rue de l'Odéon

When I chose this fragment in response to the *Cranebag's* invitation I had not reflected on the difficulties I would encounter in attempting to detach the mature man I knew from the usually penniless, tumultuous youth and young man he had been. That in 1927, when I first met him, he was now living in an atmosphere of adequate comfort and world fame was evident. The two women at his side. Nora and Lucia, were handsome and affectionate. Two other women, Sylvia Beach and Adrienne Monnier, were respectfully and wholeheartedly devoted to furthering his professional career. I had not yet met Harriet Weaver, whose London-based *Egoist Press* constituted a third essential pillar of support for the author of *A Portrait* and *Ulysses*.

Djuna Barnes is quoted as saying that, for Joyce, women hardly existed. I am convinced that this was not the case, and that the apparent indifference of the last decades may be explained by the unusually precocious experiences of the early ones. It has seemed important, therefore, both for my own needs and for possible forgetful readers to recapitulate briefly the principal events of those years before introducing my account of this all too human footnote to the literary history of this century.

It is my opinion that at a much earlier age than most men, Joyce

* Fragment from an autobiography, first published in *The Crane Bag*, Vol. 4, no. 1, 1980. In addition to this fragment, my book will contain personal recollections of Joyce's relationships with Nora, Lucia and Helen Joyce; Harriet Weaver, Carola Giedion-Welcker, Lucie Léon, Moune Gilbert, and finally, myself, MJ.

left erotic preoccupations, as he did his interest in politics, behind him. He had set himself a monumental task, the writing of *Finnegans Wake*, the rest of his life might not be long enough to finish it. Women had ceased to be for him 'the opposite sex', they were now simply other human beings, neither nobler nor ignobler than men, towards both and all of whom he was charitably and kindly disposed. For love he had Nora and Lucia, neither of whom ever failed him.

Occasionally, Joyce, who liked to shock, would ask, 'what did Christ know about life? He died at 33 and he never tried to live with a woman.' Joyce could speak. At practically the same age as Christ crucified, he had lived with a woman for nearly a decade, and had already amassed such vast knowledge of women generally that when *Ulysses* appeared, C.G. Jung was moved to comment that he knew more about women than 'the devil's grandmother' (*Letters*, III: 253). Not the devil himself, mind you, his grandmother; presumably for Jung, it takes a female – an old one at that – to know the realities of the female universe.

But how and where had Joyce acquired so young this vast stock of grandmotherly lore? From a succession of 'hers', as Kipling claimed he had? No doubt; indeed, certainly. And if we may trust *A Portrait*, details of this rake's initiation were revealed to priestly ears:

> . . .
> – With women, my child?
> – Yes, father.
> – Were they married women, my child?
>   He did not know. His sins trickled from his lips, one by one, trickled in shameful drops from his soul . . .
>   The priest was silent. Then he asked:
> – How old are you, my child?
> – Sixteen, father. (*P*: 148)[2]

Already, as far back as he could recall, Joyce had known a dominantly feminine world, composed as it was of his harassed, parturition-prone mother (15 pregnancies), the strict, bigoted 'Dante', a swarm of sisters – six! – a maid-servant, little girl playmates in the neighbourhood. And although, at a tender age, James was withdrawn from this gynaeceum, the milieu into which he was removed could perhaps be said to exemplify, as in a convex mirror, if not a feminine-dominated society, in any case, a feminine-haunted society; one in which the new authorities, although they were men whose garb resembled that of women, were part of a world community for whose members woman, with one exception, was apt to be considered 'the greatest device for suffering that God has given to man.'

During the many centuries that this traditionally Christian concept had obtained – but can we yet place it definitively in the past tense? – an implacable theological literature had kept it alive. A precocious reader, Joyce had no doubt, very young, sampled a sufficient number of these writings to decide that he would learn by experience what there was to know, and avoid entangling alliances.[3] We know too that he was much attracted by the Elizabethans who, with one exception, their own 'virgin Queen', cannot be said to have mellowed this view. Few illusions, then, as regards the feminine sex could have been inspired by familiarity with the greater part of the texts. Although his desire was great, so was his wariness. And when Emma Clery (*Stephen Hero*), whose visibly sensual response to Stephen's plea that they spend 'one night together' (*S H*: 203) was instantly masked by her virtuous protests of indignation, judgment intervened to warn of the life-long tribute he would be obliged to pay. Joyce's was a more defiant, more luminous vision: love accepted and shared in total freedom, to be governed by no law but its own. A proud, confident ideal, one that with the years was destined to be considerably buffeted, however, and eventually, under pressure, abandoned.

The complementary accounts in *Stephen Hero* and *A Portrait* (if they may be accepted as being biographically reliable) furnish informative examples of James's growing misanthropy during the period subsequent to what he calls 'the episode of religious fervour' (*S H*: 35) that followed his confession. He quarrelled aggresively with his mother, for having permitted a certain 'Father Jack-in-the-box' (*S H*: 214) to question her about him. He spoke of his father's childish foibles and more serious faults with cruel insight; he attacked 'this pest' (*S H*: 238) the Church, the attitude of women towards religion: 'their iniquities and evil influence', (*S H*: 215) which maddened him. Stephen harangues his fellow student Lynch on this topic:

> 'It is absurd that I should go crawling and cringing . . . to mummers who are themselves no more than beggars. Can we not root this pest out of our minds and out of our society . . .? I, at least, will try. . . . (*S H*: 238–9)

The essential milestones of this revolt are too well known to bear more than brief mention here, they are: in late 1902, Joyce's hard-won and meagrely lived stay in Paris; in April 1903, the paternal summons back to Dublin, where his mother lay dying. The central feminine figure of this chaotic period, chaotic in every sense – spiritually, as well as materially and affectively – was still his mother, with whom from Paris, he had carried on a less than fond, dependent correspondence. When, at her bedside, Stephen (James) refused to join the rest of the family in prayer, a legend was born, of filial rejection and ingratitude, to be justified in the name of total honesty. With the years, both tone and gestures were to become less abrasive as the definitive motto of 'silence, exile, and cunning' (*P*: 251) supplanted the earlier assertiveness.

It was during the following confused, rudderless year that James Joyce met the beautiful, free, disarmingly guileless Nora Barnacle. His emotional response was immediate, and ten years later, still with Nora, he had begun the great work that was to sacralise the date of their love's coronation: 16 June 1904.[4]

Richard Ellmann introduces this cardinal event in Joyce's life against the prosaic background of an evening passed in the company of a music teacher who, with his two daughters, had come to call. After both girls had displayed their vocal talents, Joyce roused himself from what had been an all but monosyllabic silence, to sing Henry VIII's '. . . I love, and shall until I dee.' The visitors, impressed, invited him to call. Ellmann's comment is terse and to the point. 'But for two reasons, this visit never took place. One was that he offended the Esposito sisters, the other that he fell in love.'[5]

With the assurance of the presence at his side of a beautiful, tender young woman, the lover's recently unfocused disquiet was soon canalised into detailed planning for confronting life together on the continent. In the face of daunting odds, four months later, the plan was carried out via Zürich, Pola, then Trieste, from where, ten years later, Joyce had published *Chamber Music*, finished *Dubliners*, fathered two children, written and discarded some 1600 pages of *Stephen Hero* in favour of the more mature, more perfect *Portrait*. Finally, he had started *Ulysses*. This latter undertaking was briefly interrupted to accommodate a biographically urgent creation, the play, *Exiles*.[6] That was 1914.

Meanwhile, the couple had been faring none too ideally. If the road to Dublin was a 'rocky' one, so was the road away from Dublin, for these babes in the wood. Both lovers were hopelessly feckless about finances. Nora, however devoted and well-meaning, as Joyce wrote his brother Stanislaus, could not 'cope', Joyce himself was in alternate states of self-absorbed literary gestation and green-eyed jealousy. He wrote his Aunt Josephine: '. . . Nora does not seem to make much difference between me and the rest of the men she has known and I can hardly believe that she is justified in this . . .' (Dec. 1905) (*Letters*, II: 129). He appears also to have been drinking pretty heavily.

All in all, however, these Austro-Italian years were good, often light-hearted, years, in spite of constant moves, dire poverty, countless lovers' quarrels. They were briefly broken by a frustrating banking interlude in Rome, two visits to Ireland, which allowed the young father to show off his unbaptised heir to friends and foes alike – there was even a short, highly intellectualised flirtation with a Triestine pupil, an indulgence Joyce wittily, exquisitely immortalised under the gently self-mocking title: *Giacomo Joyce*.

The August 1914 thunder-clap sent this quartette of superior-style gypsies, not back to Dublin, which would have meant asphyxiation, but to recently excitingly populated war-time Zürich. Here James Aloysius Joyce was still in exile, still silent, cunningly preparing a bomb, the explosion of which would be heard around the English-speaking world.

The neutral Swiss years were also of great importance in many ways. There was sharp intellectual ozone in the air, from which Joyce undoubtedly benefited, without the constraints of time-consuming personal contacts (I refer to dadaism, psychoanalysis, even world revolution, all three of which he skirted with . . . probably attentive . . . detachment). *Ulysses* was advancing at a rapid pace, his work was beginning to be widely discussed. Domestically, the children were receiving good schooling, the family was becoming the bulwark it was to remain.

In 1918, aged 36, Joyce had a short-lived, mildly erotic adventure with, for heroine, a Swiss woman, Marthe Fleischmann. Some thirty years later, Marthe had long since died, a small packet of Joyce's letters to her was sold by her sister to a Zürich professor, who made them public. As one reads these letters, the 'affair' appears to have been more cerebral than real and, with no evidence to the contrary, it may perhaps be considered Joyce's last 'stray impulse'. His Irish friend, Arthur Power, who questioned him closely as to what actually happened on the beach between Bloom and Gerty MacDowell, wrote that Joyce assured him: 'Nothing happened. . . . It all took place in Bloom's imagination.'[7]

Meanwhile, other women, unlike those he had known, were offering their services to further the cause of his professional career. They were: in London, Harriet Weaver; in New York, Margaret Anderson and Jane Heap (who were jailed for publishing fragments of *Ulysses* in their *Little Review*); finally, in Paris, from 1920, Sylvia Beach and her French friend, Adrienne Monnier. Separately and together, all of these women were directly instrumental in launching James Joyce's *Ulysses* on its world voyage.

It is hard to believe that the thin pale soft shy slim slip of a thing we see in the photograph entertaining the slouching gentleman with a patch over one eye, was actually the original publisher of this same gentleman's big, bawdy 732-page book. Nor is it easily conceivable that less than two years had elapsed between that July day in 1920 at André Spire's Neuilly tea-party – when Sylvia timidly asked: 'Aren't you the great James Joyce?' – and delivery to Joyce's door, on 2 February 1922, of the first printed volume of *Ulysses*. It's one of the shining stories of our time, a story that nothing can tarnish, that of a latter-day Jeanne who immediately recognised her prince among the many pretenders to the literary throne. For ten years she carried his banner, defended his cause. His only baggage was his genius, his purse was permanently empty, but she took in her stride these regrettable blemishes. Her own eventually dwindling means – originally her mother's generously contributed nest egg – were always available for his needs. Very early, to compensate, Joyce presented her with his only assets: a 600-page manuscript version of *A Portrait*, since published as *Stephen Hero*; the manuscript of *Chamber Music*; the author's corrected proof and the no. 2 copy of *Ulysses*, printed on special paper and bound in Greek-blue Moroccan leather, in which Joyce had written a poem dedicated to Sylvia and copied his original plan for the entire book. There were in addition, various pamphlets published by Joyce himself, and finally, *Gas from a Burner*, the broadside Joyce wrote on leaving Dublin for the continent, and which had become a rare collectors' item.

Sylvia shared an apartment with the talented French book-dealer, Adrienne Monnier, whose intimate, well-stocked lending library attracted the most gifted writers of the time. In 1919 Adrienne had

been helpful in the launching of Sylvia's bookshop, and soon the two
addresses, *Les amis des livres*, at no. 7, and *Shakespeare and Co*. at
no. 12 rue de l'Odéon, became the Parisian goal of writers and
knowledgeable readers from many countries.

Adrienne was hardly even then, I imagine, of the shy, slim slip
variety. Quite evidently too, it was she who wore, if not the trousers
– she always dressed in specially designed, very full, ankle-length
skirts – in any case, shall we say that it was she who wore the robe
that symbolically, as with priests and judges, confers supremacy on
its wearer. And although her knowledge of English was limited, she
accepted Sylvia's judgment, ratified by such eminent specialists as
Paul Valéry, André Gide and Valery Larbaud, that here was probably the greatest English-language writer of the century. For a decade
she too, tirelessly defended Joyce's cause: she introduced translations of his work to French readers, in her review *Le navire d'Argent*,
and she it was who initiated, supervised and published what is no
doubt the best translation of *Ulysses* into a foreign language. A
mountainous task!

Then, one day, the date was 19 May 1931, waves from the 1929
Wall St crash were still being felt, having decided that enough was
enough, she wrote the great author a letter that could not be interpreted as anything but a *lettre de rupture*: while Joyce dined luxuriously at Fouquet's, she and Sylvia were pinching pennies to buy
food; while Joyce travelled luxuriously in first-class, their only hope
of travelling would be to cling to the wheels; Joyce's every thought
was of himself, his own fame; he had imposed intolerably on them
both, but especially on Sylvia, etc. etc. In other words, a letter giving
proof, if proof were needed, that the Sapphic heart can harbour
monsters with eyes as green as any other.

(To my knowledge the actual text of this letter has not been
published. I saw the original several times, however, and can vouch
for its tenor.)

As always in moments of crisis, Joyce consulted his family and
close friends. Along with others, we were asked to call. We found
him more hesitant as to his next move than we had known him. His
father's recent death, Lucia's increasingly disquieting vagaries, the
growing resistance to *Finnegans Wake*, as the *transition* fragments
appeared, on the part of such well-disposed friends as T. S. Eliot,
Pound, Wells, even Harriet Weaver. . . . And now this churlish letter
which, while apparently designed to defend Sylvia's rights, could not

do otherwise than separate her from what was probably for her an important source of intellectual and, to a lesser degree, of affective, equilibrium. Joyce could not have been unaware of these minor considerations. If Adrienne's intention had been to rid Sylvia of an importunate suitor, she would have acted no differently. His perplexity was tinged with sadness.

But Joyce was wise . . . there was no cranny of the human heart and libido that had escaped his microscope. Finally, he made known his decision: ties with both of his Paris publishers had been severely strained, they need not, however, both be broken, his personal relationships could only be autonomous. In Vol. III of the *Letters*, Ellmann has a foot-note on the subject to the effect that '. . . Joyce treated the attack with deliberate casualness, and forbore to state grievances of his own' (274). True enough. But an entire human and professional context was involved. His decision was less casually arrived at than appeared.

After a decent interval, Joyce arranged for everything pertaining to his professional activity to be transferred to the home of his good friend the former St Petersburg jurist, Paul Léon, who carried on from where Sylvia had left off. Léon soon succeeded in bringing to a satisfactory conclusion the stalled negotiations with the New York publisher, Random House, stalled, that is, because the only figure that Sylvia advanced for publishing rights to *Ulysses* was that of $25,000!) in those days a more than prohibitive sum, especially in view of the fact that publication in the US would necessitate a costly preliminary legal action. Sylvia's statement in her autobiography, *Shakespeare and Co.* (1956), that Joyce told her he had received a down payment of $45,000,[8] was denied by the head of Random House when in New York, in 1964, having never heard this mentioned, I asked for confirmation. Here I shall open a parenthesis, for this was not my only regret on reading Sylvia's book, particularly in its French version (1962).

Sylvia's story of how, in 1935, she had been obliged to sell the mss. and other items Joyce had given her is very briefly covered and, except for the alleged payment by Random, no sum is mentioned. Several French reviewers of the book indignantly denounced Joyce's 'monstrous egotism' towards Sylvia, as did certain of our mutual friends. Was that really result she had hoped for? I feel sure that it was not. Here is a reference to the subject made by Joyce in a 1935 letter to his son and daughter-in-law, who were visiting in New

York. The letter is dated 19 February, 1935:

> . . . A propos of the S.B. sale of my MSS (of which I am still officially ignorant). I am journalistically informed that the rumour is current over there that she, by her generous sacrifice of all her rights in *U* to me, resigned herself to abject poverty. Frailty, thy name is woman. (*Letters*, III: 345)

Subtly, surely, Joyce organised his revised relationships. On those days when we remember, Sylvia was never forgotten. And when later, she organised authors' readings to be given in her bookshop, Joyce made a point of being present. I remember that we accompanied him to hear Gide, Eliot and Spender read from their unpublished works. On these occasions he did not, however, remain for the *post-mortem* palavers.

Finally, in the late 1930s, as the *Wake* was about to appear, Joyce complied with the London publisher's request for a recent photograph showing the trio, Joyce, Sylvia and Adrienne, seated around the table at 12 rue de l'Odéon. *Noblesse oblige.*

It was about at this time that one evening over dinner, chez Fouquet's, our conversation turned to a re-hash of these sad events. Someone made a harsh criticism of Sylvia's role in them. Joyce's comment: 'All she ever did was to make me a present of the ten best years of her life', put to an end to this idle talk. In the late 1950s I had the opportunity of repeating to Sylvia what Joyce had said. Her eyes filled with tears. 'He said that?' That was all. But I sensed that a deep mutation was possible, one that would purge her heart of all bitterness – a bitterness she had paid for with years of incorrigible migraine – and leave only awareness of having been elected and privileged to share in a unique undertaking.

Joyce had died in 1941, Adrienne, who suffered from a rare, interiorised hearing disease, took her own life in 1955. For some time, Sylvia had been living alone. And when, on 16 June 1962, she climbed the perilous outside steps of the Martello Tower in Dublin, to open the *Joyce Museum*, she was evidently happy: '. . . Listeners here do not have to be told that this work (*Ulysses*) is now established among the world's literary masterpieces. Its author is recognized everywhere as one of the greatest writers not only of our time, but of all time. . . .'[9] Four months later, Sylvia was found dead, presumably of an infarctus, in her rue de l'Odéon apartment. At her funeral, I was not alone to notice the startling resemblance to Joyce of the tall, unmistakably Irish stranger (his ghost?) who arrived late to join the many friends assembled in the hall of the Père Lachaise crematorium, in loving memory of Sylvia.

My attempts to form a coherent opinion of Joyce's attitude towards women, by confronting my own observations with what he himself and his commentators have written on the subject, have not been conclusive. To the question, need the man-woman relationship be a conflictual one, neither the family man nor the professional writer provides a clear reply. That for him it was an essential relationship, I am nevertheless convinced. Experience of an all-male world had bred scepticism; a closely observed all-female world had shown the fallow womb to be subject to the same storms and passions that perturb its conjugal counterpart.

That it was 'better to marry than to burn' was no doubt a tenet of his code. But that both men and women should burn as well for nobler causes than physical desire: total freedom and honesty, empathy and hope for humanity, was an exigence of the artist's sacerdotal role, that very early, it seems to me, occupied an important place in Joyce's hierarchy of values.

His most evident contribution to this discussion which, today, has become so envenomed, may well be his appreciation of the fact that biological difference need not exclude common interests and parallel action. On the other hand . . ., that familiar 'frailty thy name is woman', used without quotes in the letter to his son, could also express his more deeply rooted, instinctive response. The Joyce I knew was an essentially gentle, charitable man.

Finally, we have the evidence of Joyce's lifetime affinity for all bodies of water, the female element, *par excellence*. And this brings to mind the ancient legend according to which 'poets thought that it was on the brink of water poetry was revealed to them.'

I am tempted to add that in the inevitable clash between poet and lover, I believe it was the poet who won.

Notes

1   Richard Ellmann, *James Joyce* (New York: Oxford University Press, 1959), p. 648.
2   These details were not forgotten, as evidenced by the 1909 letters at

Cornell, and by certain passages in *Ulysses*. I recall Stanislaus Joyce's references to his brother's familiarity with the prostitute world of Dublin.

3 'Not all Stephen's trouble of mind but all his problem is economic. . . . He has never been loved by any woman, for the love of good women is more expensive than that of the other sort' (Frank Budgen, *James Joyce and the Making of 'Ulysses'* (London: Oxford University Press, 1972), p. 43).

4 Richard Ellmann, *op. cit.*, p. 548. 'My darling, my love, my queen' is how this letter to Nora begins. This is not the only example of Joyce's use of the word 'queen' in his correspondence with Nora.

5 *Ibid.*, p. 162.

6 'Understandably, the talk in Zürich turned generally on *Ulysses*, and I can remember few references in that period to his play, *Exiles*. But later in Paris, in the autumn of 1933, he referred to *Exiles* in connection with my book on *Ulysses*. The reference is important because of the light it throws on the Joycean conception of sexual love (at any rate on the male side) as an irreconcilable conflict between a passion for absolute possession and a categorical imperative of absolute freedom . . .' (Budgen, *op. cit.*, p. 349).

7 Arthur Power, *Conversations with James Joyce*, ed. Clive Hart (London: Millington, 1974), p. 32.

8 A letter from Random House dated 17 April, 1980, states: 'We paid him (J. J.) $1,000 upon signing of the contract and $1,500 upon publication of the book.'

9 *The Irish Times* 17 July 1962.

Index

Under 'James Joyce' will be found a list of references to his works; the author
himself is mentioned on nearly every page of this book.